The Figure of the C American, British, Children's Literatu

Over the past century, much attention has been paid to the literature written for adults in response to the First World War, but there has been comparatively little consideration of how the war influenced literature for young readers at the time. Based on extensive archival research, this study examines an array of wartime writing for young people and provides a new understanding of the complexities and nuances within children's literature of the period. In its discussion of nearly 150 primary sources from Britain, Canada, and the United States, this volume considers some well-known texts but also brings to light forgotten children's literature of the era, providing new insights into how WWI was presented to the young people whose lives were indelibly impacted by the crisis. Paying special attention to the varied ways in which child figures were depicted, it reflects on what these portrayals reveal about adult conceptualizations of youth, and it considers how these may have shaped young readers' own views of armed conflict, citizenship, and childhood. From the helpless victim to the heroic combatant, child figures appeared in many guises, exposing a range of adult concerns about nation, empire, and children's citizenship. Exploring everything from alphabet books for beginning readers, to recruitment materials for high school students, this book examines works from multiple genres and provides a uniquely comprehensive study of transatlantic children's literature produced during the first global war.

Elizabeth A. Galway is Associate Professor of English and Board of Governors Research Chair in Children's Literature and Culture at the University of Lethbridge, where she serves as Co-Director of the Institute for Child and Youth Studies. She has published widely on children's literature and is the author of *From Nursery Rhymes to Nationhood: Children's Literature and the Construction of Canadian Identity* (Routledge, 2008). She holds a Ph.D. from the University of Exeter, an M.A. from Durham University, and an Honours B.A. from the University of Toronto.

Children's Literature and Culture

Jack Zipes, Founding Series Editor
Philip Nel, Series Editor, 2011–2018
Kenneth Kidd and Elizabeth Marshall, Current Series Editors

Founded by Jack Zipes in 1994, Children's Literature and Culture is the longest-running series devoted to the study of children's literature and culture from a national and international perspective. Dedicated to promoting original research in children's literature and children's culture, in 2011 the series expanded its focus to include childhood studies, and it seeks to explore the legal, historical, and philosophical conditions of different childhoods. An advocate for scholarship from around the globe, the series recognizes innovation and encourages interdisciplinarity. Children's Literature and Culture offers cutting-edge, upper-level scholarly studies and edited collections considering topics such as gender, race, picturebooks, childhood, nation, religion, technology, and many others. Titles are characterized by dynamic interventions into established subjects and innovative studies on emerging topics.

Dust Off the Gold Medal
Rediscovering Children's Literature at the Newbery Centennial
Edited by Sara L. Schwebel and Jocelyn Van Tuyl

Sexuality in Literature for Children and Young Adults
Edited by Paul Venzo and Kristine Moruzi

Poetics and Ethics of Anthropomorphism
Children, Animals and Poetry
Christopher Kelen and Chengcheng You

The Figure of the Child in WWI American, British, and Canadian Children's Literature
Farmer, Tailor, Soldier, Spy
Elizabeth A. Galway

For more information about this series, please visit: https://www.routledge.com/Childrens-Literature-and-Culture/book-series/SE0686

The Figure of the Child in WWI American, British, and Canadian Children's Literature

Farmer, Tailor, Soldier, Spy

Elizabeth A. Galway

Routledge
Taylor & Francis Group
NEW YORK AND LONDON

Cover credit: "Trooper Tom – Slightly Wounded" by G.F. Christie from Blackie's Children's Annual (1915)

First published 2022
by Routledge
605 Third Avenue, New York, NY 10158

and by Routledge
4 Park Square, Milton Park, Abingdon, Oxon, OX14 4RN

Routledge is an imprint of the Taylor & Francis Group, an informa business

Library of Congress Cataloging-in-Publication Data
A catalog record for this title has been requested

ISBN: 978-1-032-04356-2 (hbk)
ISBN: 978-1-032-04358-6 (pbk)
ISBN: 978-1-003-19160-5 (ebk)

DOI: 10.4324/9781003191605

Typeset in Sabon
by codeMantra

Contents

Figures

Acknowledgements

The research undertaken for this project was made possible by generous funding from Canada's Social Sciences and Humanities Research Council (SSHRC) and the University of Lethbridge, for which I am very grateful. I must thank the staff and librarians who helped me along the way at Library and Archives Canada; University of Toronto Libraries; Osborne Collection at the Toronto Public Library; Coutts Education Library and Bruce Peel Special Collections at the University of Alberta; University of British Columbia Library; Free Library of Philadelphia; Boston Public Library; Bodleian Library; British Library; Blythe House at the V&A; and Imperial War Museum (with special thanks to Jane Rosen). I also want to express my gratitude to the team at Routledge and to my peer reviewers for their thoughtful feedback.

I greatly appreciate the research assistants who helped with this project in its early stages including Amy Bright, Courtney Killam, Jessica Ruzek, Sarah Scott, and Rylan Spenrath. I also want to thank everyone involved with the Institute for Child and Youth Studies for fostering an inspiring and supportive working environment – it is great to have the dingoes in my corner! My friends and colleagues in Lethbridge have kept me motivated when life has intervened in challenging and unexpected ways, and special thanks go to Louise Barrett, Kiki Benzon, and Goldie Morgentaler for their friendship and advice over the years.

My research in the United Kingdom was facilitated by the hospitality and generosity of Roger, Mary, and Charlotte Heath-Bullock, Carol Davies, and Andrew Bond. Closer to home, Linda and Murray McGeough helped me keep my head above water on more than one occasion.

I am grateful for the continued love and support of my family, including my siblings and my parents, Michael and Zina Galway, and I want to thank Angelina and Rosie Howey for helping me in the home stretch and for teaching me more about children's mettle and wisdom than I could ever learn from books. Above all, I need to express my love and appreciation for Kevin and Lucy – thank you for keeping the home fires burning!

Introduction

Wartime Tales of Innocence and Experience

In the morning hours of July 1, 1916, nearly two full years after Britain declared war on Germany, the British Army began the Somme Offensive. By the end of that infamous day, more than 19,000 British soldiers had been killed, and the total number of British casualties was close to 58,000. When the Battle of the Somme concluded a few months later, the total number of casualties on all sides was over 1.1 million and this attritional struggle "was a touchstone of horror" that became "the standard against which every other battle was measured" (Cook *At the Sharp End* 521–522). The numbers from the Somme are the definition of incomprehensible; how could one possibly comprehend the deaths of nearly 1,000 British soldiers per hour on a single summer day? Over the course of the war, nearly ten million military personnel would be killed along with nearly as many civilians. Throughout the conflict and the century that has followed, writers and historians have struggled to understand a war that defies understanding.

As Paul Fussell notes, the purpose of some narratives about the war is "to 'make sense' of events which otherwise would seem merely accidental or calamitous" (121). This need to "make sense" of the conflict is evident in wartime Allied literature that strives to encourage continuing support for the war effort and to assuage fears that the struggle will either be without end or will conclude in Allied defeat. Fussell and others have explored the ways in which the First World War impacted literature during and after the conflict, including how authors reimagined the years leading up to August 1914. "For the modern imagination," notes Fussell, "that last summer has assumed the status of a permanent symbol for anything innocently but irrecoverably lost" (24). Largely absent from studies like Fussell's, however, is a consideration of how the war impacted literature for young readers. If it shattered the world's collective innocence and, in turn, shaped literary and cultural expression, then an important question to ask is how it impacted the literature written for those most closely associated with the notion of innocence – children? This book will explore how a conflict that was so unfathomable was "made sense of" by adult authors of children's literature and what this reveals about how writers envisioned the young people they wrote for.

DOI: 10.4324/9781003191605-1

In her 2014 study of youth and citizenship in Britain, Stephanie Olsen remarks on the need for a study of the war in relation to literature for young readers and notes that such research would be of "enormous scholarly value and interest" (165). My book aims to take a step towards addressing this lack of scholarship and answering the question of how the First World War shaped children's literature. A more difficult question to answer is how this literature shaped the young people who read it. Comprehending the responses of real children to the war, and to the literature they read during it, is complicated. In general, their voices have not been well preserved in the historical record and accounts of their reflections on the literature they read are particularly rare. What this study can do, however, is provide a fuller assessment of how adult writers attempted to shape narratives about the war for young readers, broadening our understanding of what these efforts reveal about views on youth at the time. Young people were figured in many different ways in wartime children's literature, revealing a complex set of attitudes towards childhood and adolescence. Examining these representations may lead to a better understanding of their potential to influence those whose most formative years were lived in the shadow of two world wars.

When I first began research on this subject in 2008 there were few studies of First World War children's literature. In recent years, however, due in part to the war's centenary, more scholarship has been produced on this topic and on the subject of childhood experience during WWI more generally.[1] I add to this in two vital ways. The first is by focussing on the figure of the child and exploring in depth the question of how young people were represented in Allied children's literature.[2] The second is by providing a more comprehensive examination of literature for young people by examining works published in English on both sides of the Atlantic and by considering multiple genres and forms aimed at readers from toddlers to teenagers.

With a few exceptions, the literature discussed in this book was published in Britain, the United States, and Canada between 1914 and 1919. I focus on these three Allied nations because of their significant historical ties and close cultural connections, but also because, despite many similarities and shared experiences, there are differences that help highlight the complexities and nuances of wartime children's literature. The ties between these nations, with Canada being part of the British Empire but also sharing a unique relationship with the United States, make them logical subjects for comparative study and many of the texts discussed here circulated in more than one nation.[3] As Allies, they shared much in common, but unlike Britain and Canada, the United States did not officially join the fight until 1917. By considering children's literature from three closely linked nations that had different experiences of the war, we can gain a clearer understanding of how the conflict influenced conceptions of both childhood and nationhood.[4]

It is worth noting here that not all literature written for children from 1914 to 1919 addresses the topic of war. Many authors avoid referring to it altogether, perhaps reflecting a desire to shield young readers from the horrors unfolding around them or, at the very least, to provide them with a temporary respite from turmoil. These works are worthy of examination in their own right, but the purpose of my study is to explore a broad selection of the many texts that *do* acknowledge the war's existence and its very real presence in the lives of children. It is also important to note that the war did not cease to be a subject of children's literature when the guns fell silent in late 1918. Other scholars have done excellent work exploring the ongoing framing of the war in literature for young people over the past century, and such research helps us understand the lingering impact of the Great War. With this book, however, my goal is to better understand how writers coped with the task of portraying the conflict to young readers as events were still unfolding and immediately following the armistice, rather than on how authors addressed it from a later vantage point. Consequently, some canonical texts published after 1919, like L. M. Montgomery's *Rilla of Ingleside* (1921), one of Canada's most well-known children's texts to address the war, or Michael Morpurgo's more recent *War Horse* (1982), are not included in this study.

The works that are discussed in this book enjoyed varying degrees of fame and popularity. While I explore some texts by well-known authors and include many examples from popular works like the long-running periodicals *The Boy's Own Paper*, published in Britain, and *St. Nicholas*, published in the United States, I have also focussed attention on those that are less likely to be familiar to general readers and scholars today. Other researchers have already done valuable work on some of the better-known texts of the time, and my choice is motivated by my desire to examine more fully the diversity of ways in which the war was represented to young readers. I have thus cast a wide net, examining not just prominent texts of the era, some of which have remained in the public consciousness to some degree, but a broader sampling that better represents the eclectic range of literature children had access to during the war.

The bulk of my research for this project was conducted over a period of several years in libraries and special collections in Britain, Canada, and the United States. Like any archival research, the project is shaped in part by what has been preserved in these collections, which together hold an impressive array of diverse primary materials. My final selection represents works that reflect some of the most prevalent themes taken up by children's authors on both sides of the Atlantic, but also some that are more distinctive in form or content. Together, this material provides a more complete picture of the many ways in which authors treated the war in literature for the young. The rich variety of works discussed here includes poetry, songs, short stories, novels, school texts, magazines, advertisements, plays, ABC books, pamphlets, works that cross into the realm of games and toys, and non-fiction. The age of the intended reader for these texts varies, with works like alphabet books and simple verse often (though not always) being designed for very young readers, and other writings clearly aimed at older children or teenaged readers. Together, they reveal both commonalities and differences in the ways in which the war manifested itself within literature for young children and older youth.

Included in the discussion are materials read by both boys and girls. While some works were intended specifically for one group or the other, cross-over reading likely occurred with some frequency. Since the origins of modern children's literature in the nineteenth century, even works deliberately aimed at boys have often had a large female readership. In 1940, for example, a "survey of working-class girls aged thirteen and fourteen found that about a quarter of the adolescent magazines they read were, in fact, written for boys" and that boys' adventure stories were among girls' favourite literature (Rose 380). With this in mind, one question I ponder is how the masculine ideal perpetuated by many wartime narratives for boys may have influenced girls' own conceptions of citizenship and feminine identity at a time when roles for women were undergoing significant change.

In addition to material addressed to both boys and girls, the literature I discuss in this study includes examples intended for both working-class and middle-class readers, with publications like the popular *Boy's Own Paper* having "an audience that cut across class lines" (Rose 322). Nevertheless, despite children from different social classes being represented in some of these texts, most works discussed here tend to presume a middle-class readership, reflecting how this audience has long dominated children's publishing and influenced decisions about what is preserved in the archive. Representations of race are even less diverse. Although discussions of race are present in wartime literature, particularly in texts about empire, most of the works here are typical of much nineteenth and early-twentieth century transatlantic children's literature in that their protagonists tend to embody an Anglo-Saxon ideal (Budgen 46), and authors seem to presume a readership that, if not explicitly Anglo-Saxon, is of white European origin.[5]

Throughout the book, I have tried to ensure that the intended readership of specific works is clear from the context of my analysis, as factors like age, gender, class, and nationality are important for understanding the nuances of these different texts, but I use the terms "child" and "youth" to broadly refer to readers who were below the age of enlistment, and "children's literature" to refer to the collective body of work under discussion, which includes material intended for the youngest readers through to older adolescents.

Peering Past the Propaganda: Reconsidering the Complexity of First World War Children's Literature

Although there was a wide array of reading material published for young people during the First World War, the fact that so much of it appears propagandist or pro-war has led to the widespread assumption that it is unvarying. This view is evident in comments like the following about Michael Morpurgo's children's literature: "Unlike writers in the years of the Great War, Michael Morpurgo focuses [...] on the dark side of the First World War. The author decided to show a realistic image of war in its atrocity and unfairness" (Madry 153). These comments reveal a common notion that, during WWI, the war was presented to children in a glorified, sanitized, or otherwise unrealistic manner. Undeniably, many children's writers of the time did portray it in such ways, but there are also many examples of child readers being shown its "dark side." Similarly, the suggestion that Morpurgo's portrayal of Germans "breaks the stereotype of the brutal enemy" suggests the foe was represented in a consistently negative fashion in wartime texts (Madry 159), but as I discuss later in this book, this was not the only depiction of Germany.

I highlight these comments about Morpurgo not to single them out for criticism, but because they are representative of a tendency to see First World War children's literature as uniform and uncomplicated in its portrayal of the conflict. My research shows that it was more diverse in tone, style, and content than many have imagined. I argue that the complexities and contradictions found in children's literature from the era are meaningful and that their possible ramifications for young readers deserve consideration. For instance, while negative portrayals of Germans are more common than not in wartime children's literature, the positive portrayals that exist are important, as are the accounts that show the war's "dark side" to children. If we are to understand more fully the potential impact of literary depictions of war on child readers, we need to pay attention to their nuances and deviations from the norm.

First World War children's literature is a rich field for study and in this book, I am concentrating principally on the portrayal of 'child figures,' a term I use throughout to refer to representations of young people ranging from infants to older youths. Images of child figures were wide-ranging and often competing, and these depictions had the potential to shape young readers' conceptions of childhood, adulthood, and nationhood in various ways. The early twentieth century was a time when the concept of childhood as a period of innocence and imaginative play was prevalent in North America and Britain, yet it was also an era that witnessed violent, mechanized conflict on an unprecedented scale. When war broke out in Europe in the summer of 1914, many thought it would be over by Christmas. Instead, the world would come to witness a long, bloody conflict, the likes of which had never been seen before.

Many scholars have outlined the profound, global upheavals caused by the Great War, including its impacts on artistic and literary expression, but their studies have focussed largely on adult experiences and culture. As Michael Paris notes, even the most popular children's works of the era "have been almost completely ignored or, at best, noted only in passing in the cultural/literary histories of the war" (xxi). As I have already noted, until quite recently, discussions of First World War literature have largely excluded any detailed consideration of children's literature, with Paris' *Over the Top: The Great War and Juvenile Literature in Britain* (2004) being one of the first substantial works to attempt to fill this gap.

One of my goals is to help address this dearth of scholarship and to expand on the work started by Paris, whose study concentrates on British literature, and whose primary focus is on children's texts that "were intended to persuade young Britons to enlist for the Great Adventure" (xii). Dorothea Flothow, like Paris, examines the slanted nature of much of this material, observing that as a form "of British war propaganda, children's books of the war years presented their readers with a very limited and biased view of the First World War" (Flothow "Coming to Terms" 234). It is true that much children's literature from the period was overtly propagandist and this has led, understandably, to the belief that there was a certain uniformity in the literature available to child readers. However, by reviewing a larger body of children's literature than scholars have examined previously, and by doing some comparison of transatlantic texts, I demonstrate that wartime children's literature was more varied than one might at first presume. By examining not only how writers represented the war but also how they represented children, this study uncovers some of the nuances of this material and opens up new ways of thinking about adult conceptions of youth, as well as the potential impact of these views on children's own understandings of war, nationhood, and childhood.

The Child as the Future of the Nation: Moulding the Young Citizen

Children's literature is not only written for children but also written about them, and the manner in which authors address young readers and portray young characters reveals much about how they conceptualize childhood and adolescence. Literature produced during the First World War reflects how young people were affected by the conflict, but it also reveals the malleability of the notion of 'the child' and shows how authors imagined childhood in a range of ways. As I demonstrate throughout this book, there was no single representation of the child in literature from the period and no uniform representation of the war. Given the ways in which the war pervaded children's lives, whether they were living close to the front or further afield, it is somewhat surprising that scholars have been slow to consider the complex ways in which the cultures of young people were impacted by, and had an impact on, the conflict. One reason for this may be the prevailing association of childhood with innocence, and the seemingly inherent incongruity between the concepts of violence and innocence. As Daniel Cook and John Wall suggest, war and conflict "challenge the received, normative understandings about the 'nature' of children and boundaries of childhood" (1).

The belief in childhood innocence and the desire to preserve it have led some people to think that the only role a child can play in times of conflict is that of victim. While I do discuss this significant representation in Chapter 2, it is important to note that to see children only in this light in an effort to preserve "some notion of sheltered innocence is to commit a disservice to their experiences and actions" (Cook and Wall 1). Children engage with war in myriad ways, and are more than mere victims:

> In the disruption and destruction of the lives of children, their families and communities, childhood itself transforms and takes shape. Children, like others, are both subject to the consequences of war *and* actively involved in many aspects of conflict. They are and have been fighters, victims, refugees, peace-builders and reasons both to enter into and to end wars.
>
> (Cook and Wall 1)

What Cook and Wall identify as ways in which real children are not only impacted by but have an impact on armed conflict were true of young people in the First World War and applied to those living close to the action, but also to those on the home front, where young people made a substantial contribution to the war effort. While some wartime depictions of childhood may have ignored these realities and offered (to borrow a phrase from Marah Gubar) "a luxuriously nostalgic brand of escapism" (4), many of the works discussed in this book demonstrate that writers conceived of children as inextricably connected to the war.

Beyond the material contributions children could make by participating in activities like growing food and donating money, they were encouraged to develop values and characteristics that many adults in North America and Britain saw as crucial to strengthening the nation or empire. Children "are fascinating as political subjects because they represent the values, expectations, and futurity of citizenship, while simultaneously being denied the explicit rights and privileges afforded to adult citizens" (Weikle-Mills 214). This liminal position is worth considering in relation to wartime literature in particular, which puts great emphasis on duty, patriotism, and civic responsibility. During the First

World War, even though children did not have full legal rights, writers appealed to their patriotism and exhorted them to support the war effort, and they were certainly made aware of the shame that lay in not fulfilling the duties of citizenship.

Historian Ross Collins observes that in the United States during both World Wars, important qualities that many believed war could help cultivate included "development of civic spirit, and enhancement of moral character" (*Children* 39). Patriotism was the "hub around which all these virtues fell" and could motivate the child "toward the goals authorities would hope to develop" (39). These views were evident in Canada and Britain too, and in all three nations child readers were provided with narratives that encouraged them to be directly involved with the practical work of war and that sought to sculpt them as citizens. While some writers wanted to see young people shielded from the war, others justified their involvement, partly because child contributions to home front activities did in fact produce significant results, and partly because they viewed the war as an opportunity to mould children into future citizens of appropriate character.

In some literature for young readers, discussions of what constitutes good character are considered in the context of religious faith, as in the British text *The King's Uniform: Eighteen Addresses to Children* (c.1915). The author, the reverend Robert Harvie, proposes that there is an inherent link between the war, Christianity, patriotism, and good character. Harvie states his belief that "the cause of Britain to-day is the cause of Christ" and notes that he has "tried to state the issues simply, to the boys and girls of my own congregation" (7). Observing that "the claims of the Empire on her children to-day are the claims, at all times, of the Kingdom of Christ" (7), he clearly equates duty to Empire with duty to God.

Harvie's definition of patriotism is bound up with the notion of sacrifice as he writes, "the country is calling for men to undertake great sacrifices [...] to risk their lives for the sake of honour and right, and thousands are answering the call" (31). He presents this sacrifice as a free choice, claiming that men "may choose the valley where they will be sheltered and far away from danger; or they may choose the mountain where there is constant risk and hardship. These young men to-day are saying, 'Give me this mountain'" (31). In this case, the example of soldiers willingly risking their lives is part of the author's attempt to instil in young readers feelings of honour, sacrifice, and Christian piety, and to channel these into an acceptance of their own patriotic duty.

This focus on developing good moral character and national loyalty is present in many Allied works that encouraged young readers to support the war effort, and it was sometimes in response to underlying concerns about the rise in juvenile delinquency and the war's effect on children's moral welfare.[6] According to a 1918 report by the U.S.

Children's Bureau, in "England, France, Germany, and Russia" growing numbers of children appeared in court during the war and committed increasingly serious offenses (Lindenmeyer 145). The study attributed this to several factors including the absence of fathers who were fighting at the front, an increase in the number of mothers employed outside the home, and even

> the overcrowding of schools caused by a shortage of teachers [...]. The bureau concluded that 'when the normal life of children is broken down, when their needs are neglected by the community, children and community alike must pay the penalty'.
>
> (Lindenmeyer 145)

The contributing factors to these developments overseas, such as absent parents, also existed in America after 1917 where various programs were instituted to help curb juvenile delinquency and guard against the effects of the disruption of the so-called "normal life of children." As I discuss in Chapter 2, concerns about delinquency, legitimate or not,[7] appear to have influenced some literary depictions of child victims and accompanying calls for aid on both sides of the Atlantic, but they may have also been responsible for literature that encouraged children to be active and patriotic and to use their leisure time to support the war effort.

One means of keeping "children busy and off the streets was to provide a wide spectrum of activities more carefully organized than haphazard calls to volunteer" (Collins *Children* 69). These programs included a "recreation movement" in which communities were encouraged "to establish supervised recreational facilities [...] and other projects in order to provide a wholesome and controlled environment for children's leisure time" (Lindenmeyer 146). Efforts like the organization of patriotic "pageants" also arose from the view that inculcating "patriotic ideals was another way to deter juvenile delinquency and maintain social control. The war provided the perfect opportunity to make this preventative tactic a national effort" (Lindenmeyer 148).

From Schoolyard to Farmyard: The Importance of Children "Doing Their Bit"

Along with organized leisure activities, school was a key means by which adults could teach patriotic ideals and maintain social control. Close links between what adults deemed necessary education for the child and what they deemed essential to the success of the nation are apparent in many works. In Canada, which was automatically part of the conflict as soon as Britain declared war, schools played a role in fostering support for the empire, but they also contributed to a prominent narrative of the war as a transformative event that furthered Canada's nation-building efforts. The author of *The Thrift Campaign in the Schools of Ontario* (1919), for example, advises teachers that "by every possible means the children should be shown how they may do their duty to their country" and argues that "the aim of all teaching" is to "produce good and loyal citizens" (iii). This view is also expressed by J. O. Miller in *The Young Canadian Citizen: Studies in Ethics, Civics and Economics* (1919), in which he draws a clear connection between the education of Canadian children and a strong future for the nation. According to Miller, the "object of the education of Canadian boys and girls is to make good citizens" (79).

This idea that school was central to the development of loyal, dutiful citizens extended to many nations. Regarding schools in France, for instance, Stéphane Audoin-Rouzeau observes that

> adult demands on childhood during the war were particularly evident in the world of education. In effect, the war added an additional burden to the classic aims of the school system and reinforced the traditional mechanisms for imposing responsibility on childhood.
>
> (39)

Adding that there was a link between "schoolwork and patriotic duty" (39), he quotes a Parisian headmaster who observed in 1914 that the "'duty of schoolchildren is to be obedient, hardworking, to prepare a sound future for themselves .... This is how they can serve the nation'" (39).

A strikingly similar sentiment is expressed by the author of the *Thrift Campaign* who outlines the expectation that children will work to become good citizens in the post-war period:

> And what is expected of the youth of Ontario? That they will not waste time in school, but will be ready as soon as possible to do the most effective work as men and women [...]; that they will be loyal citizens who will take advantage of every opportunity to serve Canada.
>
> (viii)

The sense of disillusionment that infused much adult literature in the wake of the First World War is absent from this text from 1919, just as it is from many other works for children. David Budgen argues that after the war, instead of a great shift away from the wartime emphasis on the justness of the Allied cause, "works aimed at children were often marked by their sense of continuity and traditionalism" (76). While many writers from the generation that had been sent off to be slaughtered at the front came to express disenchantment and resentment, the author of the *Thrift Campaign* perpetuates the same notions of duty and sacrifice that were part of the early enthusiasm for the war.

In the above example, wasting time in school is pictured as unpatriotic, but applying themselves to their studies was not the only 'duty' children were expected to perform. As I will discuss throughout this book, children were encouraged to support the war in a range of ways. Some writers even saw childhood 'innocence' itself as therapeutic for adults, and children were asked to remain hopeful and carefree in order to ease the concerns of parents burdened with worries. Harvie is one author who advocates that all individuals, young and old, should help win the war in whatever way they can, and in his chapter "The Non-Combatants" he observes that everybody "wants to do something, and to do something which counts" but that not everyone can go to "the very front of the fighting line" because men are required for other duties, such as supplying troops with food and staying home "to guard the shores of Britain in case of invasion" (51–52). Harvie notes that all of these individuals "are doing their part to help the Cause" and that it "takes us all, working together, from the men at the front to the humblest loyal subject of the King, seeking our duty and anxious to do it, to secure a victory" (52).

In observing that many adults long to play an important role in the fighting but are unable to do so, Harvie acknowledges the disappointment and frustration that some children felt at being unable to fight on the battlefield. By noting other activities that support the military, like growing food for soldiers, he emphasizes that children's work on the home front is important and that they are "working together" with adults in ways that help the cause (52). Harvie clearly places importance on each individual trying "to do faithfully what he sees to be his duty" (52), and he remarks that when Germany is defeated, the "only people who will be ashamed in that day will be those who have shirked their duty" (52). He adds that everyone else, "old and young alike, will be able to rejoice and to feel that they have helped" bring about victory (53), reinforcing the message that children too have responsibilities and will share in the joy of victory, or in the shame of failing to serve their nation.

Texts like Harvie's show that children's literature often presented a pro-war narrative, encouraged contributions to the war effort, fostered values of duty and sacrifice, and strove to instil loyalty to the nation. Yet within this overarching narrative there were variations, complexities, and even contradictions. For instance, even as they supported the refrain that everyone must 'do his bit,' some writers considered that the child's task was to remain innocent and carefree and to thereby provide either succour to war-weary adults or motivation to help win the war. Within an overarching narrative that championed the Allied cause and cultivated notions of duty and sacrifice, child readers were thus exposed to mixed messages regarding their own capabilities and responsibilities. While literature was not children's only source of information about the war, it was the one that was most diverse in form and content when it came to teaching young people about the conflict and their potential role in it. Children's literature is thus a particularly rich source of evidence for ways in which the armed conflict, childhood, and children's participation in the war effort were presented to youth. These varied messages help to reveal that the turmoil caused by the war included upheavals in how people understood children's roles in society.

From Victims to Peacemakers: The Structure of the Book

The opening chapter of this book considers how Britain, America, and Canada were represented in wartime children's literature and explores how images of the child and the family were used to signify the changing relationships between nations. Portrayals of the connections between the three Allies were closely linked to child figures, which often served as embodiments of the state. From envisioning Britain as a caring and protective parent of loyal imperial offspring, to presenting Canada and America as youthful figures eager to make their own mark in the world, the use of child imagery and family metaphors reflects the shifting relationships between nations that were impacted indelibly by the war.

I turn my attention in the second chapter to the figure of the child victim, which was one of the most widespread representations of the child in wartime literature. I explore the different literary functions of the suffering child and consider different types presented to young readers, including orphans, refugees, and children who are injured or killed. The child victim was used in both pacifist and pro-war writing, serving as a means of demonstrating the need for peace, and as a means of demonizing the foe and justifying continued Allied involvement. One of the questions raised by these figures is how child readers may have been impacted by seeing themselves as victims. While such characters sometimes reinforced a view of children as vulnerable and reliant on adults, they also served the opposite function by suggesting children could overcome adversity, and by encouraging readers to help end child suffering by participating in the war effort.

In Chapter 3, I explore representations of the child at play. Wartime children's literature was a form of entertainment, but it also frequently *portrayed* the child being amused. Images of sporting activities and depictions of children engaged in imaginative play were common, and some texts included hands-on activities like arts and crafts. Children's literature from the war was full of images of children at play, which included hobbies like stamp-collecting and model-building, role-play as nurses, soldiers, and spies, and organized activities like the Boy Scouts and Girl Guides. In Fussell's words, "the drift of modern history domesticates the fantastic and normalizes the unspeakable" (74), and this is true of children's play during the war. Children's toys, for example, which included the ubiquitous toy soldier and miniature tanks, normalized the horrors of mechanized combat, while the war itself was often described as some type of great 'game' in literature for young readers. Despite the common image of the child at play, however, the concept of play as innocent fun was frequently undermined by a blurring of the boundary between it and work. Not only were toys shaped by the war, but imaginative play itself was often co-opted as part of the war effort. Whether pretending to be a soldier was viewed as training for military life, or purchasing certain toys was seen as a means of supporting the Allied cause, child's play was presented as deeply connected to the global conflict.

While images of children at play were common, so too were portrayals of child figures 'working' on the home front, which is the subject of Chapter 4. Growing food, practicing thrift, donating money, and making clothes for soldiers were common children's activities, and countless texts encourage participation by featuring child figures engaged in such work. In some instances, adult authors employ tactics designed to shame or coerce young readers into supporting the war effort, while in other instances they encourage young people's contributions by celebrating children's skills. Despite widespread encouragement of children helping on the home front, some authors suggest that childhood should be free from such duties, and some reinforce notions of youthful innocence by gently mocking the figure of the child helper. Together, these assorted representations reveal different views on children's responsibilities and capabilities.

Chapter 5 takes a closer look at the connection between young people and wartime recruitment efforts. It explores the chid figure as a tool used to encourage adult men to enlist and to prepare boys for enlistment. This was often done by appealing to the young reader's desire for adventure and glory, but also by promoting sacrifice as a virtue and employing shaming tactics. Girls and women played a role in these efforts, and they were also encouraged to embrace the virtues of bravery and sacrifice and make their own contributions near the front lines. Occasionally figured as combatants, young women were more commonly pictured participating in dangerous but exhilarating work as nurses and ambulance drivers. By presenting different messages about child innocence and the responsibility of adults to protect the young (and, by extension, the nation's future), children's literature raises important questions about how readers may have seen themselves and internalized messages about the agency of young citizens and their obligations to the state.

I move from considering how children's literature encouraged recruitment to looking more directly in Chapter 6 at representations of boy soldiers. Many authors went to great lengths to suggest that boy soldiers had a proud history among the Allied nations, and they cited examples from many past conflicts. The figure of the boy soldier naturalized the connection between children and warfare and, while it often embraced conventional notions of masculinity, this figure also represented a version of masculinity that was less reliant on physical strength, and more dependent on qualities like bravery, patriotism, and sacrifice. Depictions of boy soldiers were not all celebratory, however, for the praise often given to Allied youngsters was very different from the condemnation Germany typically received for its use of underage fighters. These varied figures show how adult writers could utilize the child for different purposes and they reflect shifting views of children's agency during a time of significant upheaval.

The book's final chapter examines how child figures were used to construct different images of the German foe. In any war, views of the enemy play a key role in garnering support for (or creating opposition to) military conflict and are central to most propaganda efforts. While a hostile attitude towards Germany is common in First World War children's literature, the portrayal of the enemy is more complex than one might first suspect. Some British writers, for instance, acknowledge the long-standing cultural ties between Germany and Britain, while many North American writers observe that relations with Germany have been largely peaceful. They also recognize that there have been long periods of emigration from Germany, and some Canadian and American writers express anxiety over how this could impact national unity. Consequently, while portrayals of Germany are predominantly negative and often revolve around the enemy's cruel treatment of children, there are a number that challenge this image and use the child figure to represent Germany in a more positive light, partly with an eye to fostering postwar peace. In the process of depicting Germans as alternately brutal, comical, or sympathetic, Allied writers reveal something about how they conceptualize their own national identities.

This book brings to light some forgotten children's literature from the First World War and, in doing so, explores more fully the different influences that shaped children's literature of the time. It demonstrates that child figures served several functions and appeared in many guises that went well beyond that of the helpless victim of war. As Cook and Wall argue, children "find themselves caught in the mesh of armed conflict but, unlike others, are also entangled in severely constrained images of childhood which have historical, ideological, cultural, and political origins and consequences" (1). Examining how children and childhood were envisioned by adults in a time of war, and how these visions were presented to child readers, may help us uncover how literature shaped children's own understandings of what it meant to be a child, and what it meant to be an adult. This detailed exploration of literature from both sides of the Atlantic also sheds new light on the role that children's reading material may have played in shaping lasting notions of femininity, masculinity, citizenship, and duty among a generation that would live to experience the Second World War.

Notes

1 Some recent studies include Rosie Kennedy's *The Children's War: Britain, 1914–1918* (2014), Susan Fisher's *Boys and Girls in No Man's Land: English-Canadian Children and the First World War* (2011), David Budgen's *British Children's Literature and the First World War: Representations Since 1914* (2018), Paul, Johnston, and Short's edited collection *Children's Literature and Culture of the First World War* (2016), and Celia Kingsbury's discussion of children in *For Home and Country: World War I Propaganda on the Home Front* (2010).

2 For an important study of First World War German children's literature see Zunino's 2019 book *Die Mobilmachung der Kinder im Ersten Weltkrieg: Kriegskultur und illustrierte Kriegskinderliteratur im Deutschen Kaiserreich (1911–1918).*

3 In particular, Canada imported a great deal of literature from Britain and the United States as its own publishing industry was still developing.

4 In *From Nursery Rhymes to Nationhood: Children's Literature and the Construction of Canadian Identity* (Routledge 2008) I discuss the long and complicated history between Britain, Canada, and the United States and its impact on children's literature.

5 Budgen argues that "a racial hierarchy can be seen in the works of this period" (49). He notes, for example, that while Indian troops were "frequently depicted in novels and story papers [...] they never featured as the central protagonists" (45). While the diversity of the British Empire and the Allied forces was often celebrated by authors from Britain and North America, child characters were predominantly white.

6 The number of children charged with a crime in Britain increased noticeably over the course of the war, "from 37,500 children under 16 charged each year to 51,000 by 1917" (Hendrick 113).

7 As many have suggested, each generation seems to raise these fears, and concerns about a rise in juvenile delinquency have sometimes been "created" in moments of social upheaval "because of heightened fears of a changing economic, social and political environment that appeared to threaten traditional relationships" (Wegs 603).

1 Family Ties and Family Feuds

National Identities in a Time of War

When war broke out, Britain, Canada, and the United States were bound by a complex set of relationships that had been evolving over the preceding century. Canada was part of the British Empire, but also had a strong sense of individuality and shared an extremely important relationship with the United States. Similarly, the United States was completely independent from Britain, yet it too became embroiled in what was initially considered a "European" war. The three nations differed from one another in many ways, but as allies they also had much in common. Portrayals of these multidimensional relationships were closely linked to representations of children, who often served as embodiments of the state.

As this book will show, children's literature was influenced by the overarching themes of nationhood and empire that were central to the conflict, and representations of children and childhood were clearly entwined with ideas about patriotism, citizenship, and national identity. Authors frequently employed child figures in an effort to strengthen patriotic sentiment and encourage support for the war, but in addition to fostering nationalism, many championed the collective Allied cause, highlighting similarities and connections between different countries. Writers on both sides of the Atlantic envisioned a future in which Britain's empire would still be a powerful entity, but Canadian and American writers also focussed on the growth and development of their own countries, even as they embraced their wartime alliance with Britain. Employing images and metaphors of the child and the family, children's literature served to convey a range of messages about each nation, its complicated relationships with others, and the rights and responsibilities of the child citizen.

The Imperial Child as Metaphor: Representing Imperial Relations

Prior to the First World War, children's culture had long played an instrumental role in teaching young Britons about empire. As M. Daphne Kutzer notes, "imperial imagery" was sometimes in the foreground of

DOI: 10.4324/9781003191605-2

children's stories, and sometimes in the background, but its "ubiquitous presence in children's texts is no surprise. Empire was everywhere in British culture" and played "an important role in everything from Christmas pantomimes to music hall songs to children's periodicals to advertising" (xiv). Hugh Cunningham claims, similarly, that "if anything established empire in the minds of Britain's children, it was probably not so much [...] overt efforts at propaganda as the books and the magazines that children read and the toys [...] with which they played" (181). In many ways, British children's literature from 1914 to 1919 is similar in style and content to that published in the pre-war period, and for some writers, the war simply provided a different backdrop for adventure tales that perpetuated established views on British imperialism and Britain's colonial subjects. Yet the war marked a critical turning point for the empire and much children's literature of the period reflects the changes taking place.

One manifestation of the figure of the child in wartime literature is what I term 'the imperial child,' which writers used both to glorify the British empire and to help preserve its strength in the face of widespread geopolitical upheaval. Even though the war represented a united effort on the part of Britain and its allies, there was at the same time an awareness that old bonds were loosening. Despite Germany's defeat, the war led to fundamental changes in Britain's empire, and the fact that "the British empire expanded after 1919 should not obscure that some of the key catalysts for the imperial unravelling that followed another world war crystallized" during the First World War (Grayzel 405). Indeed, the very fact that so many child readers were urged to be loyal imperial citizens betrays existing concerns that the empire's bonds were not as strong as some writers desired. It is certainly the case that within Canada, even as there were vocal pro-imperial factions, many people also saw the war as a chance for the nation to make its own mark in the world. The figure of the imperial child suggests that a strong British empire was seen as vital to defeating Germany and securing global peace, but it also shows that encouraging children to celebrate empire was about strengthening an unstable imperial identity and bolstering wavering loyalty. Young readers thus consumed literature in which the imperial child served as a symbol of unity, even as the stories being told revealed that the power and identities of different nations were being altered by participation in the war.

A vocal supporter of empire was the popular *Boy's Own Paper*, which ran from 1879–1967 and was widely marketed and read overseas, its international readership being very important to its success (Penner 641). Throughout the war the *B.O.P.* championed Britain's cause and celebrated the accomplishments of the empire. The 1914–1915 *Annual*, for example, contains the poem "The Children of the Flag,"[1] which employs the common metaphor of Britain as parent to a large imperial family. The poem's opening stanzas describe the British as a "Northern race" that has chosen to fight and die to honour its promise to safeguard "Freedom," but the poem is really about the supposed feelings of Britain's "far-sundered folk." It is the members of the empire beyond Britain's shores – the "children of the flag" – whose voices are heard throughout most of the poem. Britain's vast territories, from warm "distant isles" to "many a rugged" snow-covered peak, are described as affectionate and dutiful "blood-kin" who rush "from far and wide across the tide" to protect the parental figure ("Children").

The poet provides a classic example of pro-imperial sentiment and envisions Britain as a parent to loving "children" who are "ready to come to the roll of the drum/For Empire and the King" ("Children"). Not all members of the empire were "blood-kin" of the British, however, so ancestral connections are not enough to explain the empire's apparent strength and unity. According to this poem, it is the values of "freedom" and "honour" Britain allegedly represents that lie at the heart of the empire's supposed strength, and its offspring declare themselves ready to defend "the Flag that keeps us free" in order to save the world from German tyranny ("Children").

Another poem from the same volume of the *Boy's Own Annual* for 1914–1915 echoes this celebration of imperial loyalty by utilizing the same type of parent/child imagery. Describing Britain as a "mother" who "looked forth in sorrow" at the raging war, it asks, "Shall she be left unaided,/Fighting her battle alone?" ("Loyalty!"). The answer is clear:

> Nay! they press round, the children,
> Crying with eager tone:
> Loyalty! Loyalty! All have been ready,
> Faithfull, courageous, true-hearted, and strong.
> Loyalty! Loyalty! Simple and steady,
> In one great union peals forth the glad song.
>
> ("Loyalty!")

Here, the empire is presented as a unified whole, bound together by ties stronger than any differences of "race and creed." From "India's brave sons" to "Englishmen! Sons of fair Britain," the members of the empire are described as children of "Fair England," and their loyalty is applauded repeatedly ("Loyalty!"). As in "Children of the Flag," the child is responsible for protecting the mother and the poet inverts the traditional dynamic in which the mother is the protector of her progeny, embracing instead the idea that children must show fealty to their elders.

As Cunningham notes, children and empire

> were linked like mother and child, the empire often referred to as 'Mother Empire'. For the future of the British empire depended on its children. If they were ignorant of the imperial dream, or if they were indifferent to it, or if [...] they were hostile to it, then the future might be bleak.
>
> (179–180)

While Cunningham is referring to British children, the poem "Loyalty!" shows that the child beyond Britain's shores was also crucial to the empire's future. The metaphor of "Mother Empire" presented the colonies as symbolic children but was also designed to discourage indifference or hostility to the "imperial dream" on the part of real children within Britain and abroad.

"The Drum" by John Lea[2] is another poem published in the 1914–1915 edition of the *Boy's Own Annual* that relies on the metaphor of the empire as family to extol the contributions of soldiers from around the globe. It describes the sound of a drum rolling westward across the Atlantic to Canada, continuing across the continent to the Pacific, and crossing the ocean to "Australasia's coral bar" (315), from which point it rolls onward still:

> Thus round the world as swift as dawn,
> The message of the Drum had gone,
> And ere its earliest echo died
> Came the response in love and pride:
> "Mother of Nations, east and west,
> We gladly, proudly, give our best
> To follow afar through the pain and woe
> The freest flag that the world can show.
> We hear the call of the Empire's Drum!
> Mother of Nations, see! – we come!"
>
> (Lea)

These lines establish the empire as a vast global network of family ties. Referring to Britain as "Mother of Nations," Lea presents members of the empire as faithful children coming without hesitation to the aid of their parent.

Such images of Britain as a loving mother to doting offspring are present in innumerable works for child readers, including *The Child's ABC of the War* (1914) by Geoffrey Whitworth. The letter "C" stands "for our colonies, loyal and true/Bringing help to their mother from over the blue." The accompanying illustration by Stanley North depicts four young children approaching a seated woman, Britannia, with three of the children bearing flags marked "Canada," "Australia," and "India."

In an era when children were regularly schooled in the importance of honouring parents, this image would have spoken to the child reader's ingrained understanding of the need to show fealty to one's elders (Figure 1.1). It reinforces the lesson that children should be obedient, rendering them subordinate within the family hierarchy, but it also recognizes them as clear constituents within the imperial fold.

While Whitworth and North depict the colonies as devoted children, it is worth noting that not all imperial offspring appear to be equal members of the family. The illustration betrays contemporary attitudes towards race and highlights the fact that certain colonies enjoyed greater status within the empire than others. Three of the children are white and blonde and are identified by the flags they carry, which are emblazoned with the names of specific countries. Following behind them is a black child, who carries a plate loaded with tropical fruits, but who does not have a flag. All four children are pictured as supplicants (Canada comes bearing a boat, Australia a cannon and soldiers, and India carries a bag over his shoulder), but the last child lacks the clear identity of the

Figure 1.1 Illustration by Stanley North from *The Child's ABC of the War*, 1914. [FSU Digital Repository].

others. Without a flag, the racialized child is less explicitly connected to the ideas of nationhood and citizenship. Similarly, while all four children are drawn in profile, the white children have facial features that are clearly visible, making them more individualized, whereas the black child is presented simply as a silhouette whose dark skin is his only clear physical feature.

Whitworth's text and its accompanying illustrations reveal that while calls for support appeared across the empire,

> calculations of whose contributions most mattered and would be most effective weighed class, gender, race, ethnicity, and geography. Such unity as could be forged relied on the elevation of a potentially common, imperial identity that elided differences, often at the expense of marginalized groups.
>
> (Grayzel 393)

North's illustration of the colonies simultaneously elides the significant differences between India, Australia, and Canada – by presenting all three children as blonde and white, for instance – and elevates the importance of the contributions of those nations over those of the nameless colonies represented by the racialized child. Despite the crucial participation of black colonial people in the First World War, a "hierarchy of 'Britishness' was created in which white Britons enjoyed superior status, with black Britons from the empire/Commonwealth possessing a lesser British identity" (Jenkinson 209).

While the images in *The Child's ABC of the War* provide a visual rendering of imperial and racial hierarchy, North's illustration represents all four children as loyal, and similar claims about imperial unity are made by well-known English author Mrs. Belloc Lowndes[3] in *Told in Gallant Deeds: A Child's History of the War* (1914). In this instance, however, rather than 'the child' serving as a broad metaphor for nations within the empire, an individual Canadian child acts as a representative example. Lowndes recalls Canadian soldiers arriving in England in the first year of the war and notes that one of the "strangest" things about this group was that it included

> a little boy! He had been a paper boy, and he was so eager to come with the Canadians that one regiment smuggled him into their ship. By the time they landed in England the little chap had blossomed into a bugler!
>
> (79–80)

Lowndes describes this young participant as a strange thing to find in a regiment, but also lauds him as a symbol of imperial vigour, showing how the figure of the militarized child functioned in different ways (something I discuss elsewhere in this book). In this instance, the Canadian boy is not a victim of war, but instead has "blossomed" because of his participation. Both the empire, and the child within, are thus strengthened through participation in the conflict, rather than harmed by it.

Lowndes is full of praise for Canada's apparent devotion to the cause and quotes a song sung by some members of the Canadian cavalry in which they declare their intention "To make the Kaiser understand/He must respect our Motherland" (80). Canadians, Lowndes makes clear, think of Britain as their "mother" and proudly defend her. Such accounts of devotion would likely seem unremarkable to young English readers, not only because loyalty to Britain was so clearly and frequently promoted as a desirable and fundamental English trait, but also because representations of "mother" Britain receiving due respect from her imperial "offspring" reflect contemporary views on the hierarchal relationship between parents and children. Readers' attitudes towards imperial relations were thus potentially influenced by their understanding of their own status as subservient children.

Relying on the assumption that children accept their position as subordinates, literature celebrating imperial loyalty works to make the young reader both an obedient child and a dutiful citizen. But just as not all children happily obey their parents, not all child readers would have unquestioningly submitted to the demands of the nation. Similarly, not all nations believed in unconditional loyalty to the empire, especially if they felt that Britain took this for granted. A tendency to conflate the achievements of colonial forces with those of the British, rather than to see them as distinct accomplishments,[4] often aroused feelings of hostility, and even among "dominion citizens most loyal to Britain, resentment grew over what they perceived as British arrogance and indifference" (Robb 106). Some soldiers "bristled at the haughty and condescending manner of the British officer class" and some believed "that incompetent British commanders were sacrificing dominion troops needlessly" (106).

Class divisions and other tensions meant that even within Britain itself, unwavering allegiance was not universal. Grayzel argues,

> When popular memory/history/commemoration enshrines loss and sacrifice as the dominant experience of the war, it rarely looks back to what Britain was like before the war: to the grinding poverty, ill health, and lack of resources faced by much of the population. [...] So buried is our understanding of working- class life before and during the war that the shifts in lived experiences affected by the war—including those of [...] children—must all be contextualized across Britain, let alone its imperial outposts.
>
> (404)

These observations remind us that the experience of being a British subject differed greatly between social classes and across the empire, likely impacting readers' responses to the ubiquitous metaphor of a nurturing Mother Britain and the accompanying calls for loyalty that appeared in so much children's literature.

Growing Pains: Envisioning the Future of the Imperial "Family"

While many English children may have enjoyed examples of imperial loyalty and believed that a strong empire was crucial for defeating Germany, the same may not have been true of readers in other nations. One question to consider is how being figured as an imperial child may have affected readers' own sense of national identity and allegiance. While in some instances this literature would doubtless have resonated with children eager to display loyalty to Britain, for many the war was an opportunity for their own country to prove its merits and celebrate its achievements. In the same way that attitudes towards children and childhood were shifting during the war, varying depictions of the imperial "family" show that Britain's empire was transforming.

Children's publications praised wartime contributions by members of the empire and presented this apparent loyalty as evidence of Britain's benevolent rule, but many accounts unintentionally reveal underlying tensions. A representative example is "Lord Kitchener and the Indian Princes" from the *Jolly Book for Boys and Girls* (c. 1918) edited by Edward Shirley.[5] It celebrates India's loyalty to Britain, but inadvertently suggests there may have been cracks that Germany hoped to take advantage of:

> Every boy and every girl knows how loyal the Indian princes have been to Britain during her time of sore trial. The Germans thought that when war broke out in Europe the people of India would try to drive the British out of the country, and that we should be obliged to send many of our white soldiers to India to hold down the natives. This would use up our men and our money, and we should, therefore, not be able to fight the Germans with all our strength. But in this, as in many other respects, the Germans have been woefully disappointed.
>
> (194)

By asserting that "every boy and girl knows" about India's loyalty, the writer very deliberately brings British children into this discussion of the empire and presents them as rightly confident in its strength, but the piece also unconsciously implies there are weaknesses Germany hoped to exploit.

The author mentions Germany's strategy of sending "agents to India" to make "the natives rise against" Britain but assures young readers that this effort was doomed because the people of India "know that Britain is their best friend, and that we have always treated them justly" (194). The reference to German agents may allude to the violent *Ghadar* movement, which challenged British rule in India and was aided by "German agents in the neutral U.S. and across Asia" who "helped to channel *Ghadar* recruits and smuggle arms for the rebellion" (McGetchin 19). These happenings included an uprising in 1915, yet the author of the essay from the *Jolly Book* pays no heed to these incidents and instead presents the empire as unshakeable, crediting Britain's alleged commitment to justice. The essay constructs an image of beneficent and placid British governance and fails to acknowledge that unrest was part of the history of imperial rule in India (as evidenced by the "Mutiny" of 1857, for example), or to address the question of why Germany might have anticipated successfully fomenting rebellion. While denying that there was significant strife in India, the piece inadvertently betrays that the British were prepared to send soldiers "to hold down the natives" in instances of turmoil, undermining the assertion that the empire is harmonious and Britain kind and gentle in its rule.[6]

Although the author of this piece uses the family metaphor to describe the empire, it appears that some nations are closer kin than others. The author writes, "you and I must never forget how loyal the Indian princes and peoples have been to Britain, and we must do our best to welcome them within the family circle of the British nations" (197). This declaration clearly implies that India is not yet "within the family circle," and telling child readers "we must do our best" suggests that this effort is not easy, and success not guaranteed. Thus, although it celebrates the empire, the essay also betrays doubts and anxieties, hinting at troubles that existed in India and elsewhere and that became increasingly apparent in the war's aftermath.

Many authors seemingly attempted to reassure children of the empire's strength at a time when it was undergoing dramatic change and when the war itself had been largely caused by competition among Europe's imperial powers. Another writer who hints at the possibility of the disintegration of the British empire, even as she seeks to convince readers of its strength, is Lowndes, who declares that the Germans "were foolish enough to think when the war broke out [...] that the great Dominions [...] would seize the opportunity to desert the Empire" (78). Instead, she says,

> Irishmen of all parties rushed to enlist. A great wave of passionate loyalty swept over India. [...] Regiments of magnificent native soldiers [...] were granted the dearest wish of their hearts, namely to fight shoulder to shoulder with our white troops.
>
> (79)

By citing these and other contributions, Lowndes neatly dismisses any notion of trouble, assuring young readers of the empire's solidity.

In Lowndes's rendering, the war has strengthened and underscored the importance of Britain's bonds with other nations and has unified British society. She tells readers that "the outbreak of war seemed to bring us all nearer together, rich and poor alike" (80). Lowndes's work was first published in November 1914, but by the time the third impression was published in June 1917 there was abundant evidence that the relationships within the empire were far more complicated than the metaphor of a united nuclear family would suggest. In suggesting that fighting alongside white soldiers was the "dearest wish" of the Indian Army, Lowndes ignores the rising anger about racial injustice that helped inspire India's Home Rule movement and overlooks the fact that many soldiers of colour, including those born in Britain, saw the war as an opportunity to demonstrate their equality, not just their loyalty to empire (O'Connor 231). Similarly, Lowndes acknowledges the thousands of Irish fighters who enlisted during the war but neglects to mention that there were also Irishmen who "questioned why they should volunteer to die for a country that did not offer them citizenship or equal rights" (Pennell 184).

Many wartime authors boast about the empire but fail to acknowledge that many colonies' efforts to help Britain were motivated by the hope that participating in the war would lead to greater autonomy and equality. The idea that the war meant greater equality among people and nations is suggested to school-aged readers in a 1918 work by American writer Herbert Myrick[7]: "Black men, yellow men, white men, from all quarters of the globe, are fighting side by side to free the world from the Hun peril. That's patriotism of equality!" Indirectly touching on concerns about nations' independence that were circulating within the empire, Myrick presents the contributions of global allies not as signs of fealty, but as choices made by the equals of Britain.

Myrick's words suggest that "racialized subjects could be motivated by the overarching aim of using their wartime service as the basis for demands for equal treatment from the state" (Grayzel 389), but similar motivations can also be ascribed to Canada and Australia, where most of the population at that time was of white European ancestry. In both countries, wartime contributions were seen by some as a means of achieving a greater share of power within the empire, and by others as a route to complete independence. Additionally, both during and following the war, participation in the conflict helped to support the narrative that each of these large and diverse Dominions was, as Heather Sharp says of Australia, "a nation in its own right, distinct from Great Britain and its empire" that was "brought together" by participation in the war (3).

Some British children's writers, attuned to the ways in which war was transforming relationships between nations, did explore the nuances of British imperialism in their writing. In the 1914–1915 *Boy's*

Own Annual, for instance, which contains the very pro-imperial works that I have discussed above, there is another piece titled "Thinking Imperially" that is less about applauding loyalty to Britain, and more about considering how the empire is changing. The author attempts to define "imperialism" by distinguishing Britain from empires of old. Citing leaders like Caesar and Napoleon, he argues that their "leading idea" was to acquire territory and kill those who attempted to wrest it from them and says this "was the old imperial idea, and a very bad one." Rather than trying "to exterminate or enslave other nations," Britain should aim "to be foremost in every good work" because a strong Empire, he contends, is not built on might and aggression, but on love.

The author recognizes that change is happening, but sees this as all the more reason why it is crucial to foster bonds based on a set of common values:

> You see, by the time you boys reach middle age, if not sooner, the Commonwealth of Australia, the Dominion of Canada, the Union of South Africa, and the Dominion of New Zealand will probably have grown as great and powerful as the United States of to-day. If, by wise statesmanship, by the spirit of friendship and conciliation, by remembering that the bonds that never break are the bonds of freedom, these lusty young nations are still kept within the fold of the British Empire, what a magnificent, what a powerful empire it will be.
>
> (Old One)

Anticipating some of the changes that will result from the war, the author prepares young readers for a new reality. He is defining, or redefining, what imperialism means and he frames it as a union based on shared values, rather than on conquest and hierarchy:

> The *true imperialist* hopes and prays that the British Empire of the future shall stand for peace and justice; for all that makes life bright and cheerful; for religion, for science, for art, for letters, for beauty, for all those things which make men great and splendid.
>
> (Old One)

Although not explicitly pacifist, the article does state that armed conflict "exhausts a country, robs it of its vitality, whereas, on the other hand, peace supplies abundantly all the conditions of progress and plenty." Acknowledging that traditional imperial power dynamics are root causes of the war, the author leads young readers to envision a new type of empire in which the colonies are part of a brotherhood, rather than beholden offspring. Arguing that "a cord of love" is a "stronger unifying force" than "a ring of steel" (Old One), the author of "Thinking

Imperially" urges boy readers to embrace peace, justness, and equality, and anticipates a time "when 'men shall brothers be the wide world o'er'." He presents "might is right" as a distinctly German attitude at odds with the tenor of British imperialism, but he does not advocate for an end of empire altogether. In a bid to reframe the narrative of the British empire and preserve harmony within, the author employs the metaphor of a bond between brothers, rather than the more unequal relationship between parent and child. Revealing an awareness of the changes taking place because of the war, including increasing demands for self-determination within the empire, he asks young readers to envision new ways by which Britain's strength can be maintained.

Dutiful Offspring or Rebellious Child? Canada's Changing Role on the World Stage

One member of the empire profoundly impacted by the war was Canada, and its participation was presented in varying ways in British and North American children's literature. Some texts celebrated Canadian independence, others cited Canadian achievements as evidence of Britain's glorious rule, and many did both, often using the figure of the Canadian child to foster pride in both empire and nation. For example, "How they Honoured the Captain" by A. T. M., published in *The British Story-Book: Tales of Adventure in Canada, Australia, Africa, India, &c.* (1916), opens with the words "Three cheers for Canada!" Employing the stereotype of Canada as a wintry land, it depicts a group of children racing toboggans, including one "named the *Maple Leaf*, flying the Canadian flag." The children are enjoying an unexpected "half-holiday" because the

> papers had brought the good news of a notable battle in Europe. And of the brave Canadian soldiers who had gone to fight for right and freedom, side by side with their British brothers, Captain X, of the little town of M—, in Canada, had been singled out for special mention and distinguished honour.

This story points to the fact that Canadian forces played crucial roles in certain battles and suggests that military achievements were celebrated by Canadian children, especially when local men were involved. However, no specific details are given about which "notable battle" prompted the sudden holiday from school. If we accept Paul Fussell's assertion that terming certain moments in years of long-drawn-out fighting "*battles*" and giving them specific place names "is to suggest that these events parallel Blenheim and Waterloo not only in glory but in structure and meaning" (9), then A. T. M.'s failure to provide specific details diminishes the significance of Canadian experiences. The lack of information about the battle being celebrated, combined with the generic winter setting, contribute to the feeling that this tale is really intended for British, rather than Canadian, readers. The figure of the child rejoicing in Canada's military success is not necessarily intended to promote Canadian national pride, but rather to show young Britons that they can be proud of their empire. The description of British and Canadian soldiers as "brothers" further implies that Canadian victories can be regarded as British successes.

Another work that shows how Canadian and British identities were sometimes blurred is "A Canadian Soldier's Story," published anonymously in *Young Canada: An Illustrated Magazine for Boys* in 1916. Despite its title, this magazine was British-centric[8] and although this story mentions Canada directly, it also shows how Canadian and British identities were often presented as overlapping or interchangeable. Although the title suggests this is about a "Canadian" soldier, the eponymous hero was born and raised in England before travelling to Canada in early adulthood and is referred to as a "Britisher" by the narrator. The sketch gives an account of the "adventures" that

> befell him in the many capacities in which he was engaged, which included that of actor [...], lion-tamer's assistant, 'Buffalo Bill's' cowboy, [...] big-game hunter, a guide to a party of English noblemen through Alberta, concluding with his going with Stefansson's last expedition, in 1914.

The man experiences some extraordinary hardships while in the wilds of Canada, once even sewing-up "his own leg-wound with needle and thread," which all seem to prepare him for the next "adventure" of being a soldier. As soon as he hears news of the war, he embarks "on a two months' trek" to get to the nearest railway station where he purchases a ticket for England. He subsequently joins the British Army because "he is anxious to have a 'go' at the Huns" and the narrator remarks that the British Empire is composed of such "men who have been attracted to the ranks of the British Army in defence of liberty, honour, and humanity, and all that civilisation holds dear."

While on the surface this story appears to portray Canadians favourably, the centrality of Britain to the protagonist's identity, as well as the tale's use of familiar tropes of imperial romance (including a dangerous "Indian" character that threatens the white hero), suggest that Canada is merely an exotic backdrop where exhilarating adventures allow the intrepid Briton to prove his courage. The reliance on familiar devices of the genre suggests that this is not the "authenticated" account the narrator claims, and that Canada functions primarily as a means of showcasing the pluck of the young Briton and assuring British readers of the empire's strength.

Despite being titled the story of "a Canadian soldier," the tale celebrates the loyalty of the British-born protagonist who sets forth to defend his homeland the moment he learns of the war. His fluid identity is an example of how Canada and Britain were often conflated in children's stories, and how representations of the empire as a harmonious "family" often ignored distinct national characteristics and ambitions. The soldier's identity is flexible as he moves readily between both nations and is described as being in "the ranks of the British Army" with no mention made of the Canadian Corps, even though many Canadians did not want the nation's troops subsumed by the British Army. While Canadian soldiers took orders from the British military, there was a keen interest in keeping the Canadian units distinct that was motivated in part by a desire to "make Canada's contribution to the war effort more prominent, giving the Canadian government more recognition and influence among the Allied states" (Weir 6). Although the lack of adequately trained Canadian military personnel in 1914 meant that initially "the British chain of command made [...] Canadian Corps staff appointments with little regard for whether an officer was Canadian or British" (Delaney 936), as the war progressed "Canadian political authorities insisted that their officers be groomed for command and staff appointments in Canadian formations" (936). Accordingly, casually conflating the British Army with Canada's troops was something of a sore spot for many Canadians, and children's narratives that do so are at odds with the ongoing effort to acknowledge certain moments of combat as distinctly Canadian achievements.

One author who makes sure to highlight Canada's specific military achievements for young Canadian readers is Emily Weaver.[9] In the 1919 edition of her textbook *A Canadian History for Boys and Girls* she writes of the fighting at Ypres and paints a heroic picture of Canada's soldiers:

> In the misty moonlight, soon after midnight, 2,000 Canadians charged into the midst of 7,000 Germans, drove them from the wood and retook the guns. Nor was that all. For days the Canadians, outflanked, unsupported by heavy artillery, held grimly on against overwhelming odds till reinforcements came. The cost was enormous, but, as Lloyd George, the British Premier, put it, they stood like the Rocky Mountains, "held high the honour of Canada, and saved the British army."
>
> (Weaver 355)

What is particularly significant about this passage is its account of the British acknowledging the importance of Canada's contribution. Unlike the tales discussed above in which Canadians are described as "brothers" to, or indistinguishable from, British troops, in Weaver's text Lloyd

George himself declares that Canada "saved the British army," reflecting a widely held feeling within Canada that the nation had come into its own through its role in the war.

There has long been a popular assertion in Canada that "the war meant nothing less than the birth of the nation" (Vance 228). I think this claim is overstated and that Canadians had a strong sense of national identity and pride since at least the mid-nineteenth century, which included commemorating its participation in earlier armed conflicts.[10] Nevertheless, it is true that the First World War did bring unprecedented global attention to Canadian military achievements and that these experiences further shaped the nation's identity. Within Canada there was so much interest in the activities of the Canadian forces that "[i]t became a truism to assert that Canada gained its status as a nation through the heroism shown by its soldiers on the battlefield" (Vance 228). If the war did, indeed, spark "the awakening of a national consciousness" (228), it did so in part because of a concerted effort to foment national pride in Canadian children.

Although young Canadians were an audience for British and American publications during the war, they also consumed homegrown ones like Weaver's which show that, in addition to reading pro-imperial rhetoric, the nation's children were subject to an effort to aggressively cultivate a sense of Canadian pride and identity, and that battles like Ypres and Vimy played a central role in this.[11] While some of this material contains metaphors describing the Canadians and the British as members of a "family," it also shows a desire for Canada's independence and individuality to be recognized.

One work that envisions a future in which the nation is more independent from Britain is Edith Lelean Groves's 1917 school play *The Wooing of Miss Canada*.[12] Designed to be performed by children, the play is decidedly patriotic, its premise being that Jack Canuck wants to marry Miss Canada who has several other suitors. John Bull is Miss Canada's father, but when he expresses his surprise that his daughter has wooers, saying he considers her still "but a child among the nations" (15), her Fairy Godmother replies, "John Bull, I fear you are behind the times. Nowadays, suitors do not first consult the fathers" (16). The fairy's suggestion that Canada is no longer "a child" and that John Bull is a relic of the past, combined with the fact that Miss Canada weighs her marriage options without her father's input, all symbolize Canada's increasing independence from Britain (and perhaps echo changing gender norms during the war). As the drawbacks of marrying either Uncle Sam or Germany emerge, Miss Canada's autonomy is underscored by her final decision to wed Jack Canuck, and the union of the two solidifies the image of Canadian independence.

Miss Canada's choice is based largely on the fact that Jack Canuck is dedicated, first and foremost, to protecting Canada's interests. After

Germany threatens her, Jack Canuck (in the costume of a soldier) rushes to her rescue, saying,

> 'Touch Canada at your peril! [...]. She has men [...] brave and stalwart, ready at a moment's notice to don the khaki[13] and march away to defend her shores, should foreign foe attack. And Jack Canuck, typifying the youth of Canada, ready to shed the last drop of blood in her defence, bids Germany's Ambassador, Begone!'
>
> (29)

Significantly, Groves describes Canadian soldiers as defending *Canada's* shores, not England's, suggesting Canada's contribution to the war is more than just the performance of imperial duty.

Choosing to marry Jack Canuck, Miss Canada says,

> No longer do I care for empty titles, for crowns, for thrones, for a long line of ancestry [...]. I want a suitor who will love Canada for herself alone, who will safeguard her interests, who will fight her battles whether at home or on the fields of France or Flanders.
>
> (30)

Turning her back on "courtly grandeur" and long ancestry does not simply represent Canada's rejection of Germany, but of Britain too. This rebuff of "crowns" and "thrones" is evidence of the fact that even though loyalty to empire

> was one product of the First World War, it was not the entire story. At the same time powerful currents pushed the Empire in a different direction, highlighting local national and racial identities in opposition to an all-embracing British imperial conception of the relationship between centre and periphery.
>
> (Jackson and Kitchen 9)

By having her protagonist relegate John Bull to the sidelines and make her own decision to marry her fellow Canadian, Groves situates Canada at the centre of things rather than on the "periphery" of the British empire. In saying that the ideal Canadian man must "safeguard her interests" and "fight her battles whether at home" or abroad, Miss Canada sends a message to young children about the importance of defending Canada against its enemies and pictures the battles in places like France and Flanders as decidedly *Canadian* battles. Absent here is a sense that Canadians are fighting simply as loyal British subjects; it is Canada itself that they are fighting for.

Groves's play provides a good example of how children's literature that supported Britain's cause could, nevertheless, promote a specifically Canadian sense of pride in wartime accomplishments and a sense of national identity distinct from Britain's. The First World War "did not settle the position of the Dominions within the British imperial system, but merely produced a stronger desire that the blood sacrifices of wartime needed to be rewarded with a greater degree of autonomy" (Jackson and Kitchen 10). Groves's interest in autonomy is evident in her Epilogue, which focusses explicitly on the future of the Canadian nation:

> 'The Twentieth Century is Canada's,' and as loyal Canadians we have faith in the future of our land. We must be ever on the alert to guard well her interests, to watch the immigration and see that undesirables do not enter and to ever remember our watchword, 'Canada for Canadians'.
>
> (32)

Groves's concern about immigration echoes that expressed in earlier works of Canadian children's literature that exhibited both a desire to see Canada grow, and anxiety that "incoming population could corrupt the nation" (Galway *From* 51). She does not clarify what would classify someone as "undesirable," but given comments made elsewhere in the play it is possible that this is an expression of anti-German sentiment and fear of enemy aliens. It may also reflect contemporary reservations about immigration in general, which ranged from worries that new immigrants might not share Canadian "values," to resentment of those from non-Anglophone or non-European nations that was based on notions of race (Galway *From* 51–52). Regardless of the criteria by which Groves would deem someone unwanted, her statement "Canada for Canadians" betrays an inward-looking tendency, suggesting that the war may have been just as likely to leave Canadians feeling hostile to those outside their borders as it was to inspire in them a sense of connection with foreign allies.

Groves's comments stand in contrast to the more outward looking ones of Weaver, who says,

> before the war, a great proportion of Canadians appeared to be very much taken up with the concerns of themselves and their own country, but the war has caused both Government and people to take broader and less self-centred views.
>
> (365)

The difference in these expressions reveals the varied responses to the war among Canadian children's writers. While Weaver seems to endorse greater international cooperation and suggests the war has given Canada a more global outlook, Groves's work indicates that the war may have also prompted a retreat, with the metaphor of "the family" applying primarily to those within Canada's borders, and only to those who fit a certain set of criteria.

While Groves expresses concern about the threat immigration might pose to national unity and identity, another long-standing challenge was regionalism. Although the war saw many Canadians rally for a common cause, competition between provinces did not disappear. This is evident in *The Thrift Campaign in the Schools of Ontario: With a Brief Sketch of What Ontario Has Done in the War*. Published in 1919, this booklet emphasizes the importance of every child contributing to the efforts of the Canadian nation, but it also displays provincial bias. For instance, the author says that it is both "natural" and "right" that those living "in Ontario should think that they are citizens of the 'Banner Province' of the Dominion" (iv), and suggests the war is a source of pride for Ontario's children: "what Ontario has done should produce in every pupil, not a spirit of boastfulness, but a just pride that this Province has so nobly done what she could for the cause of civilization" ("Thrift" iv). Noting that as of June 1918 almost half of Canada's army recruits "came from Ontario" (iv), the author asks how "could the patriotism of this Province be more clearly shown than in this magnificent contribution?" (iv).

The Thrift Campaign shows that although writers appealed to children's national pride and celebrated military victories as national achievements, strong local and regional identities thrived. In this instance, the family metaphor is employed to suggest that provincial pride can be harnessed for the good of the entire nation:

> We are all Canadians. But there is a healthful spirit in each Province – a spirit which makes the nine Provinces of the Dominion act like nine sisters in the family, each of whom says to herself, "I must do as much as I can to help our mother – I must excel all of my sisters in this great labour of love." And, being one of the older sisters in the great family, this is how Ontario feels and acts.
>
> ("Thrift" iv)

In trying to inspire Ontario's schoolchildren to help the nation in the immediate aftermath of the war, the author employs a family metaphor, but in this instance, it is not Britain that is presented as the "mother" but Canada itself, with the various provinces depicted as dutiful children whose "healthful spirit" of sibling rivalry can be harnessed for the good of the whole.

In the face of internal divisions caused by responses to immigration, regionalism, and the debate over Conscription, many wartime writers envisioned the Canadian child as the means by which to secure a positive future for the nation. In *The Young Canadian Citizen: Studies in Ethics, Civics and Economics* (1919), which was published immediately following the war and designed for use in schools, J.O. Miller[14] states that the main "idea of this book is to set forth in as simple a way as possible some of the things that go to the making of Canadian citizenship" (iii), and he says that the nation "cannot [...] begin too soon to implant in the young lofty ideas of citizenship" (iv). Miller sees the child as central to the nation's success, even as he cautions that "unquestioning obedience" to the State was a negative attribute of German society that led to war (iii). Although so much wartime literature asks children to submit to the needs of nation and empire, just as it asks them to obey their elders, in his definition of the ideal Canadian citizen Miller seeks to balance obedience with a genuine desire to serve.

Courage is among the attributes that Miller uses to define the Canadian citizen and he cites the nation's soldiers at Ypres as examples for young people to follow (20), also remarking that young citizens should develop the physical strength and "bodily vigour" that Canadian soldiers embody (19). These comments show that "the healthy body of the child was an especially salient symbol" in Canada following the war and "became an indicator by which the nation's health and wellbeing could be measured [...] following the devastating years of World War I" (Moruzi "Embodying" 114). Yet, although Miller sees health and vitality as important national characteristics, he states that others are even more valuable. He declares that while the fearlessness displayed in war "is much to be admired, it is, after all, the least heroic form of courage, because so much of it is purely physical" (20). Miller observes that the "highest Courage is that which leads men to sacrifice their lives of their own free will. Such was the courage of our soldiers and sailors" (24).

Miller's argument that "free will" is precisely what makes the Canadian soldier's sacrifice heroic is in keeping with Amy Shaw's claim that "the 'citizen-soldier' was an important part of the myth of the war, and voluntary service was necessary to maintain that character of Canadian identity" (25). As the children's literature discussed throughout this book shows, there were means other than conscription by which young men were shamed, coerced, and encouraged to enlist, raising the question of whether Canadian soldiers truly had "free will," or whether Miller's assertion that they did is another form of mythologizing the war.

Despite Miller's declaration that Britain "is worthy of our deepest love" (56), his focus is on Canada itself. He writes that "soldiers on the fields of France and Flanders have made glorious the name of Canada. [...] Their sacrifice will make our country a better place for the young Canadian citizen than it ever was before" (Miller 56–57). Describing the war as a turning point, he draws a clear connection between children and nation-building, writing that the primary "object of the education of Canadian boys and girls is to make good citizens" (79). Miller declares that every child "must learn the lesson that he owes to this country, personal service, in his childhood, in youth, in maturity" (83). He suggests that military service "is only a small part of what is called national service" and that this

> means service to the State in the ordinary things of life by boys and girls [...]. It means that in a true democracy there is something at all times higher than one's personal aims [...]. It is the good of all, the gain of the nation.
>
> (Miller 83)

From Neutral Bystander to Frontline Ally: Representing the Role of the United States

In envisioning Canada's future, one important relationship writers explored was that between Canada and the United States. *The Wooing of Miss Canada*, for example, reveals that while America was an important ally in the latter part of the war, there was also a desire among Canadians to maintain independence from the United States.[15] When Uncle Sam proposes marriage, Miss Canada replies, "Canada feels very kindly towards the United States, particularly at this time when our boys are fighting side by side in France, but I think we are better friends just as good neighbors than if a closer union existed" (26–27). This speech pictures the two nations as strong allies, but Miss Canada's rejection of Uncle Sam also reveals a fear that Canada could lose its independence through too close a union with its large neighbour.

Published in 1917, Groves's play hints at concerns about the United States having too much influence over Canadian affairs, but it, nevertheless, reflects a positive response to America's recent entry into the war, something also seen in the contemporaneous "Patriotic Jack and the Beanstalk" (discussed in Chapter 4 in relation to food production efforts). This tale shows children helping to defeat a terrible Giant that is "getting ready to drop a great rock down on our soldiers in the trenches far below." Working together, the children destroy the Giant, after which Jack transmits a wireless message "through the air to our soldiers across the sea." The message reads: "We, the Children of America, are trying to do our duty by growing gardens and producing food for you, the Defenders of Liberty." The message is signed "the children of America" and they soon receive a reply that says: "Thank you, Children of America. [...] Your Big Bean Bag has knocked out our worst enemy – OLD GIANT HUNGER."

In this story, the term "Children of America" includes young people from across the continent working together to grow food, and this collective North American effort is paralleled by the troops they help to feed, who sign their return message "Soldiers of the Allies," suggesting they are a unified force composed of men from different nations. The publication in which this tale appears was copyrighted in both Canada and the United States and it portrays children from both countries working together to support the war effort. The narrator's repeated use of the term "our soldiers" when describing troops "in the trenches" and "across the sea" implies that a shared identity as "Allies" takes precedence over a specific national identity.

In celebrating North American food growing efforts, the tale includes praise for children from the United States, which is understandable given its 1917 publication date, but representations of American children participating in the war effort varied throughout the conflict. As Hew Strachan states, neutrality was "relative, not absolute" (7), and prior to its combat role America was directly involved in financial matters affecting the conflict, including the fact that some nations could raise funds in the United States while others could not (7). American neutrality was thus not uncomplicated, and children's authors from within the United States and elsewhere petitioned the nation's children for various forms of assistance with the war effort.

One English-language text that was published in France in 1915 and that suggests American children should help the Allied cause, is *French Toys*. The Introduction to this collection is addressed directly to young American readers. It asks these "children of a free nation" to "help" the people of France and includes an illustration of a doll holding a French flag and an American Flag (Hellé; Figure 1.2). This image is a visual representation of the author's hope that America will come to France's aid and forms part of the attempt to recruit child readers to the cause.

Figure 1.2 Illustration by André Hellé from *French Toys*, 1915.

As this text reveals, writers from different countries argued in favour of US involvement prior to 1917 and pictured American children as important contributors to the Allied effort. In America itself, even as some writers supported neutrality, others encouraged participation of some sort. As Anthony Pavlik remarks, "within the context of varying American views on the Great War" children's literature "of the time was largely shaped by, but in some measure resistant to, many of the dominant socio-political discourses in America during the Great War" (186). Literature for young Americans thus reveals competing attitudes towards the war, but as *French Toys* shows, it was not just American authors who offered different views on the nation's participation. The changing role of the United States over the course of the war resulted in children's authors on both sides of the Atlantic expressing a variety of attitudes towards the conflict and the role of the American child in it.

One text that highlights the complexity surrounding representations of American neutrality is George Orton's *Bob Hunt in Canada*, published in Wisconsin in 1916.[16] In this story about American teenager Bob Hunt and his friends enjoying a hunting trip in Canada, Orton refrains from proposing that America join the war but appears to defend against criticism of neutrality in subtle ways. The fact that Orton (1873–1958) himself was Canadian but lived much of his adulthood in the United States, further shows how complicated depictions of America's position on the war could be (Galway "Border" 113). In discussing the war with his friends, Bob Hunt remarks that "even the fellows that do not care to enlist are just as brave as the others when the battle comes" (Orton 180), which seems to be Orton's way of telling American readers that even though their country is not at war, "they too would be brave in the face of battle. Canadians, the author seems to suggest, are not inherently more noble or more masculine than their American counterparts just because they have marched off to war" (Galway "Border" 106). Embracing some of the same notions of manliness and bravery that attend discussions of the war in other children's literature of the period, Orton argues that American boys possess these qualities, even as he refrains from criticizing American neutrality.

While Orton appears ambivalent about the nation's involvement in the war, other writers suggest there is a role for the United States to play. For example, the American story *War Babies* by Annie Franchot (1859–1928) presents the United States as a peaceful place that offers sanctuary to European war orphans. Although Franchot was writing in 1914, she suggests that America can help, even if only by providing a place of refuge. While displaced European children benefit from travelling to America in Franchot's story, in other works it is young Americans overseas that help the Allied cause. One work that pictures young Americans contributing on the Western Front is the 1915 novel *The Boy Allies at Liege: Or Through Lines of Steel* by prolific writer Clair Wallace

Hayes. In this adventure story, American teenagers Hal and Chester are in Berlin when war starts, and the friends become embroiled in the conflict as they try to make their way westward across Europe. In one scene Chester is captured by the Germans and asked why he is in Louvain:

> "So? And yet you are not a Belgian, I take it; nor yet, French. What, then? An Englishman?"
>
> "No; I am an American," said Chester proudly.
>
> "An American! Then how comes it that you are fighting for the enemies of Germany?"
>
> "I am proud to be fighting for what I consider the right," said Chester simply.
>
> (Hayes Boy Allies at Liège 226–227)

Even though America is neutral, Chester's response shows that as a "proud" American he sides with the British cause against Germany. Unlike *French Toys* and Franchot's *War Babies*, which both posit America can help in ways that do not include combat, Hayes's novel suggests that this support can involve action near the front lines. His novel is an example of how young American readers were consuming material before 1917 that not only supported the British side but that figured young Americans as working directly to help the Allied cause (Pavlik 189).

Another example of American pro-war sentiment from before 1917 is found in the highly successful periodical *The Youth's Companion*, published in Boston.[17] The issue from July 15, 1915, contains a short article titled "The Canadian Troops" that suggests some Americans were anxious for their nation to join the fight. It offers an example of how American children's authors utilized Canada to argue in favour of participation. The article comments on the great "pride that Canada justly feels in the response of its sons to the call of the empire." While "the mere numbers of those who have responded [...] are impressive," writes the author, "far more significant are the unvarying reports that the cables and the mails bring to America of the splendid valor and high efficiency of the Canadian troops." The remainder of the article discusses the Canadian victory at Ypres, describing in some detail the difficulties that Canadian soldiers faced and how "by dogged resistance and brilliant counter-charge" they prevailed over the Germans.

The author writes that "all Canada was thrilled with the story of its soldiers at Ypres," and emphasizes the battle as a source of national pride:

> Before Ypres the Canadian troops had won special mention on numerous occasions, but that particular battle was a demonstration of Canadian valor and devotion to the cause of the empire that fills

> the whole Dominion with a solemn pride. Long after the years have lightened the burden of sorrow that lies on thousands of Canadian homes, that pride will endure.
>
> ("The Canadian Troops")

The author highlights the youth of these troops, noting that "a short year ago these heroes were in school" and were "all following the paths of peace." Through this comment, child readers are reminded of how quickly a nation and its young citizens can go from being "at peace" to being at war. This is not merely a comment on the nature of war, but a comment on the need for preparedness. In 1915, this author was suggesting to young Americans that their nation should also be prepared to go to war, and that the willingness of Canadian boys to do so is enviable. "How little cause the British Empire has to fear for the future of the English race when 'the lion's whelps' show mettle like this!" writes the author, explicitly connecting the efforts of the young people of the Dominion to the future strength of Britain.

The author presents Canadian troops as examples for young Americans to follow and, perhaps in response to criticism of US neutrality, he asks,

> Does not all this hold something reassuring for our own country? Does not the showing of the Canadian troops – in whose ranks, by the way, are hundreds of young Americans – give the world an inkling how our own young men would behave, should unforeseen necessity force us to fight in defense of our honour and our homes?
>
> ("The Canadian Troops")

The comment that "young Americans" have already joined the ranks even though their country is not officially at war, seems intended to encourage American readers to do the same and to follow the example of their Canadian neighbours. This is very much in keeping with Myrick's work from 1918 in which he cites Canadian soldiers as models of patriotism and writes,

> Of the 32,000 Canadians first to serve, only 2,000 are alive unscathed after three years' warfare. When the offer came to be relieved and sent home, these survivors of a hundred battles preferred to 'keep on doing our bit!' That's patriotism!
>
> (Myrick)

Concealing just how war weary many Canadians were by 1918, Myrick points to Canadian troops as exemplars of national loyalty that he hopes will inspire in young Americans the same spirit of sacrifice.

Although some Americans remained dubious about joining the war, a positive response to participation was widespread in American children's literature once the United States became officially involved. As with children's writers from other Allied nations, many encouraged readers to take pride in the nation's contributions and argued that these were necessary to protect certain values and ideals. Describing a "patriotism that transcends nationalism," Myrick states that his country "has no selfish purpose in the victory that must be won – no hope of aggrandizement," and that America's "men and women [...] are being sacrificed without stint for the highest of human ideals – righteousness among nations, brotherhood between humans." Like so many other writers of the time, Myrick uses a family metaphor, describing the Allied nations as a "brotherhood" to instil in young readers the idea that the war is about more than the needs and desires of any one nation, and is instead about the collective good.

Myrick appears to forestall any suggestion that American involvement is motivated by self-interest or a desire to gain power. Nevertheless, his work also fits within a post-1917 narrative that directs young readers to think about what the world will look like once war is over, and to envision the United States as having an important say in determining this future. Children's authors from many nations made some claim as to the vital importance of their own country's role in shaping post-war peace, including the place of children in this effort, and American writers were no exception. Hermann Hagedorn (1882–1964), for example, figures American children as central to the process of rebuilding the world. Titling his 1917 work "*You Are the Hope of the World! An Appeal to the Girls and Boys of America*," Hagedorn leaves no doubt as to his views on the important role young Americans will play, telling readers, "the world will look [...] to America" as a leader following the war because it will have the financial resources, "the energy," and "the youth" (18).[18]

Hagedorn is not only addressing young readers and outlining the individual role they may each play but is also characterizing the American nation itself as youthful and full of vitality and promise, unlike Europe, which is in decline. Historian David Kennedy summarizes this attitude and argues that there was

> confidence to be found in the image of a young United States rescuing decadent Europe from the burden of her feudal past, and many Americans cheerfully accepted that view of the war, with its implications of a new world order in which their country could at last take its rightfully premier place.
>
> (43)

In Hagedorn's work, this feeling emerges in his imagery of the child; in contrast to the European child victim the American child is full of life, energy, and inspiration.

According to Hagedorn, the duty of American youth is to "live for the service of democracy" and to thereby "build, out of the agony and the ashes, a better world than the sun has yet shone upon" (48–49). Unlike many other wartime writers, he does not suggest that the child's ability to serve his or her country lies in fighting on the battlefield. Instead, he writes, "To you, girls and boys of ten, twelve, fourteen, fifteen, sixteen, seventeen, is given a work every bit as grand as dying for your country; and that is, living for the highest interests of your country!" (99). Hagedorn envisions the youthful citizen as an innovative thinker and leader who can promote democracy: "Young America, ten to seventeen, [….] the world [….] doesn't ask you to enlist. The world asks you to sit down and think about […] what America stands for, what America is, and what America might be" (49–51). Picturing adolescents as the force that will drive future peace-keeping efforts, Hagedorn sees this power as the opposite of the "cramping conservatism of the elder generation" (96). He urges young readers to make use of their influence, arguing that democracy needs the "impassioned enthusiasm for freedom […] which only youth has, which only you, girls and boys, can give!" (97).

Stressing that the future is in the hands of the young, Hagedorn urges them to take charge: "If your elders […] will not volunteer to lead you, lead yourselves […]! Speak gently to Teacher, […] but if words don't wake him, RIOT, girls and boys of America! [….] Fight! Not with guns, but with your brains!" (97–99). He repurposes the wartime image of the child fighter here, presenting the older generation as the adversary that needs to be defeated. Hagedorn's piece reveals that many Americans saw themselves as "a new, youthful force in the planet's affairs" (Kennedy, D. 42), one that "was going to war not simply against Germany but against […] all that Europe historically represented in the American mind: coercive government, irrationality, barbarism, feudalism. […] America, in other words, was going to war against the past" (42). In Hagedorn's view, it is not simply victory in the war that matters; the true "goal is [….] democracy. It is a lasting peace among nations; and, as far as it is humanly possible, amity among men. Go to it! Go to it, girls and boys of America! You are the hope of the world!' (Hagedorn 99–100).

As the differing messages about American involvement in the war show, each nation's experience was unique, but no country experienced the war in isolation from others. Children's literature from Britain, Canada, and the United States reveals that the network of relationships between these three countries was frequently addressed in wartime children's literature, both directly and indirectly. A range of attitudes towards the British Empire, Canadian independence, and American neutrality (and later participation) all find expression in texts for young readers. While Allied support for Britain is a dominant theme, this was by no means the only discourse that pervaded children's texts.

The ripple effects of the conflict throughout the British Empire, as well as the impact of the United States' shift from official neutrality to active participation, are all evident in the pages of wartime children's literature. A close reading of American texts prior to 1917, for example, shows that while some were in favour of neutrality, others were eager to join the fight and often cited Canada as an example to be followed. Canadian literature, meanwhile, reflected divisions arising out of regionalism, competing views on Conscription, and differing attitudes towards the nation's relationships with Britain and the United States, but writers also aimed to cultivate and strengthen national unity and identity. At the same time, British writers simultaneously celebrated the empire – seeing the contributions of Allies as evidence of its strength – and expressed anxiety over signs of its decline amid the rising threat from Germany. In all these discussions, children played a role, both as the intended readers of such works, and as symbolic and metaphorical representations of the state. Regardless of the views on nationhood, empire, or militarism being expressed, a common thread running throughout this literature is the notion that children are the future of the nation, and that they will determine what the world will look like in the aftermath of the war.

Notes

1 For further discussion of this poem see Galway "What Shall We Tell the Children?"

2 Geoff Fox discusses some of Lea's different writing for children during the war and notes that he was "a regular contributor of verses to the *B.O.P.*" (Fox 183).

3 Mrs. Belloc Lowndes (1868–1947) began her career as a journalist and authored several short stories but was best known as a prolific novelist and author of sensational fiction whose writing was also adapted for film (Tynan 65). This text is a history of the war for children that addresses different aspects of the conflict.

4 The great costs borne by other nations are not always acknowledged by wartime writers. One work that downplays the price of loyalty is Guy Waterford's "Last Days at Gallipoli," published in 1916 in *Young Canada*. The futility of the battle in which tens of thousands of ANZAC forces were injured or killed is given a positive spin as Waterford writes that the failed undertaking,

> nevertheless gave to the world such a new and astonishing proof of hardihood and audacious bravery on the part of our troops that for the British Empire *Gallipoli* will go down in history as a name of pride almost as much as of sorrow.
>
> (233)

5 "Edward Shirley" may be a pseudonym. Although his name appears on many children's texts from the early twentieth century, I have been unable to uncover any biographical details about the author.

6 Following the 1915 *Ghadar* uprising the British "enacted repression including the 1915 Defence of India Act" (McGetchin 19), and while the revolt

failed to oust the British, it "did serve as an example of mass movement towards the eventual goal of independence" (19).

7 Herbert Myrick (1860–1927), a graduate of the Massachusetts Agricultural College, wrote a number of books about farming and became the agricultural editor of *Homestead* in 1882. From 1890 until his death in 1927 he was the president and editor-in-chief of the Phelps Publishing Company (Strahan).

8 Published in London and Toronto, this is typical of children's literature published in Canada in the nineteenth century and early-twentieth century in that its title is designed to appeal to Canadian readers, but it is in reality a very British publication. (Galway *From* 44). Even though the title is *Young Canada*, the title page describes this as "An Illustrated Magazine for Boys Throughout the English-Speaking World" and there is limited mention of Canada within the text itself. For an overview of this publication during the war years, see Stephen Dale's *Noble Illusions* (2014).

9 Weaver emigrated from England to Canada as a young teenager and authored several works of fiction and non-fiction. Galway's "Border Crossings" provides further discussion of this history text, which was first published in 1900 and was followed by several revised editions.

10 Canada's military involvement was limited before 1914, but events like the War of 1812 and the Boer War provided earlier writers with fodder for fostering pride in military achievement. The First World War undoubtedly saw Canadians involved in warfare on an unprecedented scale and its sheer scope made it very different from previous wars, but it was an event that further solidified a sense of national pride and identity that had, in fact, been emerging steadily for many decades (see Galway *From Nursery Rhymes to Nationhood*).

11 Douglas Delaney argues that popular histories have had long-lasting effects on "the Canadian collective memory of the Great War" and created the false impression "that Canadian soldiers with Canadian ideas were responsible for the victory at Vimy and every battle the corps fought after it" (933).

12 Groves (1870–1930) published three volumes of verse and wrote more than twenty patriotic plays to be performed by children in Canada's schools. She was a teacher and a long-serving member of the Toronto Public School Board of Education who assisted in founding several schools in the city, one of which was later named after her ("Edith").

13 The willingness to don khaki and fight is presented as a fundamental characteristic not just of Canadian men, but of Canadian youth, making this play a clear example of literature that encouraged young people to participate directly in the war.

14 John Ormsby Miller (1861–1936) was the principal of Ontario's Ridley College and the author of texts on Canadian history and other works for students (Bothwell 159).

15 For a further discussion of how the relationship between the two countries was presented to child readers, see Galway's "Border Crossings" (2015) from the *Lion and the Unicorn*.

16 Galway's "Border Crossings" provides an extended discussion of Orton's novel and its representation of American neutrality.

17 Established in 1827, *The Youth's Companion* ran until 1929 and was one of the most popular magazines in America, publishing works by many famous

authors and reaching a circulation of more than half a million at the end of the nineteenth century (Tebbel 104–105).

18 Elements of my discussion of Hagedorn's work were originally published in "The Hope of the World? The Figure of the Child in WWI Children's Literature," which appeared in *Politics and Ideology in Children's Literature* (Eds. Áine McGillicuddy and Marian Keyes).

2 'What Have We Done?'

The Vulnerable and Victimized Child

Children are among the most vulnerable populations during armed conflict and their portrayal in First World War literature was used to support both pro-war and pacifist arguments. Depictions of the child victimized by war raise questions about how adults conceive of children and childhood and how these portrayals might shape children's understanding of themselves. For instance, it is possible that depictions of child victims might foster feelings of fear and helplessness in child readers and contribute to a prevailing hierarchy in which children are reliant on, and subordinate to, adults. Alternatively, however, the figure of the child victim may be cathartic or empowering, teaching child readers that they are not alone in their fear and suffering and presenting them with examples of other young people overcoming adversity.

When considering wartime portrayals of young victims, it is important to remember that the vulnerable child was not new to children's literature. From Jim Hawkins to Anne Shirley, endangered, orphaned, and neglected characters were a staple of Victorian and Edwardian fiction. In the context of the war, however, when real children faced challenges on an unprecedented scale, the figure of the suffering child became even more poignant and likely resonated with young readers of the day, aware as they were of the traumas inflicted by the conflict. Various types of child victims – including those orphaned, displaced, injured, or killed – populated the pages of children's literature, each achieving different effects and serving different functions in the politically charged atmosphere of war.

As Harry Hendrick observes in his work on the history of childhood, from the early nineteenth century onwards many laws have been "concerned with protecting children from forms of neglect and abuse [...]. In nearly all of the legislation the rhetoric has been that of the child as helpless, as being acted upon, usually in some kind of damaging manner" (7). Hendrick argues, however, that sympathy for child victims was accompanied by "suspicion of what they might become" if they were not protected (7). As he astutely notes, the

> child victim was nearly always seen as harbouring the possibility of another condition, one that was sensed to be threatening to moral

DOI: 10.4324/9781003191605-3

> fibre, sexual propriety, the sanctity of the family, the preservation of the race, law and order, and the wider reaches of citizenship.
>
> (7)

Hendrick is not talking specifically about child suffering caused by war, but his remarks are relevant to the way in which adults regarded young victims of the First World War (particularly those untethered from the nuclear family) with a mixture of sympathy and fear and wanted to contain any threat they potentially posed to social stability. When the war caused the widespread suffering of children, their possible threat as delinquents was more obvious and they became signifiers of the nation's misery and decline. One function of child victims in literature was to suggest that this conceivable social menace could be mitigated by helping young people impacted by the war.

Some authors submit that the best way to help children is to end the conflict and they utilize the figure of the young victim to bolster anti-war sentiment. Overall, however, there is a lack of pacifist sentiment in children's literature from the period, and Catriona Pennell argues that in Britain, this resulted less from censorship laws and more from widespread popular feeling in favour of the war, which helped to suppress objection to the conflict (7). While there certainly are examples of British and North American authors using the figure of the child victim to present anti-war arguments, a much more common function of this character is to convince readers of the importance of the Allied cause. In such instances, authors intimate that the only hope for children is Allied victory and these child figures serve to garner support for the war effort.

As Susan Fisher observes in her study of Canada during the First World War, the "violated child became a simple, irrefutable, and enduring justification for the war" (9). Paradoxically, however, child readers were taught that they themselves could actively come to the aid of 'helpless' child victims. At the same time that the child within the text was presented as vulnerable, child readers were encouraged to think of themselves as capable of helping. These multiple functions of the child victim reveal the varied ways in which writers imagined both their young characters, and their young readers.

Threatened and Threatening: Conceptualizing Childhood

On both sides of the Atlantic, various policies and fund-raising efforts showed that people were deeply worried about the war's psychological, emotional, and economic impact on children. In the United States, for example, "the federal War Labor Policies Board prohibited the use of government contractors that employed children" (Yarrow 3), and the federal Children's Bureau, established in 1912, drew attention to concerns about the war's effect on young Americans, including the impact of milk shortages and the worry "that public health nurses, vital to the agency's plan to reduce infant mortality [...] would be removed from child health duties and called into war work" (Lindenmeyer 72). The Children's Bureau also feared that "increased demands for women's labor might encourage mothers of young children to take jobs in booming war industries" (72). Such concerns were not limited to the United States. In Britain, for example, the Save the Children Fund was "formed in 1919 to provide food for child victims of the post-war blockades in Austria and Germany" (Baughan 117). Interest in children's welfare was widespread across the allied nations and influenced policy throughout the war years and beyond.

Concern about young people's well-being was evident in policy discussions but also in prose and poetry for adults, often embodied in the figure of the victimized child. Published in 1918, "The Plaint of the Children" by Canadian poet Archibald Sullivan[1] captures the kind of imagery commonly associated with the child war victim:

> What has our childish world of little things
> To do with Princes, Emperors, and Kings?
> We know the flowers are dead and no bird sings -
> What have we done?
>
> Oh, by the pleading of our little hands,
> Lifted above the turmoil of these lands,
> God of the wretched – God who understands –
> What have we done?
>
> [....]
> Pain travels quickly. We are tired and small,
> And Hunger crouches by each shattered wall;
> Death is our playmate – he will end it all.
> What have we done?

The children depicted by Sullivan are helpless, and their vulnerability is highlighted by his use of repetition, with the phrases "little things," "little hands," and "tired and small" emphasizing the children's diminutive stature and physical weakness. The recurring refrain "What have we done?" further underscores that the children are wholly innocent and bewildered by events over which they have no control.

Sullivan is writing for adults, but his representation of the innocent child is similar to imagery that also appeared in literature for young readers, much of which utilizes the child to symbolize hope, futurity, or the devastating toll of war. The common use of the term 'boys' to refer to British, Canadian, and American soldiers, for instance, helped to capture the idea that they were loyal offspring of their nations and to garner a widespread feeling that the nation (or Empire) was a cohesive entity held together by familial bonds. There was also a sense that the generation of 'boys' waging war in the trenches represented the nation's future.

This future was alternately imagined as bleak or hopeful in children's literature of the period. For example, in Hagedorn's *You Are the Hope of the World!* (1917), the author refers to European soldiers as "boys" in order to highlight the devastating loss of life and potential. Writing for young Americans, Hagedorn observes:

> In Europe, boys of your age are dying daily by hundreds, by thousands! Millions lie dead or wounded [...]. Boys who might have been leaders of men [...]; boys who might have been great scientists, great poets, great tellers of tales, great inventors, great merchants, great physicians, great preachers. Europe does not know yet what she has lost. [...] Europe will call for new poets, new tellers of tales, new scientists, new inventors, new merchants, new physicians, new preachers. *And no one will answer.* No young heroes will appear. And then Europe will know at last how much she lost in the terrible years of the Great War.
>
> (1–4)

In Hagedorn's work, the lost "boys" are not all literal children; rather, the image of a vanished generation of boys symbolizes the long-term consequences of the devastation in Europe. Hagedorn reads the overwhelming loss of so many in the prime of life as the forfeiture of an entire continent's future potential. According to Hagedorn, the misery and destruction of a generation of young men will impede the progress of civilization in Europe, exemplifying the latent threat to the social order that the victimization of young people represented.

Another writer who uses the image of the young war victim to represent widespread devastation is E. Maxtone Graham (1862–1952).[2] In Graham's *The Sword of Peace: A Play for Children* (1918), published in Edinburgh and sold for the benefit of the Scottish Women's First Aid Corps, various nations are represented by child actors. In using young performers, the playwright relies on familiar conceptualizations of children and gender to put forward her views on the war's causes and on the relative merits and faults of the opposing sides. The play is described in its Preface as "a short patriotic play in three Acts, for children of various ages" (2), and the stage directions indicate that the roles of Germany and Austria are to be played by boys, whereas the nations viewed as victims of German aggression are to be represented by girls (3). Exemplifying that children's literature "encourages child readers to perform specific versions of childhood" (Nodelman 193), these stage directions show that in Graham's drama the child actors literally perform both gender and childhood.

By specifying which nations are to be portrayed by girls, and which by boys, the playwright exploits notions of feminine weakness and passivity to promote the claim that Germany and Austria were the sole aggressors in the war, and to highlight the heroic status of nations like Britain and America, parts played by male child actors. Whereas Austria and Germany are described as "big, strong, rough boys" (Graham 8), Belgium is presented as a "*little* girl" (emphasis original) (5), and this contrast between Belgium who is "so little" and Germany who is "so big" is in keeping with the common portrayal of Belgium as a victim of German aggression (5).

Although Graham relies on conventional notions of gender and childhood, she also challenges some stereotypical representations of children. While innocence and vulnerability are qualities commonly ascribed to children and are used in the play to present Belgium as blameless, they are not the only qualities Graham assigns to the young, for "big, strong, rough boys" represent violence and belligerence. The instruction about casting boys explicitly associates the male child with these traits (in contrast to the female child embodying innocence), but using any child actor as a signifier of aggression acknowledges that children possess this quality. These boys thus suggest that children are not simply weak and passive, and the play provides an example of competing constructions of childhood in which the figure of the child embodies both victimization and threat.

Hagedorn's work and Graham's play reveal how the image of the child could be used to explain both the causes and the potential outcomes of the war to young people, but they are just two of many texts in which the image of the child victim appeared. Countless stories, articles, poems, and advertisements informed child readers of the toll the war was taking on people their age. In the British publication *The Kiddies' Magazine* from May 1918, for example, there is an advertisement with the heading "A Deadly Blow" that calls for financial contributions to the National Children's Home and alludes to the war's impact on British children:

> The continuance of the War has struck at the happiness of the rising race. The death of Father or of Brother – and in many cases of both – has flung a heavy shadow over thousands of infant lives. In addition, the cost of living and the scarcity of certain foods are beginning to militate against their health and well-being. The fathers wage a righteous war, but the children – in substance and in sorrow – pay the price.
>
> ("A Deadly")

Like Sullivan's poem, this piece suggests that children are the ones who "pay the price" of a conflict that they have no control over, thereby highlighting their status as innocent bystanders.

The appearance of this advertisement in *The Kiddies' Magazine*, a long-running Methodist magazine published in London, means that it would have drawn the attention of young readers to child suffering, but the fact that it is also addressed to adults is evident in the following plea: "Remember your own childhood and do what you can to bless that of others by sending a gift" to the National Children's Home ("A Deadly"). In asking readers to remember their own youth, it draws on childhood nostalgia and implies that 'true' childhood is a time of peace and pleasure. This advertisement asks readers to look back to an idyllic childhood that supposedly existed before the war and has since vanished. Perry Nodelman observes that numerous "texts for children express [...] nostalgia for a better world that never actually existed; they describe a childhood more sweet and innocent than most if not all children ever experience, far from the bitter complexities of adulthood" (220). Such nostalgia is evident in this fund-raising campaign, which argues that adults have a duty to help young war victims experience a supposedly normative childhood; the kind that some writers imagined existed before the war.

In this work and others, the war is pictured as an anomaly – something that has disrupted the supposedly normal patterns of childhood. Many wartime depictions of children suggest they have no control over the momentous events occurring but "pay the price" for actions taken by adults; this price is the loss of what authors define as a 'real' childhood. Such works hearken back to Romantic notions of youthful innocence at the very same time that they suggest this innocence is under threat. The call for funding for the National Children's Home perpetuates the belief that war is at odds with a natural state of childhood, not only impacting children's health and safety but threatening to destroy childhood itself. The need to protect children therefore goes beyond saving the individual child, and the young war victim is used to suggest that the very notions of 'the child' and 'childhood' are under attack.

While many texts express concern about the loss of childhood, Hendrick cautions that when it comes to social policies designed for children and adolescents, we need to "recognise just how much of so-called protective legislation has been concerned with their presence as threats rather than their suffering as victims" (7). In other words, mourning a specific vision of childhood that has supposedly been disrupted by the war is not solely about concern for children, but about concern for adult society. Prior to the war, reforms that protected children were frequently motivated "by a fear that, left unnurtured, the child would fail to be a worthy citizen as an adult" (Olsen 19), and this can be seen in things like the introduction of compulsory schooling, which helped alleviate concerns that uneducated children "might not cast their votes in a responsible way" when they grew up (Cunningham 141). Hendrick notes that

> children who were seen as threats were so primarily by virtue of their victim status, that is, their neglect or cruel treatment led them

> into situations or forms of behaviour that in some way or another were deemed to be threatening to the social order.
>
> (12–13)

Anxiety about children's welfare does not simply give rise to a desire to insulate the young from the hardships of the adult world but can result in a desire to see children take on some of the responsibilities associated with adulthood. As one study of children in 1980s America suggests, "the absence of a real economic role for young people is often associated with delinquency; if children had 'meaningful' work opportunities, it is proposed, these problems would diminish" (Medrich et al. 133). Such views were also current during the First World War, when stories encouraging young readers to help relieve the suffering of victimized children did not simply show anxiety about the welfare of individual children but expressed fears about the future stability of society.

In the preface to his 1918 collection of stories for children titled *Not Only Men*, George Bedborough (c.1868–1940) suggests that literature for young readers could potentially harm the nation. He expresses concern that stories of the war's horrors, while perhaps necessary for preparing children for challenges they may one day face, might also imperil the future. Consequently, he encourages parents to share stories "of noble deeds in this war" with children (9), suggesting that these "would be by no means confined to one side" (9), and arguing that they could "suggest ways of helping the coming generation to be a kinder, more humane, more loving race than our own" (7). Both the experience of being directly victimized by war, and the act of reading about such victimization, were thus seen by some adults as posing a risk to individual children, as well as to childhood and society more broadly.

The Child Refugee

The idea that war puts childhood itself at risk is taken up in non-fiction and fiction alike. The 1914 children's story *War Babies* by Annie Wood Franchot[3] is one example of an American text in which young European victims of war figure prominently. In this tale, French siblings Jacque and Jacqueline are war orphans and refugees, and in her portrayal of them, Franchot draws on notions of childhood innocence and implies it should be preserved. She describes their adventures as they flee their home and makes clear from the outset that the war is directly responsible for their status as orphans and refugees:

> Jacque and Jacqueline were playing in the lovely old walled-in garden of their home in Verdun in Northern France, while a great battle

> was raging between the allied armies of England and France against Germany.
>
> Again the guns – Bing! Bang! Ping! and everything seemed to shake; even the ground trembled and windows crashed and the children's mother came rushing from the house calling, "Jacqueline, Jacque, come quickly," but the words had hardly passed her lips when a bomb exploded in the garden path and she fell dead before their eyes.
>
> Frightened and bewildered, the children ran from the garden calling for their father, but their father – the poor children did not know until later – had fallen early in the day, killed by a German Uhlan's lance while fighting to defend his city.
>
> (Franchot 1–2)

The children's transition from playing innocently in their garden to witnessing first-hand the violent death of their mother drives home the devastating nature of the war. With both parents killed, the protagonists become the eponymous "war babies"; they are the offspring of the violence that surrounds them.

The depiction of the terrified and confused children running "wildly on an on" until they reach the edge of the city is designed to elicit the full sympathy of the reader:

> Clasped in each other's arms, they sat huddled in a corner of the doorway. Jacqueline rested her curly head against her brother's shoulder, sobbing. Jacque sat looking out with great scared eyes, wondering what all the noise meant and when it would stop. He could see the flames of fire all over the city, and the smoke made his eyes smart and ache.
>
> (Franchot 2)

The helplessness, terror, and confusion of these children suggest that warfare and violence are out of keeping with normative childhood experience. By contrast, the image of the "walled-in garden" in which they play at the beginning of the tale seems an appropriate metaphor for idealized childhood, symbolizing a place of protection.

In her study of the development of free kindergartens for the British working-class in the early twentieth century, Jane Read observes that the garden was conceived of as the appropriate play space for young children: "Romantic notions located the child not in the gutter of a city street but in the natural environment of field and forest. In the context of the city, relocation of the child was to be within a garden" (422–423). In Franchot's novel, the garden is similarly pictured as the appropriate space for children, but its tranquillity is disrupted by the violence of war. The narrator describes the garden as both "lovely" and "old," suggesting it belongs to the past – to a time before the war. Like the garden in which the children frolic at the tale's opening, childhood is imagined as a realm of play that is walled-off from the harsh realities of adulthood until war violently intrudes and the children are cast out into the dangerous world. The protected space of the garden stands in sharp contrast to the image of the children huddled in the doorway of an unfamiliar building, surrounded by smoke and flames.

Franchot's depiction of the orphans perpetuates a view of children as disempowered beings in need of saving by adults. She emphasizes the siblings' vulnerability, but never suggests that the trauma they have suffered has made them more self-reliant or worldly. Forced to flee their home, Jacque and Jacqueline remain passive participants in their own adventure, swept along by forces beyond their control. At heart, their tale is about their need to find a new, safe home and return to the domestic realm, considered by Franchot the proper space of childhood. The novel illustrates that childhood "and a childlike point of view are [...] constructs of adult minds that adults work to impose on children, in part by means of children's literature" (Nodelman 193). In the version of childhood that Franchot presents to young readers, innocence and passivity are sacrosanct. Rather than their victimization forcing the orphans to take responsibility for their own survival, their security is instead achieved through the children's close connection to Nature and the help of adults.

The first adult to come to their aid appears as they sit huddled on the steps of a church on the outskirts of their city, a setting which symbolizes hope for the children's salvation. They spot "a strange, great flapping thing with big wings and a man's body, and the man" stretches out his "big, strong arms" and lifts the siblings "into the place beside him, strapping them safely to the seat" (3). This "bird-man" (4), as the children call him, is a German pilot and the first of several adults who play a role in saving them. The portrayal of the pilot is at odds with the predominantly negative representations of Germans that appeared in wartime children's literature (something addressed in detail in Chapter 7) for he protects the children, transporting them across Europe and instigating a series of fantastical adventures that conclude with a journey to America.

The help the siblings receive suggests that these child victims depend on adults for their survival, but they also receive support from the animal kingdom, intimating a close connection between children and Nature. This occurs in the most fanciful episode in the story when they travel from Europe to America. They begin this journey by boat but fall overboard and are rescued by a whale. The whale then transports them to an island where they are retrieved by a giant Eagle that flies them the rest of the way to the United States. The eagle symbolizes America, and Franchot clearly utilizes the figure of the child war victim to construct a vision of that nation as a place of salvation, freedom, opportunity, and hope. Ultimately, the children's safety is ensured by their arrival in the United States, where they are reunited with their maternal Grandmother.

America becomes a land of peace and protection for the victimized European child in Franchot's text. Although she was writing in 1914 and perhaps did not expect that the nation would ever enter the war, her tale anticipates a later discourse in which Americans saw themselves not only as the saviours of war-torn Europe, but of democracy and civilization throughout the world. Like Hagedorn's work, in which outlining the destruction of Europe's youth situates American boys and girls as "the hope of the world," Franchot's tale reflects what historian David Kennedy describes as America's view of itself as "savior to a decrepit old order" (42). It is only once they arrive in the United States that the European orphans are truly safe. Yet Franchot's stance on the war itself appears neutral; Germans are not portrayed as villains and are, in fact, among those who help the French orphans escape.[4] She seems less concerned with assigning blame and more preoccupied with demonstrating the devastating impact of war on children. She argues for the preservation of a particular vision of innocent childhood – one that sees the natural world and the domestic realm as the proper spaces of childhood – and she pictures America as a land of peace where this childhood can be realized.

Another work that features the figure of the displaced child is Angusine Macgregor's *Mrs. Bunny's Refugee* (c. 1918), published in London by Blackie. The title is a nod to the many accounts of war refugees (particularly those from Belgium) that circulated during the war. Whereas Franchot's text celebrates America as a land of peace but presents a fairly neutral view on the war, Macgregor's story aligns itself clearly with the Allied cause, assigning more blame to Germany, and the displaced child serves slightly different functions. Franchot's very passive child characters perpetuate a view of children's helplessness, but Macgregor's display agency as well as innocence. Her illustrations are reminiscent of those by Beatrix Potter and the story involves interactions between human and animal characters (in this case, a family of rabbits). Through the inclusion of both human and non-human children, Macgregor presents a more complex, and at times contradictory, construction of children and childhood.

The eponymous refugee is a human child who embodies innocence and vulnerability. Meanwhile, Mrs. Bunny's anthropomorphized offspring represent these same qualities but also suggest that children may wield some power, albeit limited. The experiences of the rabbits mirror the realities many families faced during the war, including the absence of husbands and fathers. Mrs. Bunny (also referred to as Mother Bun) is the head of the household, responsible for looking after the welfare of her rabbit children who are vulnerable to war's dangers:

> The baby bunnies were sitting round the fire, waiting for Mother Bun, who had gone out to find them some supper. They were feeling nervous, because every now and then they kept hearing the most awful bangs, and every bang meant a gun going off.
>
> They all gave quite a start when the door flung open, and Bobbin, their black cousin, half fell in amongst them.
>
> They all clustered round him while he told them he had seen a soldier quite near. "Oh dear, I hope nothing will happen to Mummy!" said Bunty, the youngest bunny [...].
>
> (Macgregor)

The absence of a father, the proximity of fighting, the sight of soldiers, and concern for the safety of their mother are all experiences that child readers in Britain and elsewhere might have shared with these anxious, anthropomorphized rabbits.

The absence of Mother Bun from home is a further reflection of wartime reality when increasing numbers of women worked outside the domestic sphere to support the war effort and to provide for their families while men were away. While this work often had a positive effect on the family, including providing important household income, there were also concerns that much of the work women engaged in was having "a disintegrating effect on home life" in Britain (Andrews and Hobbs 199). In their 1918 study of the effects of the war, Irene Andrews and Margaret Hobbs claim that lengthy workdays and "the increased employment of married women [...] at a distance from their homes have all contributed to this result" (199). Wartime Britain "witnessed a marked rise in juvenile crime" (Hendrick 113), which was sometimes blamed on changes taking place within the domestic sphere. In America too, the disruption of "normal home life" caused by the military participation of fathers and the "entrance of mothers into industry" were seen as putting children at risk and contributing to "juvenile delinquency" (Lindenmeyer 146). The disruptions to domestic life caused by the war are represented in Macgregor's story in which the father is absent, and the young rabbits are apprehensive of their mother's departure from the home.

The bunnies' fear for their own and their mother's safety is alleviated when she arrives home with food, symbolizing the comforting return of the female to her traditional place within the domestic realm:

> There was Mother Bun with her arms full of things. "There!" she said, with a triumphant smile, "that is not bad for war rations."
>
> There was a tin of milk, two beautiful red apples, and a loaf of bread nearly a yard long. "Won't we have a fine supper!" cried Bunty.
>
> (Macgregor)

This scene is inspired by some of the daily hardships faced by families of the period, including war rationing, and may have functioned as a form of wish fulfilment for young readers whose own desire for scarce little luxuries may be represented by the food Mother Bun secures.

Unfortunately for the rabbits, this pleasant episode does not last long, reflecting the pervasive unease and uncertainty that children of the time faced:

> Suddenly Mrs. Bun said, "Hush! what's that?" and crept to the door to listen; and all of them got quite scared again. [...] First they all armed themselves. Bobbin seized a saucepan, and Bunty had a Belgian ribbon tied round him, which made him look very martial, while the others took whatever they could find (Macgregor).

Unlike the passive French children in Franchot's novel, Macgregor's little rabbits take on the role of defenders as they arm themselves, suggesting the possibility that children can be active participants in war, not merely victims. This difference may be explained by the nation of origin of each text. Whereas Franchot's American readers were living in a neutral country that at the time had no plan to enter the war, Macgregor's British readers were already living with the expectation that they might eventually need to fight as soldiers.[5]

Although Macgregor hints at the possibility of child empowerment in this scene, perhaps as a means of preparing young readers to go to war, it is undercut by the haphazard nature of the "weapons" the young rabbits grab hold of (including a saucepan), and by the fact that Bunty's donning of the ribbon clearly shows the rabbits' affiliation with Belgium, a nation regularly portrayed as a victim of German aggression whose utter helplessness necessitated the involvement of Allied troops. This gesture of patriotic pride implies the rabbits are not just acting out of self-preservation but in defence of the nation, but their status as Belgians highlights their vulnerability, undermining the suggestion that children may be capable of defending themselves or the state.

The possibility that the armed bunny children wield real strength is further undercut by the sudden appearance of Marcel, a human child who embodies the same notion of helplessness that dominates Franchot's tale. Rather than suggesting that children can defend themselves, the small human boy instead represents complete vulnerability:

> They had not gone a yard, when they saw the forlornest little boy, sitting on the roots of the big tree under which Mrs. Bun had her home.
>
> They were all rather frightened at first; he was so very much bigger than they were. But when Mrs. Bun saw it was only a tiny boy, and that he was crying, she sent all the bunnies home again.
>
> (Macgregor)

The crying child is clearly suffering, and the assessment of him as "only a tiny boy" is concomitant with the idea that he does not pose a danger to the rabbits. By extension, this undermines the possibility that the bunnies, who are themselves tiny children, could pose a danger to anyone or successfully defend themselves. Like the human child, they are helpless in the face of the threats that surround them, and in this tale, it is adults who must come to the rescue of children, be they human or *lapin*. Recognizing the boy's inherent defencelessness, Mother Bun performs the role of maternal nurturer and protector, kindly taking "him by the hand" and leading "him gently to her hole under the tree" where there is "a lovey fire, where he warmed his little cold hands" (Macgregor). The artwork depicting Marcel echoes the description of the children from Franchot's *War Babies*, with his child status conveyed through a cherubic face and a head full of toddler's curls (Figure 2.1).

Through the combined portrayal of the human child and the young rabbits, Macgregor presents a more complex construction of childhood than Franchot. While Marcel embodies vulnerability, the story,

Figure 2.1 Illustration by Angusine Macgregor from *Mrs. Bunny's Refugee*, c.1918.

nevertheless, suggests a possible identity for children beyond that of helpless victim. While the episode in which the bunnies arm themselves with common household objects suggests they might not be able to adequately defend themselves, it does show their *desire* to do so, and the story implies that there are ways in which they can make their own situation, and Marcel's, better. Rather than simply sitting and crying as Marcel does, the rabbits are eager to help a fellow child when they see his distress. Gladly following their mother's instructions, they do what they can to make the little boy comfortable:

> And didn't the baby bunnies set to work for their little guest! They scuttled about, put the best china on the table, and cut some bread and butter from the long loaf. Then they all sat round him while he had his supper.
>
> (Macgregor)

The bunnies, whose youth is emphasized by the word "baby," are doing their part to help another young victim of war. While their ability to fight may be limited, this tales suggests there are other ways in which children can help, including by coming to the aid of refugees like Marcel.

The figure of the displaced child was common in literature of the day and Mother Bun refers to Marcel as an unfortunate "little refugee," speculating, "I suppose he has lost his mother – probably had his home burned down." Demonstrating her bravery, she shakes "her paw angrily at the imaginary enemies" that displaced Marcel and sets out on a quest to help the child. Outside the safety of the rabbits' den, signs of war are everywhere, and her leg is "struck by a bit of shell." While binding up her wound with her handkerchief, she overhears voices and stumbles upon Marcel's mother and siblings, who are sobbing and "looking very sad indeed." Mother Bun reunites Marcel with his family, and she and her offspring watch as the humans "set off in the cart, which was to carry them to safety; while Bunty the Baby waved the bedspread, which was made out of a bit of a Belgian flag." The reference to the Belgian flag, along with the illustrations that depict Marcel wearing the wooden shoes worn by working-class Belgians at the time, indicate that Marcel and his family are Belgian refugees. During the war, the plight of Belgium was often cited as the primary justification for a declaration of war against Germany, and Bunty's waving of the bedspread, made from the flag, is a show of solidarity with the Belgian people in this British text.

Wartime literature from North America and Britain presented Belgium in a sympathetic light and tales of German atrocities committed against Belgian children served to increase support for the war effort.[6] As Catriona Pennell observes, such accounts, some of which were conveyed to the public by refugees in Britain, included claims of children having their hands and ears chopped off, and babies being bayoneted (129). She notes that British children "were not spared the gruesome content of the atrocity stories" and gives accounts of children hearing these from their schoolteachers (129). Literary representations of the victimized Belgian child were part of a dominant narrative that cited Belgium as the justification for war against Germany, even as feelings on the ground towards refugees began to shift. As Pennell notes, in Britain a "common reaction to refugees, after the novelty of their arrival had worn off, was one of annoyance. Many people complained about them being ungrateful" (137). Yet, despite whatever annoyance may have been felt, the displaced Belgian child remained a galvanizing figure in literature and one that was used to help justify the Allies' fight against Germany.

In 1914's *Told in Gallant Deeds*, Lowndes draws attention to the plight of Belgian refugees when speaking of the effort that women and children on both sides of the conflict were making to provide warm winter garments for their troops. She wonders if the

> devoted German mothers and wives [...] ever give a thought to those Belgian women who, homeless wanderers owing to Germany's ruthless inhumanity, can provide nothing for *their* sons and brothers, but have to rely entirely on the kindness of their Allies and of America.
>
> (257)

Lowndes also draws her young readers' attention to the plight of children in other war-torn nations of Europe, and to the assistance that has been provided by America:

> The poor little Belgians, and those French boys and girls whose homes have been destroyed by fire, shell, and shot, are not likely to have any Christmas presents this year. Neither are the children of the other combatant nations likely to have a very happy Christmas. So a kind American editor bethought himself that here was a chance for the boys and girls of America. The American Government entered very heartily into the project of sending what is now known as the Santa Claus ship to Europe with Christmas presents for the children of the warring nations, and they offered the use of a United States battleship.
>
> (Lowndes 257–258)

While Lowndes begins by talking about Belgian and French children, she observes that German children are also victims of a war over which they have no control and notes that America sends them Christmas gifts too (258). Though she refers to German "inhumanity," this account of the Santa Claus ship[7] suggests that the children of all nations share a common innocence and are all, in equal measure, victims of a conflict instigated by adults. Lowndes thus conceives of childishness as a quality that supersedes national characteristics, and the negative qualities often attributed to the German enemy are not ascribed to its children.

Child Victims and Righteous Allied Soldiers

Representations of child victims were often a means of celebrating Allied soldiers, which is exemplified by the front page of the November 1916 issue of the British publication *Work and Play*. This contains an image of a soldier carrying a young girl (Figure 2.2), and the accompanying note states:

> In the villages captured by the British desperate hand-to-hand fighting often takes place [...] and the lives of [...] civilians [...] are [...] in great danger. Our picture shows a Highland soldier carrying a terrified little French girl to a place of safety.
>
> (Front Page)

Figure 2.2 Image by Fortunino Matania of a Scottish soldier carrying a French girl to safety, from *Work and Play*, 1916.

Like the French children in *War Babies* and the Belgian child in Macgregor's text, this child victim appears dependent on the help of other people – in this case an adult Allied soldier – and projects a clear image of vulnerability. The masculine soldier is figured as her protector, and the child in distress serves in this instance as a means of celebrating the work of these troops. Here, the image of the vulnerable French child is used to justify the Allied cause and to argue that fighting is necessary to protect young, defenceless victims of war.

Another piece that uses the suffering of European children to celebrate the actions of the Allies, specifically the British, is "A Covert from the Tempest," the fifth chapter in Rev. Stuart Robertson's 1919 book *The Red Flowers: Sermons from the Front to the Children at Home*, published in London by the Religious Tract Society. Through recounting some of his experiences in France, Robertson, an ex-chaplain, justifies British involvement in the war by presenting an image of the British soldier as a friend to the European child. He recalls "a little French boy who ran away from home to live with the British soldiers" and who would not go home because his mother kicked him (31). When asked "were you not afraid the British soldiers might kick you" the boy replies in the negative "in a voice that was full of trust, and a little angry that anybody should think such a thing of his soldier friends" (32). Robertson says that Britain's troops "are brave and cheerful, and many fine things can be said about them, but I think the finest thing of all is to say [...] the children of France love them" (32). Robertson uses the child to highlight the goodness of the British soldiers, elevating them in the boy's affections above his own mother, and establishing them as the friends of the weak and powerless.

In addition to using the figure of the suffering child to celebrate the British soldier, Robertson uses it to argue that the Allied cause is righteous. Many overtly Christian children's texts were stridently supportive of the war, and Robertson suggests the Allied cause has been sanctioned by God, recounting an episode he witnessed during a rainstorm in a French village:

> One of these sudden deluges had come down and everybody was making for shelter. Among them was a group of five little children.
>
> Do you know where they sought and found shelter?
>
> Under the rain-cape of a British soldier. He had one of those big, wide, sleeveless waterproof cloaks, and the children ran to him and crept in beneath. The rain splashed on his steel helmet and dripped from it on to his cloak, running down in streams, but they were sheltered and dry and happy. "A man was a covert from the tempest."
>
> (Robertson 30)

Robertson quotes here from *Isaiah 32:2* and describes this incident as a "beautiful thing" (30). He surmises that when the war is over, and the British soldiers return home, "the French children will be sorry: for they have found the British soldier always kind and friendly to little folk" (31).

Beyond what it suggests about the goodness of individual British soldiers, Robertson's reference to suffering children highlights the righteousness of the Allied effort. He elaborates on the need to fight Germany, which has waged war "on the weak":

> Its armies have slain women and children: their path has been marked by broken hearts and little graves; and children lie dead in Belgium and France, in England, and in the deep salt sea because the cruel hand of Germany struck them dead.
>
> We are fighting against that, for the weak against the strong. The flag of our navy and our army is a shelter against this terrible tempest; and the soldier sheltering the children under his rain cloak is this big truth told in a little parable. [...]
>
> When I saw the children sheltered under the wide wings of the cloak of the British soldier, it was to me a parable of that Man Who, the prophet said, would be "a covert from the tempest"; and I want it to be so to you as well, that in the storms of life you may turn to Him with as sure a trust and find as sure a shelter, as the children did in the storm at Aubigny.
>
> (Robertson 32–34)

Employing images of child vulnerability to celebrate British soldiers and their cause, Robertson depicts the Germans as murderers of the defenceless who do not hesitate to slay little children. By contrast, he presents Christ as being on the side of the British in their role as protectors of the weak.

Wise, Brave, and Helpful Child Victims

Although many works of literature from the First World War contain images of child vulnerability, others evoke another element of the Romantic vision of the child – one which suggests that children have a certain wisdom or insight that adults lack. An example is the young girl in Robert Henry Newell's poem "The Sergeant and the Child," which appeared in *The Third Golden Rule Book* (1918) in Canada, an assorted collection of poetry and prose excerpts for children designed to be used in Ontario schools. The title page describes this as part of a series that embodies "a Graded System of Moral Instruction" recommended for use in Ontario schools and libraries "by the Minister of Education."

Newell's poem describes an encounter between "a sergeant old and gray" and a young girl that takes place when soldiers are marching through a village and are met with the cheers and applause of its residents (141). Most of these villagers see only the surface pageantry and glory of the troops and not the reality of war, but in the midst of this scene the sergeant notices "a little maiden weeping" (142), sitting apart from the rest of the village. When he questions why she is crying when everyone else is cheering she responds,

> But think–O Mr. Soldier, think, –
> How many little sisters' brothers
> Are going far away to fight
> And may be killed, as well as others!
>
> (Newell 142)

Whereas the adults see glory, the child alone sees the cost of war, and the sergeant, whose experience as a soldier means that he shares her insight, remarks that it is "left for little ones like thee / To find that war's not all a blessing" (142). Here, amid a scene of pageantry, the little child alone weeps because of her true understanding of the soldiers' duty. The child's awareness sets her apart from the rest of the village:

> And still the ringing shouts went up
> From doorway, thatch, and fields of tillage, –
> The pall behind the standard seen
> By one alone of all the village.
>
> (143)

The little girl is the only villager to see "the pall behind the standard," as the adults around her are blinded by misguided notions of glory.

Newell's representation of the child combines conventional symbols of innocence with an appreciation of the child's wisdom. She is described as a "baby beauty" and a "little maid" who speaks softly and has a headful of "curls" (142), yet she is the only one in her village wise enough to see what war really means. This poet is employing the "device of looking at the world through the eyes of a child [...] to reveal and expose the follies and vices of humanity" (Pattison 126). The child's understanding in this poem contrasts some of the glorification of duty and sacrifice found in other works presented to child readers during the First World War. In Newell's verse it is the child who is sage, while the adults celebrating around her fail to recognize that the soldiers represent death and suffering. The astute child serves as a critique of war and, as the sergeant notes, it is left for little children, who suffer helplessly, to realize that war is not all "a blessing."

Newell was a widely known nineteenth-century American humourist and his poem was originally published with the title "Picciola" in his 1864 collection *The Palace Beautiful and Other Poems* (published under his pseudonym Orpheus C. Kerr). It was written in the context of the US Civil War and is not about the First World War at all. Newell's political satire of the American Civil War became increasingly caustic and moralistic as that conflict progressed (Glass 817), and the fact that this poem was included in a 1918 Canadian school anthology may reflect growing cynicism about the First World War. In her study of Civil War literature, Alice Fahs notes that although literature written by Newell and others "did not constitute a literature of bitter disillusionment like that produced in England in response to World War I, it nevertheless criticized wartime culture in pointed terms" (204). Fahs further notes that Newell,

> skewered the inflated rhetorics and falsified patriotism that he found almost everywhere he looked within war culture. Over and over again Newell attacked the rhetoric of heroism and nobility that surrounded the war, including the Victorian fascination with death and bloodshed.
>
> (205)

Given that Newell was known for "puncturing prevailing heroic ideas of war" in his own day (Fahs 204), the choice to include his poem in this 1918 anthology suggests a similar tendency may have been emerging in literature produced for Canadian children towards the end of the First World War.

Nevertheless, while the weeping child in Newell's poem serves as a caution against glorifying war, other child victims serve as examples of brave and dutiful citizens supporting the cause and function as inspiration for children and adults alike. An example can be found in Lowndes's *Told in Gallant Deeds* (1914), in which she refers to a brave young French girl injured in the bombing of Paris:

> The first words which Denise said to the policeman who lifted her up after the explosion were, "Surtout ne dites pas à maman que c'est grave." ("Above all, don't tell mother that it's serious.")
>
> But alas! her mother had soon to know the worst, for brave little Denise had to have her leg cut off. When she awoke after the operation, she found by her bedside [...] a gold medal, and what do you think was engraved on it? Her own brave words to the policeman [...].
>
> (Lowndes 211–212)

In Lowndes's story, the child victim is not an object of pity as much as she is an example of fortitude. Unlike the French siblings in *War Babies*, she shows "pluck" and strives to protect her mother from worry (211), earning the admiration of adults and serving as a role model for them, as well as for young readers.

In addition to exemplifying bravery, child figures can also play an active role in helping other child victims of the war, just as the little rabbits from Macgregor's tale try to help the refugee, Marcel. This dual role of the child – victim and saviour – appears in numerous children's texts from the period, highlighting the complex and multifaceted nature of the image of the child. One representative example is found in the British publication *The Boys' Journal* from September 12, 1914 in a section titled "The Boys' Social League. The President's Weekly Chat. What B.S.L. Members Can Do in Time of War." This short piece asks readers to think about what will become of "the wives and children of the men who are killed in battle" as well as those "of men who are unable to provide for their children because of the war" (27). Raising the possibility that such children could starve "because there is no one in the home capable of earning bread-money" (27), the author presents children as helpless victims. At the same time, however, the boy readers he addresses are told that they can help ease the suffering of their peers by contributing financially to a relief fund.

The writer encourages his readers by saying that every donation, no matter how small,

> will be valued, and although you may only send a sixpence or a shilling, you will have the knowledge that you have subscribed according to your means, and that your subscription will be the means of supplying some poor family with a much-needed meal.
>
> ("Boys' Social" 27)

Here, the image of children suffering because their fathers are killed or incapacitated is invoked in order to convince the child reader that he has both an obligation and an ability to help other children who have been victimized by the war.

Another example in which children are simultaneously figured as victims and helpers is an English school-story titled "How the War Came to Fountainbury" by Hailey Bury. Published in the 1915–1916 *Boy's Own Annual*, the story simultaneously presents children as powerless victims and as heroes. It tells the tale of a boys' school on the edge of a village named Chalfont that suffers from a Zeppelin attack. As the characters stand on the school grounds watching the attack in the distance, a teacher remarks, "The fiends! [...] Helpless non-combatants murdered in their sleep. Women and children –" (Bury 596). The adult character describes children as "helpless," yet the events of the story suggest otherwise as one of the boys at the school, Young Dick Sims, ends up playing an important role in avenging Chalfont.

A quiet, bookish, "spectacled" boy who spends much of his time reading scientific books (595), Young Sims is gently mocked by some of his peers for his quiet ways. On the night of the Zeppelin raid, however, his bookishness pays off. As the bombs fall on the village the masters and pupils stand "powerless" and are merely "passive spectators of the drama of the air" (596). Sims, however, who "had read that [Zeppelins] sent and received signals by wireless telegraphy" (596), discovers that a wireless message is being transmitted to the German enemy from the school itself.

Sims is both a helpful individual and a traditionally vulnerable child figure who, overcome by the strain of the evening, bursts into tears after making this important discovery. Yet, with the encouragement of his school master, who pats "the sobbing boy gently on the shoulder" and bids "him be calm, for on his ability to read the signals much depended" (597), this seemingly "insignificant small boy" is able to decode the message and help the village (597). Although Young Sims is "shaken by the magnitude of his discovery" (598), he works to overcome his fear, even going so far as to pursue the fleeing spy. He breaks the school rules to do so, but in his mind the "injunction to go to bed had seemed to him a childish termination to a night of adventure" (598).

There is a duality in this child figure, as Sims is unnerved by the night's events but also rejects the notion that being a child should restrict his ability to act in service of his community. After witnessing "the horrors of the raid and the suffering" of the children and adults of the village "the small boy had determined on revenge" (598), and his efforts save the day. His adventures take their toll on him, however, and after he faints from the strain he is "hurried back to the school, where he lay delirious in the sick room" (598). Young Sims recovers, but the depiction of him fainting allows his character to remain childlike which, rather than undercutting him, renders him an effective example of bravery for child readers to emulate. In this story, British children are "non-combatants" innocently murdered by the Germans, but the British boy who helps catch a spy is also a figure whose knowledge, perseverance, and sacrifice enable him to come to the defence of those around him.

The above examples are just a few of the many depictions of children as innocent victims found in juvenile literature, and they demonstrate some of the varied ways in which authors utilized such figures. Whether to argue for an end to the fighting, to cultivate support for the war, or to present a particular image of different nations involved in the conflict, the child victim was a prominent figure in North American and British children's literature, and its various manifestations reveal some of the possible ways in which children and childhood could be conceptualized. Child readers encountered images of young war victims who were reliant on adults for their survival, but they were also presented with the possibility of doing their part to help win the war and defend not only themselves, but their peers. The figure of the child victim simultaneously reinforced notions of child vulnerability and suggested that children could demonstrate agency and contribute in some measure to the events unfolding around them.

Notes

1 Canadian-born Sullivan found success as a writer of poetry and prose in both London and New York (Caswell 265).

2 Graham was the author of several texts for adult readers including the historical study *Children of France* and several works on Scottish history and genealogy.

3 Annie Wood Franchot (1859–1928) was a resident of Olean, New York and the author of several children's books ("Women").

4 Franchot's positive depiction may reflect the fact that this book was published when the United States was still officially neutral, as well as the fact that America had a large population of German ancestry.

5 The possibility that children themselves could take up a defensive role was explored by many writers at the time and is discussed at length in later chapters.

6 For a detailed discussion of both the veracity of atrocity claims and the myths and propaganda surrounding them (including the potent image of the mutilated Belgian child), see John Horne and Alan Kramer's *German Atrocities, 1914: A History of Denial.*

7 The Santa Claus Ship was the *USS Jason*, which left the United States in November 1914 "loaded with 8,000 tons of gifts comprising 5,000,000 separate articles that had been donated by American children and were destined for British, Belgian, French, German and Austrian children whose fathers were away fighting the war" (Tait 45).

3 The Child at Play

Blurring the Boundaries between Children's Pastimes and the Business of War

During the First World War, even though many authors represented childhood as a period characterized by play, innocence, and imagination, it was evident that children were unavoidably impacted by the conflict. Rather than viewing children merely as victims, however, many writers suggested that young people had the ability to help the war effort and that they could do so in part through their play. As the long tradition of toy soldiers attests, connections between children's play and warfare pre-dated 1914,[1] and First World War children's authors were continuing a familiar practice when they drew parallels between adult warfare and children's pastimes. Sports, hobbies, imaginative free play, and the activities of formal children's organizations became ways of cultivating interest in warfare, engendering patriotism, and preparing young people for military service and other duties. Children's play took on greater significance as it was co-opted as part of the war effort, and it was a prevalent theme within children's texts.

Portrayals of children participating in games and other amusements countered the image of the young, suffering war victim, but these figures served as much more than embodiments of a carefree and imaginative childhood. The wide variety of representations of the child at play reflects the fact that the word "play" "stands for a category of very diverse happenings" (Sutton-Smith 3). The line between amusement and work was often blurred, with different forms of play frequently presented as either a metaphor for adulthood or as practical preparation for it. The view of childhood as a training ground has long roots and, during the war, the leisure activities children engaged in were widely considered a means by which values like teamwork, as well as physical and practical skills, could be instilled in children, laying the foundation for the future of both the individual child and the nation.

"The Mimic War": Preparing Boys for War through Sporting Activities

One activity that served as a metaphor for adulthood was team sport. This had long been a popular subject of boys' literature, but while

DOI: 10.4324/9781003191605-4

sporting opportunities for girls had been increasing since the Victorian period and were a topic of some texts, depictions of girls engaged in sport "remained circumscribed by outworn social values" (McCrone 133), including "anxiety around the female sporting body and maternity" (Enever 667). For boy readers of everything from poetry to prose, however, sport was ubiquitous and was used to explore themes of masculinity, sacrifice, and more. One British poem that employs sporting imagery is Frank Ellis's "The Next Man In!" from the *Boy's Own Annual* 1915–1916, which goes far beyond simply celebrating the joys of cricket:

> You're the next man in, remember that!
> Put on the pads, and take the bat.
> Go to the wicket with smiling face,
> If you're feeling nervous, show no trace.
> There's only another to follow you,
> And all will depend on what you do.
> Your side may lose, or they may win:
> Which shall it be? – You're the next man in!
> [....]
> The old school-times will be done some day;
> There's another match that you've got to play.
> In the game of life you must take a part,
> Will you side with the right with a noble heart?
> For youth is passing, and manhood's near;
> Go into the field with hope and cheer.
> Grip tight – play straight, then you're sure to win.
> Are you ready? Then, come – you're the next man in!
>
> (Ellis, "Next" 227)

Using the image of a cricket match, Ellis[2] leads young male readers to think ahead to adulthood, when the "old school-times will be done." The child reader he addresses is, literally, the man of the future – "the next man in" – and Ellis suggests that sports are both a metaphor for life's struggles (what he refers to as "the game of life") and an actual means of preparing for the challenges of adulthood. These, as suggested by the poem, include being responsible for the well-being of others ("all will depend on what you do"), being brave ("If you're feeling nervous, show no trace"), and being morally upright ("Will you side with the right with a noble heart?"). Ellis's depiction of boys playing cricket thus serves to present an image of noble, masculine citizenship.

There is a long-standing and prevalent notion that children can learn and develop through different forms of play, and the pervasiveness of sporting themes in Victorian and Edwardian boys' literature reveals the widely held view that sport is particularly useful in aiding the development of the male child. While sport could contribute to this maturation in several ways, it was frequently linked to the development of soldierly skills, for there was a "strong current of militarism in pre-World War I Edwardian Britain" (Moss 25), and in numerous works of prose and poetry athletic activities serve as a metaphor for the military duty boys would be expected to embrace as adults.

The use of football as a metaphor is clear in Annie F. Freeman's "The Old Eleven," published in the *Boy's Own Annual*[3] 1915–1916:

> Laughingly, chaffingly, on they came, through the splash of the rain and mud,
> Eleven men of the football team, till the ball with unceasing thud
> Was whirled 'cross the field to a waiting goal, and the distance re-echoed wide
> With the frenzied shouts from a hundred throats that cheered for the winning side.
> And they played for the honour of records past, the pride of the school to uphold,
> Unheeding the rain as it stung the cheek, the lash of the wind as, cold,
> It swept o'er the field; they were out to win! then, met by a cheering throng,
> Eleven men of the winning team in triumph were swept along.
> And they waved on high with a conquering shout, in ever unbroken rule,
> THE CAP OF THE SCHOOL!
>
> (Freeman, "The Old" 174)

The tone here is triumphal, with the players full of laughter as the crowd cheers them on. The second stanza clearly mirrors the first, but images of schoolboys at play are replaced by those of men at war:

> Readily, steadily, on they came through the gun-fire's increasing roar,
> Many a man who had fought a fight for his school in the days of yore;
> And, far o'er the guns with their smashing might and cannon's wild thund'rous roll,
> They heard the shouts of the football field, and a voice in their hearts cried "GOAL!"
> As they pressed their way through the thickest fight, through deathly explosion's blast,
> To fight for King and Country's sake, the honour of records past.

They were out to win! And when victory brought the enemy
swift retreat,
There were comrades still who were near at hand, the
conquering team to greet,
And they waved on high, with a shout that made the wakening
echoes ring,
THE CAP OF THE KING!

(174)

The clear parallel between the two stanzas delivers the message that the same loyalty, pride, and desire to "honour" the past that readers display at school should be applied to "King and Country." By suggesting that the costs and rewards of football are the same as those of battle, and by presenting victory as assured, Freeman glorifies war in an example of propagandist literature in which "honour," "triumph," and "victory" are celebrated, and the horrors of battle minimized. The image of youth at play is used in this instance to convince young readers that they too can, and should, press their way "through deathly explosion's blast" to fight for their nation.

A similar poem is John Hogben's "Jack in Khaki," published in the same 1915–1916 annual.[4] Its subject is a young soldier who "leapt at Kitchener's commands" and "donned the drab disguise" of the khaki uniform (Hogben "Jack"). Like the boys in Freeman's poem, he is pictured as having been prepared for war by his sporting days at school:

He was the Captain in the field,
When raged the mimic war;
The first to dare, the last to yield,
When helping up the score.
The tug of war, long jump or high,
Cricket, or race, or gym,
Or making golf-ball climb the sky –
'Twas all the same to him!

Hogben's use of sport as metaphor is clear in his term "the mimic war." The qualities of daring and perseverance, which made the boy the "Champion of his school," are the same qualities that make him the ideal soldier who obeys "his country's call" and plays the "sterner game" of war. Like Freeman, Hogben downplays the costs of such obedience, but he, nevertheless, suggests that participation in real warfare will mark the end of boyhood:

To him, O never fear, shall come
A happy warrior's joy;
He shall return (God willing) home,
But nevermore – a boy!

Sports and school days may prepare one for adulthood, but it is war, suggests Hogben, that truly makes one a man.

Hogben distinguishes between the "boys" who are playing football at school and the "men" who will eventually fight in battle, but both Freeman and Ellis use the terms "man" and "men" throughout their poems. Even though soldiers were commonly referred to as "boys" in First World War literature, the term is absent from these British poems. Instead, both describe schoolboys as "men," perhaps to encourage young readers to look ahead and start thinking of themselves as adults or, more specifically, to "groom readers to accept the need for boys to head for the battlefields" (Reynolds "Words" 266). The fluidity of terms like "men" and "boys" in wartime children's literature reveals that the images and language used to signify the child depended on the effect each author hoped to achieve.

The frequently interchangeable use of "boys" and "men" may also reflect a way of thinking about citizenship that does not exclude the child. While many wartime texts suggest that children must prepare to take on the role of loyal citizen in adulthood, others conceive of children as already having obligations to the state, despite not having the privileges that citizenship affords. In the case of the poetry by Freeman and Ellis, it is the individual's responsibilities, rather than his rights, that are underscored, and the child reader is encouraged to think of himself as sharing the same abilities and duties as men and to prepare, in part through playing sports, for his role as a fighter for "King and Country."

The Importance of Having a Hobby: Cultivating the Child's Interest in the War

While sport was a popular topic in boys' periodicals and well-suited to militaristic themes, even seemingly innocuous children's hobbies became imbued with the flavour of war. In an article on stamp collecting published in the *Boy's Own Annual* (1915–1916), for instance, F. W. Burgess[5] (1855–1945) outlines the war's impact on this pastime when he remarks that he finds it "a pleasure" to see that "stamp-collecting has been as popular as ever" (707), and that these "are special times when there are opportunities for obtaining certain varieties" of stamps (708). He divulges how even a relatively innocuous hobby is profoundly affected by the war when he notes that several "colonies once belonging to Germany are now using stamps on which is the head of King George" and observes that "some portions of European territory [...] have been compelled to use stamps which [...] tell that the enemy is within their gates" (707).

Unlike the sporting poems discussed earlier, Burgess does not utilize this hobby to inspire militaristic sentiment in readers and it appears his purpose is simply to impart advice to collectors, but his serious treatment of this pastime shows how children's hobbies could be viewed on level with work, evincing Steven Gelber's claim that "stamp collectors transferred to the leisure sphere the discourse that defined the meaning of industrial capitalism and used the language and images of the marketplace to legitimize both work and leisure" (743).

The tension between dismissing children's pastimes as frivolous, and respecting their skills and interests, is evident in "An Amateur Censor" by Ellis Parker Butler (1869–1937). Published in November 1917 in *St. Nicholas*, a few months after the United States had declared war, this short story by this prolific American author[6] casts the child philatelist in the role of war hero and echoes Burgess's respect for this hobby as a serious undertaking. It is set in the London office of the censorship bureau, the "wonderful organization England had created to censor the mails" (Butler 32), where a Belgian refugee named Professor Kampf is employed. One day, his wife allows their son Henri to visit him at work, even though prior to the war "she would never have thought of trusting a twelve-year-old boy alone in such a big, crowded building, but every boy seemed to become more self-reliant after the war began" (33). The notion that the war has helped to change children (and adult attitudes towards them) by making them more self-reliant and mature, is borne out by this tale in which the young Belgian boy plays an important role in helping England.

Initially, Henri is keen to visit his father's office because he hopes there will be some war envelopes with stamps that he can add to his collection. The narrator observes that these are "the envelops with the censorship marks, the military franks and the Red Cross and other war-stamps on them. They are interesting things to collect, and Belgian boys are great collectors. Practically every Belgian boy is a stamp-collector" (Butler 34). Henri's love of stamp collecting, described here as a popular pastime among Belgian boys, is central to the story, and his father shows him four sheets

> of the sort stamp-collectors and dealers know as 'approval sheets.' Each sheet had a blank space at the top, and below this was printed fifty squares [...], each big enough to hold one postage-stamp. [...] On the four approval sheets in this letter every space bore a stamp. (34)

Mr Kampf explains that the man responsible for sending these is Lieutenant Monson, a Belgian soldier interned in Holland, and that every batch of "mail from Holland for America has ten or twenty of his postcard appeals. [...] He must have a list of many of the stamp-collectors in America, and to them he writes his post-cards" (34). In these cards the soldier explains, "to pass my weary days I am getting together a collection of postage-stamps for my children at home. Please send me any duplicates you do not want" (34).

The Lieutenant's claim that he wants stamps for his children at home clearly suggests stamp-collecting is a child's pastime, and because this hobby is burdened "with the stigma of childhood play" (Gelber 756), the soldier's letters escape the otherwise careful scrutiny of the censorship bureau. Henri's father remarks, "Ah! you know the fun of collecting stamps, my little son! [...] Perhaps you would like to send some stamps to poor Lieutenant Monson some day, yes?" (34), and he passes the sheets to the boy. The professor's comments represent the "rhetoric of play as frivolous" in which play is categorized as opposite to, and lesser than, work (Sutton-Smith 11). By regarding the stamp collecting simply as a source of "fun" that his "little" son enjoys, the father relegates it to the realm of child's play and misses the stamps' true significance. Conversely, it is the seriousness with which young Henri treats his hobby that allows him to see the stamps for what they really are – a coded message.

Henri's careful methods reflects the tendency among practitioners to regard "stamp collecting as a science" and have made him familiar with many stamps (Gelber 756). He notes that the ones in the soldier's envelope are the "commonest ones. [...] And all mixed up" and remarks, "If I used an approval sheet, I would arrange the stamps by countries, as the dealers do" (Butler 34). His disciplined approach allows him to

Figure 3.1 Illustration by Reginald Birch from "An Amateur Censor" in *St. Nicholas*, 1917. [University of North Carolina at Chapel Hill – Digitized by Internet Archive].

realize that the stamps are, in fact, a cipher and leads to the discovery that Lieutenant Monson is really a German secret agent who has been using this code to forward news from America to Berlin. This discovery solves the mystery of how information had been reaching Germany about ships carrying platinum for England's munitions factories, and thanks to young Henri's discovery, "there were no more special attacks on the platinum carriers" (36). The child becomes the hero of the hour as a direct result of his "child's play" (36), which is elevated from something frivolous to work of great importance (Figure 3.1).

Gelber remarks of adult stamp collectors that by "making their leisure like work, they could bring to it all the honor accorded productive activity in a work-oriented society" (743). Similarly, the seriousness with which Henri regards his pastime enables him to solve a mystery that the professional adult censors could not. Rather than merely being a victim, like so many other Belgian child refugee characters, Henri enables the capture of a German spy, protects England's munitions factories, and receives "an Order of Merit for notable services to the king and nation" (36). This portrayal suggests that children have been underestimated by adults and that they possess unique and valuable skills. In this instance, American child readers, whose nation had been at war for seven months, are assured that they can play a part in the war, not merely by stepping into more adult-like roles, but also by embracing some of the very traits and forms of play that help to define their status as children.

War in the Nursery: Toys, Crafts, and Imaginative Play

Stories that show children at play often incorporate the "rhetoric of play as progress" that Sutton-Smith defines as the belief that children "adapt and develop through their play" (9). He says educators "have so needed to represent playful imitation as a form of children's socialization and moral, social, and cognitive growth that they have seen play as being primarily about development rather than enjoyment" (9–10). According to this view, play's central function is to help children learn, and in wartime literature, it is the child's development into a useful citizen and enthusiastic supporter of the war effort that is most frequently emphasized in representations of children at play.

The outbreak of war in 1914 saw military themes enter the child's consciousness on a new scale, affecting the activities of even the youngest girls and boys. The British *Collins' Children's Annual* of 1915, for example, contains illustrations by Phyllis Cornish of very young children engaged in pastimes like knitting items for troops and war victims, or pretending to be soldiers. "The Martial Spirit" depicts four small children marching in line, with one girl beating a drum and a little boy playing a whistle (Figure 3.2).

Figure 3.2 "The Martial Spirit" by Phyllis Cornish from *Collins' Children's Annual*, 1915.

The last and smallest figure in the frame is a barefoot toddler, clothed in a simple pinafore, who marches proudly behind the other children. Although, historically, boyhood in particular was shaped by war play (Cross 39), girls and their pastimes were equally affected by the First World War and Cornish's depiction of female and male children shows that militaristic play cut across boundaries of both gender and age.

Two other illustrations by Cornish are titled "The War Game in the Nursery: Germania Objects to Her Part" and "The War in the Nursery: 'Charge'!!" The first of these depicts the youngest of four children in tears at having been made to dress up and play the part of the German enemy (Figure 3.3). In the other illustration, all four children are united in their "charge" against the foe, represented by a small puppy standing on a box labelled "I am the enemy." One child waves the British flag and blows a bugle, while the others rush at the "enemy" with makeshift swords (Figure 3.4). These illustrations reveal the ways in which warfare could be transmuted into a form of child's play with even very young children mimicking the actions of soldiers, displaying their hatred for a foreign enemy, and demonstrating pride in Britain.

It is difficult to ascertain the extent to which such depictions merely reflected what British children were already doing, or encouraged them to behave in a certain way; that is to say, such images of the child at play may have been intended to shape the play of real children, not merely to depict it. As Rosie Kennedy puts it, toys, games, "and juvenile literature show us both what images adults wanted children to have

Figure 3.3 "Germania Objects to Her Part" by Phyllis Cornish from *Collins' Children's Annual*, 1915.

Figure 3.4 "'Charge'!!" by Phyllis Cornish from *Collins' Children's Annual*, 1915.

about the war and also what they felt children would enjoy" (*Children's War* 52). If understood in this way, these illustrations can be read as another means by which children were encouraged to engage in militaristic play without it appearing to be adult-driven, the implicit belief being that it would help foster patriotism, solidarity against the enemy, and martial spirit in a way that made these seem like natural conditions of childhood.

Another British work that shows the war's influence on children's play is "How to Make War Models from Matches and Match-boxes," an instructional piece from the November 1914 issue of *Work and Play*. Although the periodical's title could be interpreted as presenting work and play as opposites, they are approached as interrelated and concurrent activities here. This piece is an example of the "enthusiasm" with which British children and adults "looked to the themes of war as a source of amusement for children" in the early months of the fighting (Kennedy "How Merrily" 226). Complete with illustrations, the article includes detailed instructions on how to make a model transport cart and field-gun and ends with the promise that later issues of the magazine will describe some of the "countless other models" that can be made (50). Similarly, the *Children's Painting Book: Paint Your Own Picture Post Cards* (c.1917)[7] shows how arts and crafts activities were shaped by the war. One of the illustrated cards to paint is titled "Playing Soldiers" and it depicts four little children dressed in costumes, pretending to be troops. The caption reads: "This army game is fun,/Come quickly and enlist, and bring your gun." Here, war is clearly depicted as amusement and children are encouraged to "enlist" in the game of "playing soldiers."

There are countless such examples of children "playing soldiers" in British children's literature from the period, including the short story "Dad's Soldier Boy" (1918) by Harry Golding,[8] illustrated by Charles Robinson. In this, Billy and his sister Mary witness the departure of adults from their community, including their Uncle Ned, who "met a hero's death in Flanders" (9), "the baker's man" (9), "the greengrocer's man" (10), "the nice young lady in the sweetshop [...] and quite a number of others" (10). Once his own father enlists, Billy spends his precious money on "a khaki cap" and a "pop-gun" because "Daddy was to be a soldier – it was only right and proper that his son and heir should be a soldier too, and as like him in every way as possible" (12). The boy does not view his subsequent activities of constructing a sniper's post (18), transforming the spare bedroom into a trench (15), and building a tank out of "the rain-water barrel" and the baby's perambulator as a game (19), but rather as serious work. In one scene, for example, the narrator remarks that Billy was usually the one

> who started the games [...], but to-day he told Wallie sternly there was 'no time for fooling about.' It appeared a 'push' was to be made, and the enemy (invisible to the others) were in great force and strongly entrenched.
>
> (19)

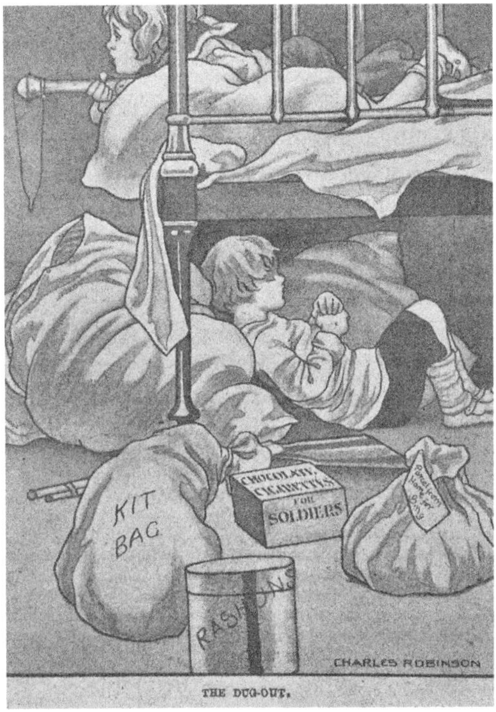

Figure 3.5 Illustration by Charles Robinson from "Dad's Soldier Boy" from *Wonder Book*, 1918.

Billy earnestly performs the role of soldier in his imaginative play, but the fact that some of the other young characters are not as invested in these games is a reminder that the image of the child fully immersed in play is a construction by the adult author (Figure 3.5).

When Billy tells Wallie they need a tank, for instance, their differences are clear:

> 'What tank?' asked Walter, who was not very imaginative; 'do you mean the one on your roof?'
>
> But Mary nudged him to be quiet, for she could see by the look on her brother's face that he was thinking hard.
>
> (19)

Wallie is less imaginative than Billy, and Mary observes her brother's game with some objectivity and detachment. Although she participates, she is less captivated and more pragmatic, stealing out of the spare room "trench" to get tea ready "like a good girl" when needed (15), and being rightfully wary of some of Billy's riskier games. These different approaches to imaginative games reveal that the widespread image of the child happily engrossed in war play may misrepresent the extent to which real children enthusiastically embraced military themes.

Depictions of children enjoying war games are products of the adult's imagination, and in the caption for the illustration "Playing Soldiers" discussed above, the declaration that the "army game is fun" comes from the adult writer. This leaves open the question of how much "fun" real children may have had playing war when so many adults around them were being maimed or killed. Cornish's depiction of a child crying after being cast in the role of the German enemy – a part that is subsequently assigned to the children's pet dog – suggests that war play was not always pleasurable and could potentially traumatize the child. As Celia Kingsbury observes, in a time of global warfare,

> it might seem psychologically sound to protect the young from violence, to grant them whenever possible the liberties childhood normally offers. Instead, children were expected to go along with the group and play war games in which hating the enemy became great fun.
>
> (169)

Depicting child figures enjoying martial-themed play can be understood as one means by which child readers were manipulated into accepting warfare as a legitimate pastime for both adults and children.[9]

One fictional work that shows children immersed in such play is *At War!* (c. 1916). Written and illustrated by Swiss-born French author and artist Charlotte Schaller and initially published in French, it uses colourful drawings and simple language to show how one little boy makes sense of the war. It begins with an illustration of little Bobby reading a newspaper and coming to terms with the fact that the war is a reality:

> Bobby can't believe his ears ... he has been told of a great war. Certainly he has already seen lots of soldiers start! His dear papa, also, has gone off in his beautiful uniform... Could it possibly be true? Let us try and find out. Ah! here is a paper – let's read it! ... Oh! Yes! it must be really true, as it is written in the paper.
>
> (5)

Even though his father has gone to fight, Bobby is only fully cognizant of the war once he reads about it. Given the extent to which news was censored and influenced by propaganda, the claim that something is "really true" because it appears in the paper is dubious, but it establishes the written text as a legitimate source of information for young readers and thereby validates Schaller's own pro-war narrative.

Once Bobby absorbs the fact that the war is real, he assembles his toys and play-acts the role of soldier, demonstrating his bravery and a sense of duty:

> All his soldiers, gunners, Cuirassiers, Zouaves; his rifles, his cannon and his aeroplane are thoroughly well cleaned and dusted [...] and Bobby, dressed up in his fine uniform, astride his battle horse, his great sword in his hand, holds a review of his troops. Their good looks and their splendid appearance inspire him with the greatest confidence. The Boches (Germans) can come ... Bobby awaits them unflinchingly.
>
> (Schaller 6)

The accompanying illustration shows Bobby in uniform on his rocking horse, with all his toy soldiers lined up before him (Figure 3.6).

The depiction of him "astride his battle horse" conjures up an outdated image of warfare and does not acknowledge the new horrors of mechanized warfare that produced such a shock at the time.[10] In this

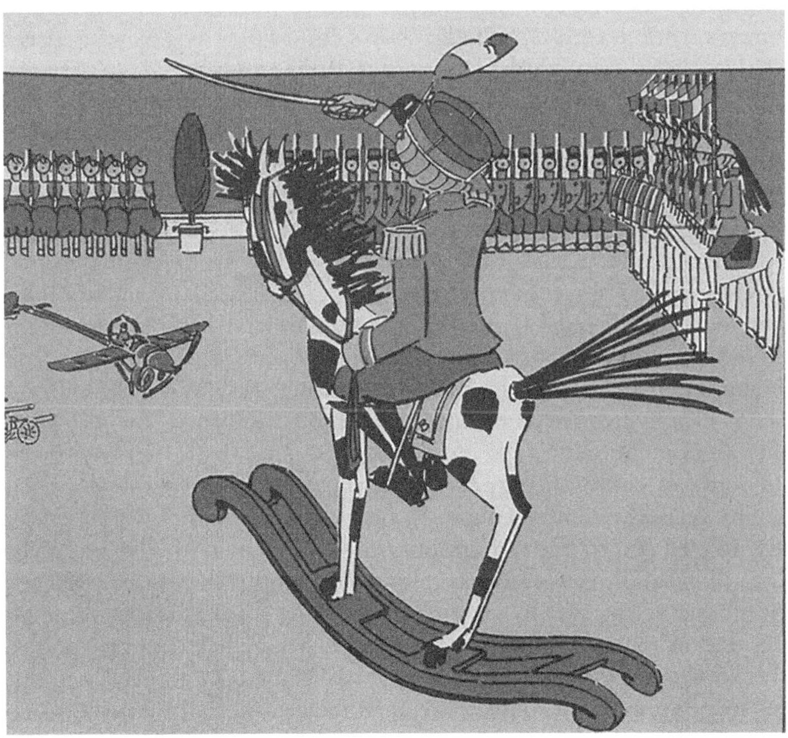

Figure 3.6 "Bobby Astride his Battle Horse" from Charlotte Schaller's *At War!*, c. 1916. [BnF].

instance, however, it is not the technical skills required by modern warfare that the author is interested in cultivating, but rather a specific set of ideals. The adjectives that accompany this account of Bobby's game include "good," "ready," and "splendid," and he prepares to meet the imaginary enemy with "confidence" and without flinching. This shows that his nursery play helps cultivate certain traits adults deem necessary for the contemporary soldier.

In Schaller's story, play is structured along gender lines. While Bobby pretends to be a soldier, his sisters Zezette and Jacqueline imagine themselves as hospital nurses. When war first broke out in Britain "the only military sphere in which women were accepted was their traditional role of caring for the sick and wounded" (Gould 116), and Schaller's tale is in keeping with the gendered nature of wartime games and toys, for it was frequently "the caring, nurturing role of wartime nurse that girls were offered by toy makers and parents" (Kennedy "How Merrily" 232). Zezette and Jacqueline reveal their expectations of what nursing entails as "they go round to their little friends and fetch beds, mattresses, blankets, pillows" and "carefully clean the brightest and prettiest room in the house" (Schaller 8). Reflecting the traditional notions of gender that prevailed at the outset of the war, as well as the increased demand for women's work as nurses, Schaller shows child's play as a way for girls to practice roles they might be expected to fulfil as adults.

In addition to understandings of gender, Schaller's narrative may have shaped young readers' attitudes towards national identity and Allied relations. It was published in both French and English, and its positive depiction of French children may have helped to solidify a sense of Allied identity in Anglophone readers. That cultivating a sense of solidarity is one of the primary goals of this book is evident from its inside cover, which is covered in writing that says "Long live Canada! Long live India! Long live the Allies! ... Long live the Highlanders! Long live Belgium!" and so forth (this is written in French in the original version of the text). The story concludes with the children shouting, "LONG LIVE THE ALLIES!" (32), which further underscores the book's focus on celebrating unity among nations.

A sense of common purpose is conveyed throughout the story, and "Bobby feels very courageous [...], because great and powerful friends have arrived [...] to fight the common foe" (Schaller 10). The accompanying illustration celebrates the close relationship between France and Britain during the war by showing two young soldiers standing side by side, one in the blue uniform of the French labelled "Bobby" and the other in the khaki uniform of the British labelled "Tommy," a ubiquitous term for British troops. Having Bobby paralleled with the British soldier in this way renders him an embodiment of his own country, suggesting that both soldier and child hold the key to the nation's future. While France and Britain had a long history of going to war against one another, this story focusses on the common goals of Allied nations, demonstrated in Bobby's admiration of "the brave and heroic Belgian Army. Courageously led by her young King, she has not hesitated to attack the giant" (12).

In employing the metaphor of the giant, a fictional figure familiar to child readers, Schaller fuels abhorrence of the German foe. Much like Cornish's illustration of children playing in the nursery, in which young "Germania objects to her part," Schaller reveals the deep aversion many felt to aligning themselves with Germany, even in play. After hearing of the Victory of the Marne, for example, "Bobby also wants to feel the emotions of a great battle, but how is it to be managed? Nobody will act the nasty Boches" (Schaller 16). He solves this by transforming his inanimate toys into the enemy; he drives a nail "into the ninepins, and there are the 'Pointed Helmets' all in a line" (16). He then enjoys the pleasure of destroying the German troops through a game of bowling. In this way, children in the story avoid adopting the loathsome identity of the Germans which, even in make-believe, they regard as a form of defilement.

There have long been adults who have attempted to promote peace and civility and "to preserve childhood innocence" by rejecting war toys and play (Cross 39), but Schaller's story reveals that not all adults believed the preservation of innocence was possible or even desirable. Some envisioned militaristic play as ideal for promoting civic spirit, and though most of Schaller's tale depicts children at leisure, it also shows them performing various tasks that support the war effort. Bobby helps "to wind the wool with which his mother and his little sisters knit gloves, mufflers, jerseys and caps" and he "slips into the parcels packets of tobacco, cigars, cigarettes, pipes and matches, which he buys with the pennies out of his money-box" (26).

Bobby and his sisters also take special care to "write every day" to their father with "never any fault in the spelling, nor the least blot" (30). They try to keep up his spirits by telling him about Bobby's "army, always in fine trim" and about the imaginary "wounded that they are caring for" (30). The same self-sacrifice that the children enact through their play is displayed in their writing and they "put their best into their letters, for they know what pleasure it gave Papa who was fighting so bravely to protect them" (30). As Lee Talley has shown in her work on child evacuees during the Second World War, young people were both "giving voice to or silencing emotions and/or analyses of the war" in their written communication (29), and acts of self-censorship are evident in children's letters. Bobby and his sisters' determination to remain positive and boost their father's morale by writing to him about their play can be seen as an act of self-censorship, as they do not even allow a spelling error to disturb him. It is worth remembering, however, that the children in Schaller's text are fictional creations, and thus their efforts to suppress their emotions may reflect adult expectations, rather than children's own impulses. Through the depiction of Bobby and his sisters writing letters, child readers are taught that one way to ease the wartime burden on adults and maintain morale is by being their very "best" selves and suppressing their own concerns, fears, and faults.

Another book that encourages the child to consider the needs of others and that draws a clear connection between the war and child's play is *French Toys*. Published in Paris in 1915, it is illustrated by André Hellé, a well-known artist of the period, and shows how children can help the war effort through the play they engage in.[11] The Introduction explains that the text is intended for American readers and addresses them as follows:

> Children who will see the future for which are dying the sons of France, this book has been written for you. If you love the toys made in France, if you adopt them, you will help us to find work for the widows, the orphans, the wounded of the most terrible war.
>
> (3)

This passage declares that the very toys children play with matter and that American children can help France by choosing to purchase French toys.

Published prior to American involvement in the conflict, the narrator addresses this collection to the "children of a free nation" in a direct appeal for aid (3), and various tales in it reveal an attempt to cultivate support for the war among American children. What differentiates this from other texts demanding children take part in the war effort is what it tells them about the *way* in which they can do this. While many authors encourage children to engage in work akin to adult labour (growing food, sewing, knitting, and so forth), this book suggests that children can help through child's play itself, and the purchasing of toys becomes a way for American children to help the cause.

One story in the collection is "The Leipsic Soldiers: Beware of the 'Made in Germany'" in which French historian Frédéric Masson gives a history of the lead toy industry in France and laments the fact that Germany has taken over an industry that his French "forefathers invented" (12). He criticizes the work of the "Nuremberg toy-makers" and observes that their soldiers were "painted all over with what was declared to be 'harmless paint'" (15), implying that the Germans knowingly painted their toys with toxic colours and lied about it. Masson declares that the French must "become once more the 'workers' in those trades we have let slip into the hands of this terrible, methodical organiser next door. *He* has no scruples" (16). Warning readers to "beware of the soldiers of Leipsic!" (16), Masson makes the case that supporting the German toy industry is tantamount to supporting the German army against France.

Pierre Mille (1864–1941), a journalist and popular French fiction writer from the period, also authored a story in this collection titled "The Wonderful Adventure." In it, the young American protagonist, Lilly, is awakened by the sound of Father Christmas in her nursery calling for help: "They are fighting, my little Lilly. Even these dolls are fighting, your playthings, those of Germany against those of France. I cannot manage them, it is awful" (38). As in Masson's piece, the German toys are portrayed negatively and embody the enemy's flaws:

> There was the Zeppelin [...] which never could fly save once when [...] it scratched nurse's eye and [...] burst [...]. There were the leaden soldiers so badly painted that whenever Bob plays with them he gets a stomach-ache. There was the railway with the carriages that bend if one lays the tip of one's finger on them [...]. Lastly there is the Emperor who says "*mein alten Gott*" as soon as one pulls his string and who distributes iron crosses!
>
> (Mille 38–41)

Mille subsequently contrasts these German toys with the French toys, which are described in much more glowing terms.

In using toys to represent the warring factions, Mille constructs a negative image of Germany for young American readers. While "stories focusing on Germans as despicable" became prevalent in Edwardian Britain in response to the South African War and Germany's increasing presence as an imperial threat (Francis "Meanest" 153–154), the United States had a less antagonistic relationship with Germany prior to WWI and was still two years away from joining when *French Toys* was published. Nevertheless, such works held the potential to shape the attitudes of American child readers and could potentially persuade them that their nation should join the Allied cause.

In Mille's story, Father Christmas tries desperately but unsuccessfully to end the toys' squabbling. He says to Lilly, "They'll smash up every thing. You see they cannot agree, my little Lilly. You must get rid of one of the camps. Choose" (44). Lilly replies, "I had rather get rid of those that come from Germany; they are so ugly while the others are pretty and they are quite good, too, when no one teases them. It is the fault of the Boches" (44). Mille draws a clear parallel between the war and the squabbling of these toys, picturing Germany as the instigator in both instances. The use of the derogatory term "Boche" is repeated when the narrator reports that Lilly "took the Swiss farmer's wife who is Boche, the Zeppelin, the Emperor, and the whole set and flung them out of the window" (45). In Mille's story, Lilly clearly serves as an example for young Americans to follow as she declares her allegiance to the French and severs her ties with the Germans. She, and by extension the child reader, is asked to take a political stand through her play.

Preparing Children for War through Organized Play: Boy Scouts, Girl Guides, and the Junior Red Cross

The belief that children's pastimes could help support the Allied cause or prepare children for future military duties was perhaps best exemplified by the youth organizations that flourished during the war. One study of organized children's activities suggests that these can be "valuable investments in the future child" but can also "reflect and perpetuate many undesirable cultural qualities, including social inequality [...] and sex stereotyping. Viewed from either perspective, organized activities are more than just fun and games" (Medrich et al. 158). During the First World War, organized activities included uniformed youth groups, suggesting "an underlying adult view of youth as a problem that required a solution. Such youth groups were often designed to keep working-class boys off the streets and provide them with a pastime that promoted middle-class values" (Hay 270).

The Boy Scouts and Girl Guides are two uniformed organizations that have been seen both as both "investments" in the child and as perpetuating "undesirable cultural qualities." With their emphasis on skills-development and discipline, they clearly mingled play and work, and some scholars argue the Boy Scouts organization was explicitly designed to prepare "the next generation of British soldiers for war and the defence of the Empire" (Springhall 935). Founded in Britain in 1908 by Robert Baden-Powell (1857–1941), the group was popular around the globe[12] and the Scout was a common figure in wartime children's literature, but historians "have ardently debated whether or not, and to what extent, Scouting was a movement defined by militaristic goals" (Crotty 74). While some contend Baden-Powell had "the peaceful object of making better future citizens of [...] boy members" (Warren 376), the organization certainly had "a distinctly military flavor" that included uniforms and ranks (Crotty 76), indicating that children's 'play' was aligned to some extent with the military roles they might assume in adulthood.

The connection between childhood and future military duties is evident in a note from the editor in the April 1917 issue of *Work and Play* announcing the magazine's absorption by the weekly paper the *Scout* (founded by Baden-Powell). This quotes Baden-Powell's declaration of what the *Scout* will offer readers and presents a clear picture of the masculine ideal he wants boys to aspire to:

> In these Scout yarns you will read how brave men contrive to stand up to danger with a smile on in tight places, how they sacrifice themselves for others, how they make themselves [...] big, fit, and strong, to go through their hardships successfully.
>
> ("Important")

This is followed by a tidy summary of the view that Boy Scout activities will help turn boys into ideal adult citizens:

> Boy Scouts, as you know, go in for learning how to do [...] things while boys, so that they may, as their motto says, 'Be prepared' to do their duty as men when the time comes. They learn through games to 'play the game' [...].
>
> ("Important")

According to Baden-Powell, childhood is a time to prepare for the duties of adulthood, and the Scouts organization has an important role to play in this training.

A similar message is evident in Edward Shirley's "Boy Scouts in War-Time" from the British anthology *The Jolly Book for Boys and Girls* (c. 1916). He remarks that "Scouts, whose motto is 'Be prepared,' have done splendid work during the war. They have [...] guarded waterworks, level crossings and bridges, and have been watchers on the coast. [...] and in a hundred other ways have tried to be of real use during the great struggle" (230). What might have been dismissed as a form of play prior to the war is here described as "splendid work" by the author, who talks of Scouts wanting to "be of real use" on the home front.

In discussing an accompanying illustration of a Scout "acting as a War Office messenger" (230), Shirley further emphasizes the child's desire to be taken seriously and acknowledges that Scouting can prepare one to be a soldier:

> You will notice that he is a very distinguished scout; his arm fairly bristles with badges. I have no doubt that he is longing for the day when he will be old enough to enlist and fight for his country. He is bound to make an excellent soldier, for he has already learned to obey promptly, to keep his eyes open and observe what he sees. He has a high sense of duty, and he never allows a single day to go by without doing a good action.
>
> (230)

In this instance, the Scout figure serves the clear didactic purpose of instilling in boy readers "a high sense of duty," inspiring them to "good action," and teaching them the value of prompt obedience, so central to military life.

The international reach and popularity of the movement meant that there were various iterations of the figure of the Boy Scout in children's literature from different nations. One British example is *Defenders of the Empire*, a "Postcard Painting Book" published c.1914. Its illustrations of horses pulling military carts and wagons, guided by able-bodied young Scouts, seem far removed from the grim realities of trench warfare, during which more than eight million horses died, and show readers that children can be part of the events unfolding around them. The war is thus pictured as children's "work" but is simultaneously converted into a form of play as the postcards are designed for children to colour, punch out, and mail to their friends. Child's play, children's literature, and young people's labour in support of the war effort thus become intermingled.

While some texts imply that the war could have a permanent negative impact on children and cause an irretrievable loss of innocence, others propose that the disruption of childhood is temporary, and that 'normal' childhood can resume once peace is restored. For example, in "Doing His Bit," published in London in *Collins' Children's Annual* of 1916, the poet suggests that the contributions made by British Scouts on the home front truly are work, but that child's play can resume after the war:

> Little Boy Scout, will you signal to me
> If there's an enemy crossing the sea?
> On the bleak headland you're watching our coast,
> Doing 'your bit' without murmur or boast.
>
> Cricket and football no yearning inspire,
> Century records you do not desire.
> The world has grown stern with war's bitter strife,
> Games seem no longer the chief thing in life.
>
> Brave little laddie, when tumult shall cease,
> And joy-bells announce the glad news of peace,
> Back to your games you can go with a zest,
> Feeling that staunchly you helped with the rest.
>
> (F.M.G. 88)

The poet embraces the notion that children have a special resiliency; though the "world has grown stern" and the child has abandoned his usual games, there is hope that these can be easily resumed after the work of war is completed.

The assumption that labour does not normally belong to childhood and is the result of extraordinary wartime circumstances represents a particular construction of childhood rooted in middle-class values. It was not uncommon for working-class children to be employed in prewar Britain, so the expectation that young boys will go back to their games "with a zest" after war's end reveals how conceptions of childhood were shaped by class bias. Unlike Hogben's suggestion that war marks childhood's end and the warrior will be "nevermore – a boy," F.M.G. suggests that Scouts helping the war effort are experiencing only a temporary change from typical childhood play.

As American writer Bennett Chapple's[13] verse "A Twentieth Century Paul Revere" shows, British children's writers were not the only ones to portray the Scout as a valuable participant in the war effort. Chapple's poem appeared in 1918 in the magazine *Boys' Life* (published by the Boy Scouts of America) and in the American anthology *Patriotic Selections for Supplementary Reading*. In it he compares a young Scout to Paul Revere, celebrated hero of the American Revolution:

> Listen, my children, and you shall hear
> Of a Twentieth Century Paul Revere;
> Of a brave young Scout on a valiant steed,
> Who rode a race for his Country's need.
> He heard of his Country's call for men;
> He heard of their sacrifice, and then –
> He heard of the need for money, too;
> For food and clothes to help them through.
> He wanted to help though he could not fight,
> He wanted to serve in the cause of right.
>
> (Chapple 155)

In this first stanza, the boy's youth and desire to help are both emphasized. He cannot yet be a soldier, but there are other ways in which he can serve "his Country's need," and the comparison to Revere establishes the Boy Scout as an emblem of American identity and patriotism (155).

One way to help is by collecting donations, so the boy mounts his horse and rides throughout the land calling for support:

> Gather your nickels! Gather your dimes!
> Help the Nation! Prepare, these Times!
> Lend Uncle Sam a part of your pay!
> Store up! Store up! for a rainy day.
>
> (Chapple 155–156)

Children in America, as well as Canada and Britain, were encouraged to support the war effort financially and this Boy Scout provides an inspiring example to follow. Though too young to fight, he can "spread the call of his Country's need" and rally the people of his nation (156). This is explicitly referred to as 'work' when he addresses his "valiant steed" at the end of the poem: "Our work is done [...] Old Man – The Nation's roused to a War-Thrift Plan" (157). Chapple transforms the activities of the Boy Scouts from organized play into meaningful action worthy of celebration in verse.

The notion that Scouts were working, rather than playing, is also evident in "The Dream of Boy Scout Bliss," published in the Canadian/American anthology *Mother Goose's Garden* (c.1917) (Figure 3.7).

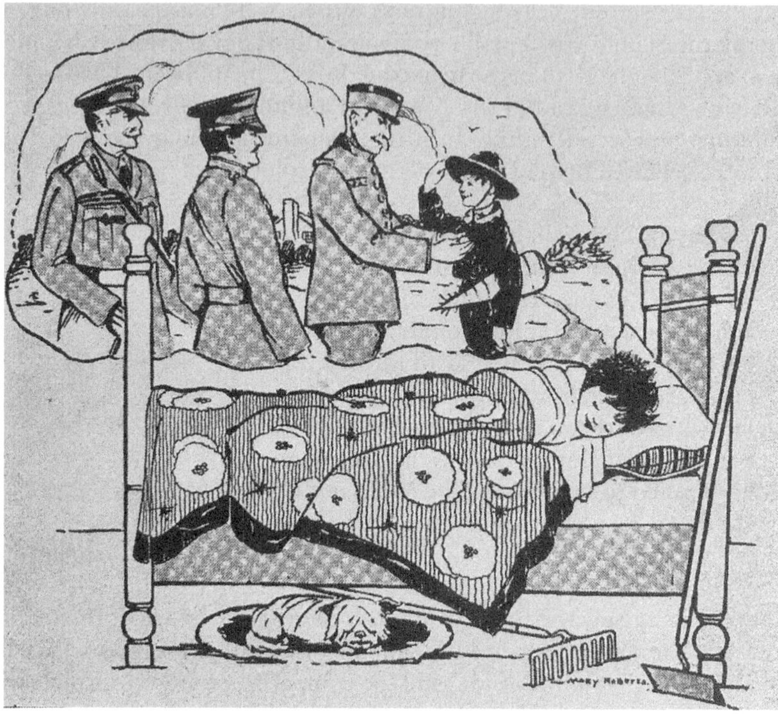

Figure 3.7 Illustration by Mary Roberts from "The Dream of Boy Scout Bliss" from *Mother Goose's Garden* c. 1917.

It highlights the food production efforts of Billy Bliss, a Scout who is "very tired" at the end of "a hard day's work in his carrot patch." His mother says, "You deserve a medal for the way you have stuck to your duty to-day," and when the exhausted boy falls asleep, he dreams of being awarded a medal by three "very famous generals" who praise him and his peers:

> "He's a fine little fellow," smiled the American General. A good sample of the Garden Army of North America that is working so hard to produce food that we may win the war.
>
> "That is the kind of a boy," remarked the English General, "upon which we base our faith that the Anglo-Saxon family will win and maintain the freedom of the world."
>
> ("The Dream")

The generals describe the children's gardening as vital, and their strong work ethic as evidence of cultural values shared by Britain and North

America, described here as an "Anglo-Saxon family."[14] The author shows child readers that they can help win the war, but also uses this tale of the Scout to create an image of Britain, Canada, and the United States as wartime allies united by common ideals and ethnic ties.

Though less ubiquitous than the Scout, the Girl Guide was also a figure in wartime children's literature and the Guiding movement remained popular throughout the war. A letter by founder Agnes Baden-Powell (1858–1945) from the August 1914 issue of the *Girl Guides' Gazette* reveals that girls were encouraged to put to use the skills they had learned as Guides:

> Now that we are faced with such a grievous calamity as actual warfare, I wish to explain to you that though we have no connection with military work, there is still a vast field of usefulness for you Guides.
>
> Grown up Guides may volunteer as Nurses [...], but our girls have no such vocation and are not yet fully trained. They are learning still.
>
> And I watch with great pleasure the progress they are making in Ambulance work, Nursing and invalid Cookery.
>
> (Baden-Powell, Agnes "Miss" 1)

The claim that there is "no connection" between the Guides and military work is echoed in a later publication that states "Guiding is not a military movement. Most of the training is done by games, stories and hikes" (Guides 10). The apparent desire to distance this uniformed organization from the military not only echoes the view that childhood and warfare belong to separate spheres but seems designed to reassure readers that a separation between women and militarism is being maintained. Nevertheless, the letter reveals that the movement is interested in the "training" of girls and that the games Guides have been involved in have prepared them for wartime. The words "*actual* warfare" (italics mine) acknowledge that the Guides have employed war metaphors in their activities prior to 1914 and are now faced with the real thing.

Agnes Baden-Powell tries to reconcile traditional notions of femininity with the new roles for women emerging during the war; a difficult balancing act that many children's writers grappled with. In addition to the ambulance work and nursing that she cites as areas where older Guides can be of use, she notes other tasks that involve girls' traditional, domestic duties:

> Go and see the anxious ones in their homes, take care of their children or mind their babies, wash up for them or do a little mending.

> One of our chief duties is to maintain discipline, no great work can be achieved without perfect order, discipline and obedience.
>
> Prompt obedience to orders is what every soldier has to learn, and it is instant, cheerful obedience which helps to make everything go smoothly.
>
> If troops require helping, parties might be got up for assisting in cookery, washing, sewing [...], lighting fires in the open, and many other services. So, you see, your Camping experience will come into use. [...] We are not called into the fighting line, but let us put forth all our strength to help others to be resolute and hopeful, confident that good will come.
>
> (Baden-Powell "Miss")

This passage recalls the familiar nineteenth-century view that women are to be obedient, cheerful, and hopeful influences within the home, and the suggested tasks include girls' common domestic duties. Even the reference to camping, which may at first seem to encourage adventure, is cast in a domestic light.

Robert Baden-Powell

> explained camping and woodcraft for girls not as thrilling adventures, but as sensible pastimes that would teach them femininity and domestic skills while appealing to their 'natural' maternal instincts. Spending time in nature, he claimed, would develop 'the soul and character of the future mothers of the race' while improving girls' all-important home-making skills.
>
> (Alexander 112)

Both Agnes and Robert Baden-Powell thus saw the Guides movement as one that would prepare girls for traditional roles in the domestic realm, but in drawing a parallel between girls and soldiers, noting that obedience is required of both, Agnes Baden-Powell aligns the Guides with male troops, complicating traditional views of gender.

One piece that portrays the Guide as equal to her male peer is "A Guide We Are Proud Of," published in the *Girl Guides' Gazette* in 1914. It recounts the achievements of ten-year-old Alice Barnes who, while paddling on a river, quickly responds to the cries of a Scout who his "sinking in the mud and unable to do more than shout for help" ("A Guide"). Alice does not hesitate and "at great risk to herself" she rushes to the boy's aid and saves him. If it were not for the girl's "pluck and presence of mind the Scout would have been drowned" ("A Guide"). This tale maintains that girls can display just as much "pluck" and skill as their male counterparts and reiterates the notion that through their leisure activities, girls can develop practical skills and important traits like bravery.

While the Girl Guides and Boy Scouts were organized separately according to gender and thus reinforced traditional roles, wartime representations of organized play also made manifest newly emerging gender expectations. As Margaret Higonnet observes, "political upheavals facilitate the mobilization of children in wartime and [...] social chaos unsettles gendered identity formation" ("Girl" 8). Throughout the war, children's literature reflected both a desire to preserve traditional notions of gender, as well as an urge to acknowledge – and even celebrate – war's role in destabilizing these. These shifting views emerge in the above account of Alice Barnes, but they were also evident in co-ed organizations like the Junior Red Cross, which was established in Canada in 1914 and the United States in 1917.[15] "The Junior Red Cross," published in *St. Nicholas* in November, 1917, outlines American children's contributions to making clothes for the war effort and refers at one point to a New York school where boys demanded "equal rights with the girls – that is, knitting-needles, yarn, and instruction; and shortly thereafter they were making equally good articles" (26). This account clearly shows how the activities of organized children's groups contributed to changing attitudes towards gender.

The need for every individual to help secure Germany's defeat contributed to the erosion of distinctions based on gender and age. Just as boys were needed to take on duties like sewing that were traditionally assigned to girls, and just as women had to step into positions normally held by men, children had to take on a level of responsibility previously reserved for adults. The demands of the war effort meant that adults reevaluated the abilities of children and taught young readers to think of themselves in a new way; one that recognized their significance and abilities. This is evident in "The Junior Red Cross" when the writer remarks on the high quality of the work American children produced, recounting that when inspectors examined boxes containing 1,500 hospital garments, "not one of them required the slightest correction" (25). They assumed the sewing had been done by adults, but the items "were not sewn by women at all" but were "made by the girls of the eighth and ninth grades of the Buffalo schools" (25).

According to this article, this incident directly contributed to the formation of the Junior Red Cross in the United States, which arose out of a demand made by children:

> The Red Cross was forced by the boys and girls themselves [...] to admit them to the organization on special terms. As soon as the war came to America, numerous plans were suggested to the Red Cross authorities for giving a [...] membership standing to boys and girls. But the national organization was loath to do this. It savored too much of seeking juvenile members for the sake of the fees they would

> turn into the Red Cross coffers. [...] But the work of boys and girls for the Red Cross turned the scales in their favor.
>
> ("Junior Red" 25–26)

The inspectors' initial supposition that the sewing was done by adults reveals an assumption that children are less skilled, but the high-quality of their work changed this perception. Similarly, the discussion of fees suggests that worries about exploiting children gave way to an appreciation of their ability to help. This article suggests that the wartime activities of youth organizations were instrumental in shifting attitudes towards children and were viewed as more than frivolous pastimes or a means of keeping children out of trouble. As with other representations of children's play, depictions of children engaged in organized activities figured them as capable and responsible individuals who could adapt to the changing needs of their nation and transform their leisure activities into work of vital importance to the Allied cause.

Spies and Spy-Catchers: Espionage and Child's Play

Different accounts of children's organizations reveal the uncertain boundaries between work and play, and between adulthood and childhood, but this ambiguity is also evident in tales in which the activities of groups like the Scouts spill over into children's independent play. This blending of formal and imaginative play emerges in different ways but is particularly evident in the figure of the child engaged in espionage. Spy tales were incredibly popular during the war, with children's writers often depicting children playing at being spies or catching spies, just as they showed them pretending to be soldiers or nurses. Many also suggested that children could really participate in espionage, and several stories featuring Boy Scouts suggested that the "training" received through the organization made them particularly adept at this. Others, meanwhile, suggested that all young people, not just Scouts, needed to practice their surveillance skills and "be prepared."

One story in which child's play transforms into real spy-catching is "On the Other Side of the Wall: A War-time Adventure in an Old Castle" by Captain Charles Gilson (1878–1943),[16] which underscores the value of schoolboys being prepared for the business of war. Young Dick and his friend Roy are spending their school holiday at Dick's home, a large Elizabethan property that includes the ruins of a medieval castle rumoured to be haunted. Hearing the ghost story inspires the boys to amuse themselves by exploring the ruins for signs of the spirits. What starts off as a game suddenly turns real as the boys hear the sound of footsteps and immediately display their level-headedness and courage. Roy declares he is "not going to turn tail" while Dick announces that they "had better be prepared for anything" and promptly picks up two solid pieces of wood to carry (451). His foresight proves beneficial when the boys stumble into the secret hiding place of a German spy who has been using the castle ruins as a hidden wireless telegraph station.

Gilson's story ends by suggesting that the traits of bravery and preparedness that characterized Dick and Roy's play as they hunted for ghosts, and which quickly became the real work of successfully capturing a spy, have since been put to different use by the pair who are no longer school aged: "all this happened more than a year ago; and they are now in Flanders, in the trenches, taking their part in the great struggle against Germany" (452). This story shows how the amusements of childhood can be co-opted by authors to serve a didactic purpose; in this case, to teach readers that their play can prepare them for their future duty as soldiers. It also suggests that the transition from childhood to adulthood can happen abruptly in wartime, as in a little more than a year the protagonists go from being school children entertained by ghost stories, to men fighting in the trenches. Tales in which children outwit and apprehend professional spies further suggest that the boundary between child and adult is hazy. This ambiguity had real-life consequences for boys who were bombarded with propaganda urging them to enlist the moment they came of age, and many of whom enlisted early (something that will be discussed at further length in Chapter 5).

Although tales like Gilson's encouraged young readers to prepare themselves to meet the enemy, some authors were less earnest and used the spy genre to more humorous effect. As David Budgen notes, the motif of the German spy "was so widespread that it was almost immediately ridiculed in some publications" (67), and some authors similarly mocked the figure of the heroic child spy-catcher. One example is "Rough Luck! The Story of a Boy Scout and a Spy" by Eustace Drew. Set in a quiet seaside resort shortly before the outbreak of war, it is the story of "a chap rising fourteen" who finds his summer holiday to be "just a bit too restful." The subtle implication is that this boredom may be a contributing factor in the boy's overzealous pursuit of a German spy, which he engages in as a means of keeping himself entertained.

Narrated in the first person by the eponymous Scout, it begins by showing how his Scout's training allows him to spring into action when, while out swimming, he fortuitously discovers a secret underwater cable being used to send information to Germany. This seemingly heroic accomplishment is undermined, however, by his eventual realization that the British military had discovered this many weeks earlier and had replaced the cable with one they were monitoring. The Scout's public declaration of his discovery upends these efforts and one angry Lieutenant remarks, "the whole thing is bust up by that poisonous imp of mischief. [...] those Boy Scouts are too jolly efficient" (340). What begins as a tale of a Boy Scout helping to catch a German spy thus turns into a humorous account of his discovery that his efforts have hindered, rather than helped, the cause.

The difference between Drew's comical presentation of his boy hero and more laudatory depictions of child scouts, spies, and spy-catchers demonstrates the artificiality of the heroic child character who always saves the day. Though clearly intended to amuse, Drew's story is also something of a cautionary tale that may have taught young readers to question what they read. In mocking the child sleuth, Drew may be gently rebuking the countless tales of child spies that filled the pages of juvenile literature throughout the war. Child readers are invited to laugh at the imperfect resolution of the heroic fantasies indulged in by the young protagonist, who serves to remind them that tales about glory being heaped on children were not always to be trusted.

Another possible function of such humorous depictions is posited by Emer O'Sullivan in her discussion of German children's literature. She argues that comic representations of children playing at war go beyond simple entertainment and could have actually provided "psychological relief for adults" (209), suggesting that humorous tales can "transform adult fears in the face of war by presenting it as simply child's play" (209). According to O'Sullivan, comic episodes "reduce the frightening complexity of war to a game" and allow readers to engage "free of fear and even pleasurably, with the topic of war" (209). In O'Sullivan's view, humorous stories like Drew's spy tale "transformed a serious and threatening subject into something that both children and adults could laugh at" (209).

While humorous accounts of children playing different types of war games may have been a means of reducing fear and providing comic relief at a time of great anxiety, works that undermined the image of the heroic child sometimes had a darker edge. One satirical critique of the "boy hero" figure appears in the *Boy's Own* (1915–1916) in a poem by Felix Leigh, a frequent contributor to the magazine. Leigh's "Warranted to Wear: Or, The Serial Boy Hero" draws attention to the unrealistic depictions of child heroes that dominated wartime children's literature:

> Down a trench he stole on tiptoe, with intent to scotch a Hun,
> But the Germans had him captured at the close of Chapter I.
> Did we feel at all uneasy? Rather not: for well we knew
> He'd escape and join our fellows ere we'd got through
>   Chapter II.
> [....]
> In the Chapters that succeeded he was shot against a wall –
> He was swallowed by a quagmire near the Yser, horse and all –
> He was trapped in burning houses – he was Zepped, and he
>   was gassed,

But he always turned up smiling, and, no doubt, in Chapter
Last,
He'll be calling out, "Hands up, Sir!" to the villain, Fritz
the Spy,
Who will thereupon surrender to The Boy Who Cannot Die!

Leigh's rendering of the young hero who captures the German spy and always escapes death shows how artificial this figure was. Leigh invites child readers to laugh at such representations, but his poem may also prompt them to question what they read. The title "The Boy Who Cannot Die" draws attention to the lack of realism that enabled much children's literature to function as a form of propaganda, for the boy character who could not die was an illusion – one that stood in stark contrast to the millions of real young men who would never return home from the war.

Higonnet argues that at the time of "the First World War, children were initiated into the culture of war everywhere through dressing up as well as visual culture, toys, and narratives" ("War" 119). Yet this war was unlike any that had come before, and it ushered in a new era of modern warfare in which the rules of conduct seemed to be constantly changing. From the introduction of tanks to the horrors of gas attacks, war looked very different from the type that children had traditionally acted out in their play. In a world turned upside down, there may have been something reassuring for children in structured play that followed clear rules, in imaginative play over which they asserted control, and in play with war toys over which the child could "claim mastery" (Higonnet "War" 120). Play could thus provide a realm in which children could exercise some agency at a time when they were surrounded by chaos, but it could not be entirely separated from the world of adults, who established and shaped youth organizations and largely determined the toys and games children had access too. Depicting play in children's literature was also a means by which adults could help determine the form that children's play took, including the extent to which it was transformed into war "work." Although some writers from the period expressed concern about politicizing or militarizing children's activities,[17] throughout the war many continued to exploit the child's sense of the importance of his or her play and showed readers how their pastimes could contribute to the Allied cause.

Tales of children helping the war effort on the home front through their leisure activities may have helped children accept the notion that they had both the ability and the duty to contribute to the war effort. While at times the child's innocence is highlighted and authors try to preserve the image of childhood as a safe and imaginative space far removed from the horrors of war, many embrace the idea that children have a duty to their nation and suggest that this can be performed in part through play, arguing that the activities of the young are not frivolous or self-indulgent, but serve the greater good. The notion that the actions of children could have a meaningful impact on the community was widely taken up in wartime children's literature as authors represented children as active figures who could make a positive contribution to society.

Notes

1 The popularity of war toys, including toy soldiers, varied between nations and Cross argues that these "were far more acceptable in Europe than in the USA in the 19th and early 20th centuries" (40).
2 Ellis, a frequent contributor to the *Boy's Own*, is possibly the author of *'Somewhere in France' and Other Poems*, published by J. W. Frings in 1918.
3 Several stories by Freeman were published in the *Boy's Own*.
4 Hogben's poetry and prose appeared in different periodicals during the war. In 1919, a collection of these war-themed works was published as *The Highway of Hades* and dedicated to "Jack in Khaki" (Hogben *Highway* vii).
5 Frederick William Burgess authored the 1913 text *Chats on Old Coins* and other books on antiques and collecting.
6 Butler authored more than thirty books and two thousand short stories but worked full-time as a banker ("Ellis Parker").
7 This series is clearly imbued with British patriotism. The back page reads, "The 'Little Patriots' Post Card Pictures are entirely British productions. The pictures are by British artists, the reading matter is by a British writer and the printing is done by a British firm who employ only British labour" *(Children's Painting Book)*.
8 Golding was a "prolific Ward Lock writer, editor, and compiler, best known for a popular series of 'Wonder' books and mass-market compilations" (Reynolds *Left Out* 42).
9 Rosie Kennedy notes the difficulty of ascertaining how children felt about such play and of determining its role "in shaping their understanding of the real war, or their sense of themselves" (*Children's* 52). She asks:

> Did games give children an opportunity to confront fears about absent fathers and brothers? Did children use the war-themed toys they were given in the way that was intended, or did they subvert their use for something else? All this is very difficult to know because of the essentially private way in which children play.
>
> (52)

10 This image of Bobby on horseback resembles a traditional form of commemorative war statuary that for many served as "a reassuring vision of [...] fitness and manhood" (Wingate 28), and "subscribed to the ideals of individual heroism and aggression" (33).
11 Hellé was "the penname of André Laclôtre (1871–1945), an illustrator and maker of toys and furniture for children" (Brotons Capó 62). He also wrote the plot and constructed the sets for Debussy's ballet *La Boite à joujoux* (67).
12 Scouting is "the most successful youth movement in world history" and has "more than thirty-eight million Scout and Guide members worldwide" (Proctor "Building" xxvii).
13 This may be the same Bennett Chapple (1879–1962) who worked for Armco Steel Corporation and published verse in the *Armco Bulletin*.

14 This image of the "Anglo-Saxon" child does not represent the diversity of Canada and the United States at the time, but by emphasizing a shared English heritage, the author envisions an Allied identity that incorporates the United States, which had only recently aligned itself formally with Britain.

15 The youth section of the British Red Cross was officially established in 1924 but

> young people played an active role in supporting the work of the British Red Cross during the First World War. One of the most important tasks they undertook was collecting sphagnum moss, which was made into dressings for the wounded. In 1918, the British Red Cross supplied nearly two million dressings for wounded soldiers.
>
> ("Junior")

16 Gilson was a soldier and a prolific author of books for boys, writing several wartime short stories and novels, including many works of fantasy.

17 As early as 1915 "support for war as a theme for children's play was not universal" in Britain and when the war's "mass casualties began to be reflected in children's toys, objections were raised by those alarmed by the glib way in which children were being encouraged to accept the human consequences of war" (Kennedy "How Merrily" 231).

4 Tinker, Tailor, Farmer, Thrift-Maker

The Child Contributor on the Home Front

Although images of innocent and victimized children abound in literature from 1914 to 1919, many authors suggest that children are more than just passive witnesses to the war who have no role to play and who must wait to be rescued by Allied forces. Instead, they argue that children can help themselves, other young victims, adults in the community, and soldiers on the front lines. At school, at home, and at play, children learned it was their duty to contribute to the war effort. In some instances, wartime literature was empowering, encouraging the participation of young readers by appealing to a sense of pride and suggesting children possess inherent qualities that make them valuable citizens. In others, writers shamed children into participating in activities on the home front by questioning their honour, their appropriate performance of gender roles, or their loyalty to the nation. Whatever the approach, the image of the child as a dynamic, helpful figure on the home front stood in contrast to the image of the helpless child that was also prevalent throughout the war.

Children's authors often celebrated the achievements of adult men and women, but they also urged child readers to do their part in helping to win the war. Common activities for young people included practicing thrift, donating money, growing food, and sewing or knitting. To encourage children to help win the war, writers provided fun and entertainment through both non-fiction and fiction, but they also appealed to the child's sense of patriotism and national identity, exploited the child's yearning for empowerment, invoked both traditional and progressive notions of gender, and appealed to feelings of shame, honour, and duty.

Mother's Little Helper: The Child at Home

While many works of children's literature contain an adult narrator or adult characters who urge children to help the war effort, the eager child who requires no prompting is also a recurring figure. Many works portray children as feeling frustrated about not being able to fight for their countries, and authors seek to assure readers that every child has some role to perform. The departure of fathers and older siblings to the front

DOI: 10.4324/9781003191605-5

lines, and the increasing absence of mothers as they entered the workforce, altered the dynamics of family life and the everyday realities for many children. These shifts meant that the child's role within the family changed, sometimes resulting in a greater burden of responsibility. The extent to which individual children actually felt an increased sense of duty and obligation is difficult to ascertain, but literature from the period shows that adult authors were either actively trying to cultivate a sense of responsibility in child readers, or were reflecting the feelings of contemporary children in their writing.[1] Some authors seem to address a genuine desire on the part of children to feel needed, and they attempt to reassure readers that every individual has an important part to play.

One poem that touches on these concerns is Lillian Gard's "The Lad Who Was Left Behind," published in the 1915–1916 *Boy's Own Annual*.[2] It is about a little boy whose father has gone to war and left him with the "honoured task" of looking after his mother and siblings, which he performs faithfully:

> And when he saw "the Mater" (whom "Pater" loved so well),
> With forehead wrinkled gravely, he'd bravely, blithely, tell
> Of all the brightest war-news – till fear would stand at bay:
> He knew "the Dad" would wish it – and he was far away!
>
> And when "the kids" would grumble (as "kids" of seven and
> eight
> *Do* grumble), then the laddie, grown manly and sedate,
> Would point out how all soldiers "stuck" hard things, every
> day –
> He knew Dad hated discontent – and Dad was far away!
>
> And on the little things of home the laddie kept his eyes;
> (Those blue eyes bright with twinkles where a flash would,
> sometimes, rise):
> And all the little cares he'd dress in merry hope-array,
> Till Dad came back and shook his hand – that Dad who went
> away!
>
> (Gard 340)

Gard's verse implies that one way in which the war impacted children was by making them more mature, for although the boy is "just a careless laddie" at the start of the poem, he grows "manly and sedate" in his father's absence.

In this poem, it is the male child's responsibility to step into the role of father, and he takes on the tasks of reproving his siblings when they grumble and teaching them the lesson of quiet perseverance. In something of a reversal of their roles as parent and child, he also assumes a paternal role towards his mother, striving to relieve her anxiety by keeping up a "merry" demeanour and focussing on only the "brightest war-news." His ability to alleviate her suffering lies in his performance of childhood innocence; despite his awareness of the gravity of the war and his father's absence, he plays the part of the happy, hopeful child in order to cheer his mother. It is not a vicarious pleasure in the child's supposedly innate optimism and innocence that alleviates the mother's worries; rather, it is the child's conscious *performance* of these traits that comforts the adult.

At first glance, the poem's title seems to suggest that the child "left behind" feels abandoned or left out of the important work of war, but the verses convey another meaning; that the child has been "left behind" to serve as a protector of the family in his father's stead. The boy's important responsibilities within the home include being a conscientious guide for his siblings, a mindful comfort to his mother, and a brave and selfless lad worthy of his father's trust and respect. The poet suggests that keeping his eyes "on the little things of home" is the boy child's primary responsibility, and the family home the space where the child rightfully belongs during the war. The poet acknowledges child readers' desire to help achieve victory but persuades them that this can be done within the domestic sphere.

Children's apparent longing to have adults consider them helpful appears repeatedly in wartime children's literature, often in works that adopt the child's perspective or employ a child narrator. For instance, in "The Littlest One," published in the American periodical *St. Nicholas* (1918), poet Edith Price assumes the voice of the child to express this yearning:

> My daddy he's a Captain,
> My brother is a Scout,
> My sister is a Camp-Fire Girl –
> But I am just left out.
> They each have uniforms to wear.
> And different things to do.
> Oh dear! I do so wish that I belonged to something, too!
>
> My mother tells me not to mind;
> She says, "Why, don't you see?
> Because you are the littlest one
> *You* just belong to *me!*"
>
> (Price 851)

This poem appears in a section titled "For Very Little Folk" and suggests that the precise nature of the role children can play in the war effort is dependent on their age. While only older children can be Scouts and Camp-Fire girls, younger children can still serve a function, and in this case, it is childishness itself that is a valuable source of comfort for the mother.

In the final stanza, the poet switches focus from the young child's yearning to have "things to do" to the mother's desire to keep her child close. An accompanying illustration shows the father and older siblings dressed in various uniforms, while another shows the mother embracing her very young son (Figure 4.1). Taken together, the poem and illustrations convey that while children may have a role to play in the war effort, the home is still the most appropriate sphere for the very young. Price acknowledges the child's desire to be part of the great events unfolding in the world, but also draws attention to the mother's longing to be near her child. At a time when so many families were sending older sons and daughters off to the theatre of war, Price, like Gard, suggests that one duty of the younger child is to give his mother a sense of security. The poem expresses an adult wish for the child to remain innocent, protected, and within the safe domestic sphere, even while acknowledging the child's desire to move beyond this realm. Child readers are thus presented with multivalent images of what it means to be a child, and of how children might best comfort or assist the adults around them.

Other poems in the same section of this American periodical further suggest ways in which even very little children can help the war effort without leaving home or losing their presumed innocence. "Her Sacrifice" by Mattie Lee Hausgen, for example, is accompanied by artist Decie C. Merwin's depiction of a small girl holding a doll and looking

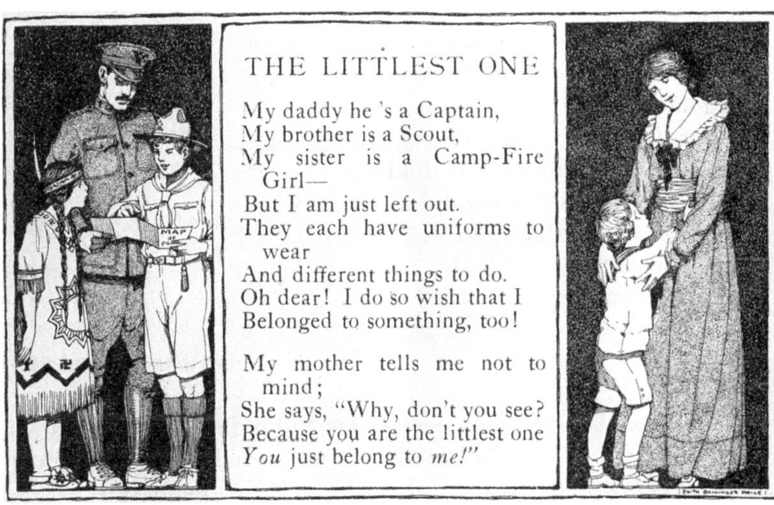

THE LITTLEST ONE

My daddy he 's a Captain,
My brother is a Scout,
My sister is a Camp-Fire
  Girl—
But I am just left out.
They each have uniforms to
  wear
And different things to do.
Oh dear! I do so wish that I
Belonged to something, too!

My mother tells me not to
  mind;
She says, "Why, don't you see?
Because you are the littlest one
You just belong to *me!*"

Figure 4.1 "The Littlest One" by Edith Price from *St. Nicholas*, 1918. [University of North Carolina at Chapel Hill – Digitized by Internet Archive].

thoughtfully at a large wooden crate. Like Price, Hausgen adopts the voice of the child and writes:

> I've kept my snuggle doll for night,
> But all the rest I packed up tight
> For children o'er the sea;
> And in the box are games and toys
> For little Belgian girls and boys,
> As sad as they can be.
>
> (Hausgen "Her" 852)

This poem shows how, in 1918, writers were still employing the image of the Belgian child victim to elicit the sympathy of children whose nations were fighting against Germany and to involve readers (young Americans in this case) in the war effort. This is a good example of the duality of the child figure as the poem references both "sad" child victims of Belgium, and helpful, self-sacrificing American children who, by donating toys, are aiding those afflicted by the war (Figure 4.2).

The very young are also pictured as capable of helping the war effort in Hausgen's poem "Doing Her Bit," also published in *St. Nicholas* in 1918, in which the poet once again assumes the voice of a child:

> I cannot knit a scarf nor sweater,
> Nor write a soldier boy a letter,
> For I am only five, you know,
> And have not learned to write nor sew.
> *I* know, though, I must "do my bit,"
> So, when my mother starts to knit,
> I hold the yarn, stretch wide each hand
> And very, very still I stand
> Until she winds it in a ball,
> And never say I'm tired at all!
>
> (Hausgen "Doing" 852)

In this instance the little girl's declaration "*I* hold the yarn" reveals her pleasure and pride in being able to help in some small way. By never complaining of being tired, the small child shows her willingness to selflessly serve others.

While many authors sought to inspire sacrifice in their young readers by presenting them with such exemplary child characters, others depicted less idealised and more humorous young figures striving to help on the home front. For instance, in "A Little Red Cross Helper" by American artist and poet Maude M. Hankins (1876–1968), which

·HER·SACRIFICE·

VERSES BY
MATTIE LEE HAUSGEN
PICTURES BY
DECIE C. MERWIN

I 'VE kept my snuggle doll for
night,
But all the rest I packed up tight
For children o'er the sea;
And in the box are games and toys
For little Belgian girls and boys,
As sad as they can be.

·DOING·HER·BIT·

I CANNOT knit a scarf nor sweater,
Nor write a soldier boy a letter,
For I am only five, you know,
And have not learned to write nor sew.
I know, though, I must "do my bit,"

So, when my mother starts to knit,
I hold the yarn, stretch wide each hand,
And very, very still I stand
Until she winds it in a ball,
And never say I 'm tired at all!

Figure 4.2 "Her Sacrifice" and "Doing Her Bit" by Decie C. Merwin" from *St. Nicholas*, 1918. [University of North Carolina at Chapel Hill – Digitized by Internet Archive].

appeared in *St. Nicholas* in 1918, the child is full of good intentions but is easily distracted:

> I'm awful busy working for
> The soldier-men in France;

> I mean to make them lots of things
> If once I get a chance.
> [....]
> And I started on a sweater –
> I would have got it done,
> But Ethel May showed me her scarf,
> And then I started one.
> [....]
> I've started wristlets and a cap,
> Some woolen stockings too, –
> I think it's very int'resting
> To start off things – don't you?
>
> (Hankins 373)

While Hankins' representation of the young girl includes a degree of idealised innocence, the child is not faultless; her efforts are haphazard and not particularly efficacious. She abandons projects like the sweater and relies on her "auntie" to complete the scarf, telling the reader "she finished it for me." Despite the light-hearted tone in which the poet presents these failings, this verse has the potential to persuade young readers to be more effective "helpers." For instance, the child narrator finds it interesting to "start off things" and asks the implied child reader, "don't you?" The inference here is that beginning things is not enough; to truly help, one must show perseverance and dedication to the cause.

The Power of Innocence: The Child as Moral Enforcer

Another work that humorously suggests children are not always effective helpers is the British text *The Peek-a-Boos in War Time* (1916), illustrated by Chloë Preston (1887–1969) and written by May Byron (1861–1936).[3] It depicts the adventures of Jemima, Jane, and Washington, three childlike creatures called "Peek-a-boos," as they learn how citizens are contributing to the war effort (Figure 4.3).

Although their efforts to help with different tasks often have comical results, these figures, nevertheless, play an important role as moral enforcers, teaching young readers the importance of every individual trying to help and underscoring that it is shameful not to participate in the war. For instance, when they pay a visit to some friends, they find them away "on war work" and Jemima decides that they "shall have to get busy on war work too." The idea that it is disgraceful to do otherwise is introduced immediately:

> "I've noticed," said Jane [...] "that the busiest people have got something on to show how hard they work. Aprons, you know; Pinafores, Leggings, Overalls –"

> "And bibs, I suppose?" said Washington scornfully. "No, thank you. If I can't be busy in ordinary clothes, I shan't be busy. – I shall just slack. [...]" At this moment, four [...] friends dashed past in a motor-car, chatting gaily. They were every one of them clothed in coloured overalls. And, seeing Washington in his usual ordinary unprotected clothes, they pointed the finger of scorn at him [...] and shouted – "Slacker! Yah, boo! Slacker!" This hurt Washington's feelings so much that he rushed into the nearest draper's and bought several overalls with feverish haste.
>
> (Byron)

Being taunted by these friends has an immediate effect on Washington, and Byron endorses the power of such shaming tactics by going so far as to provide her young readers with clear instructions as to how to point the "finger of scorn," noting that it "is the third finger of the right hand, with all other fingers doubled under."

Mary Hillier notes that during the First World War *The Peek-A-Boos* series "showed, predictably, a wartime flavour" but argues that these books "were for very young readers and in the nature of a charade, so that none of the plump figures in military or naval clothing would ever meet with disaster" and there was never "any hint given of the realities of war" (27). Nevertheless, although *Peek-a-Boos in War Time* is light-hearted, it contains a didactic lesson about patriotic duty. The message that it is shameful for any citizen not to support the war effort seems

Figure 4.3 Illustration by Chloë Preston from *Peek-a-Boos in Wartime*, c. 1916.

particularly intended for males as the story emphasizes the scorn directed at Washington.[4] This humiliation influences his decision to buy overalls, even though he and the others do not really understand what they are used for:

> "By the way," said Jane, as she was paying for the overalls [...] "what do people mostly wear these for? [...] I mean, what kind of work do they put them on for?" [...]
>
> "Munitions work, mostly, madam," said the assistant.
>
> "What's munitions?" asked Jemima.
>
> The shop assistant [...] said, "Well, shells, you know."
>
> "Oh, I see. Work by the seaside. How jolly!" said Jemima.

This conversation shows that the naïve creatures do not have a clear understanding of what war entails, but what they do understand keenly is the feeling of disgrace caused by not working, which prompts them to act.

The Peek-a-boos eagerly seek work at a munitions factory but find it "tiring" and "very dull." When they prove to be more trouble than help, they are "turned out" and told not to come back. Quite happy at first to do nothing, they soon feel that

> this was not what they had meant when they bought the overalls. There was a heap of work waiting to be done, and hardly anyone to do it: it said so in the newspapers every day. So they [...] drove off into the country to look for jobs.

This reference to "the newspapers" indicates that the childlike figures have absorbed certain lessons from reports of the war and that their reading has shaped their behaviour and their perspective on the conflict. In this case, their reading has prompted them to search for opportunities to help on the home front, and Byron may have intended for her text to have a similar effect on child readers.

As the Peek-a-boos seek work in the country, the story reveals the hostile attitudes towards British men who were perceived as shirking military service. When the naïve characters attempt to work at an ironmonger's shop, for instance, they announce "patriotically" to the shopkeeper "'We are ready and willing to work, [...]. So that you may go to the Front.'" This comment does not go over well with the ironmonger, who "went flaming red, and threw the things he was holding [...] at the Peek-a-boos. He then leaped over the counter and rushed at them to drive them out" (Byron). The simple Peek-a-boos unwittingly shame the ironmonger by suggesting that they should do his work for him so that he may fight, and this scene repeats itself when they offer to work for the man who sells petrol so that he too "may go to the Front." They witness a similar reaction as he "stared at them with goggle-eyes; and then he hastily marched off, – not to the front, but to the back, – and shut and fastened himself into a shed" (Byron). Rather than emphasizing British heroism, Byron represents the adult male in a way that underscores the shame associated with failing to live up to the heroic ideal by refusing to enlist.

Throughout these exchanges, the Peek-a-boos retain their childlike innocence. They never understand or scrutinize the reaction they provoke but, to borrow a phrase from Deborah Thacker, they challenge the reader "through ironic counterpoint" to question the actions of these men (20). The failure of the Peek-a-boos to comprehend fully the world around them shows their peripheral position in the social order; one like the tenuous position children hold within society. Yet their marginality also allows them to observe things with a degree of detachment and, through their naivety, they throw into relief the failings of adults. The anger they provoke when telling men to "go to the Front" suggests that shaming could be a powerful force, and that the young could be effective moral enforcers. Although the Peek-a-boos' humorous adventures consist of a series of bungled attempts to engage in war work, their tale itself succeeds at conveying the lesson that even small, inexperienced people should do whatever they can to help win the war and that to do otherwise is dishonourable.

The popular image of the child as innocent and carefree is complicated in wartime literature that actively elicits feelings of guilt in an effort to secure children's loyalty to the nation. Not only could adults shame young readers, but tales like Byron's suggest that shame could be wielded by children themselves to persuade their peers to contribute, as well as to provoke adults into performing their duty. Childhood's supposed purity "served as an example to an unfit adult citizenry, whose shortcomings were both physical and moral" (Olsen 20), and Byron's story presents this purity as potentially capable of persuading adults and children alike to act patriotically.

The Child Worker: Celebrating Child Labour

Although the Peek-a-boos' attempt at munitions work fails, other texts show young people successfully employed in wartime industry. In a 1917 issue of the British periodical *Chums*, for example, there appeared the first instalment of a series of articles recounting the experiences of a thirteen-year-old boy from northern England working in a munition factory. "The Boy Munitioner: A Real Story of Life in a Great War Factory" is introduced as "the true story of the daily life of a boy munition worker" told "in the boy's own words" (A Boy 73). This work is at odds with the views of many who felt that children did not belong in the workforce, and it stands in contrast to contemporaneous efforts in North America and Britain to exclude children from industrialized labour. Despite long-standing concerns, employing children to work in factories was not uncommon and this piece mirrors wartime reality in Britain when "the greater need for manpower led to many children leaving school early to enter employment on farms and in the munition factories" (Sherington 74).

The article states that each one of the thousands of boys working in war factories across Britain is "doing his bit towards the making of a cartridge or the building of a submarine" (A Boy 73), and the young narrator explains that he was "fairly itching to leave" school because he "wanted to do a bit to help in the war" (73). This apparently first-hand account presents child labour in a positive light, even though concerns were raised at the time about the negative impacts of such work on children, including lost educational opportunities. H.A.L. Fisher, who was appointed President of the Board of Education in 1916, estimated that "by 1917 600,000 children had left school prematurely – at 13 years of age or less – to work" in jobs related to the war effort (Perkin 238). In 1917, Fisher made a proposal for a post-war Education Act that he described as

> prompted by deficiencies which had been revealed by the war; it is framed to repair the intellectual wastage which has been caused by the War; and [...] it will put a prompt end to an evil which has grown to alarming proportions [...] – I allude to the industrial pressure upon the child life of this country.
>
> (Quoted in Perkin 238)

Despite the concerns of Fisher and others, the view that child labour should be further limited and access to education improved was not universal. As the piece from *Chums* shows, child readers were presented with literature that wholeheartedly embraced the figure of the child worker and supported one side of the debate about education and child labour taking place at the time. The editorial comment at the start of the article states that one aim is to dispel what are termed "very hazy ideas" that "exist about these boy munitioners," including that they "work almost day and night" or "that they are sweated and browbeaten by bullying foremen" or even "that they are simply allowed to run wild" (A Boy 73). The writer seeks to dismiss such concerns by presenting what is described as "the true story of the daily life of a boy munition worker" that champions children's work, declaring that the reader "will be doing a national service by making this story known to all your friends" (73). Presumably, this "service" will be in the form of inspiring other children to take up war work by following the example of the boy who gives a cheerful account of factory life.

A Penny Saved: The Thrifty and Generous Child Citizen

Although some literature encourages children to work in wartime industries, a more common way in which children could help was by practicing thrift and making monetary contributions. The importance of being thrifty was underscored repeatedly and a typical example is a short piece from 1916 that appeared in the British periodical *Work and Play* in the section titled "Chats with My Nieces," by Aunt Margery. She celebrates the generosity of British children, acknowledging "the money which has been raised all over the country to help the poor Belgians in their need" and the food that has "been sent from the homes of the poor [...] that the soldier boy might have a feast" (14). Reflecting on how "it took the war [...] to teach the children, and many of the grown-ups too, to be thrifty, to be generous, to be self-denying" (14), Aunt Margery sees in the war a silver lining and teaches British child readers that through both thrift and munificence they can improve their character and make a difference to the lives of soldiers and civilians alike.

North American children were also encouraged to make financial contributions, as seen in *The Thrift Campaign in the Schools of Ontario* (1919). As the author explains, even though the fighting has ended, "the cost of the war is still to be met, war's ravages must be repaired, and for these purposes money must be saved by all citizens, children as well as adults" (ii). Designed to improve the sale of War Savings Stamps,[5] the book explains that "patriotism and sound business instincts demand that every citizen's savings be lent to the Government of Canada to be used for the nation's needs" (ii), and that "the help of every [...] boy and every girl, will be urgently required" (ii). Arguing that even small savings will have a big impact if part of a collective effort, the author notes that if each student in Ontario "will economize sufficiently to buy a Thrift Stamp every week during the year [...] the aggregate of these savings will be a magnificent sum" (*Thrift* ii). In this way, the text outlines a practical means by which children can patriotically serve Canada as it recovers from war.

Like Aunt Margery, who suggests that it took the war to teach people the importance of thrift and charity, the author of the *Thrift Campaign* does not look back on the pre-war period exclusively with nostalgia. Instead, he suggests that before 1914 Canada was at risk from the "very real danger" of "rapid growth and remarkable prosperity" that meant "improvidence and extravagance took the place of the foresight and thrift which were typical of Canadians in the earlier days when conditions were hard and money scarce" (*Thrift* 40). Prudence is presented here as the natural inheritance of Canadian youth that had been in danger of being forfeited. By reclaiming it, Canadian children are not only helping the recovery effort but strengthening their character and re-establishing fundamental Canadian values that were corrupted before the war. The author writes that in "sacrifice and in self-denial, in resisting the allurements of unnecessary pleasures [...], comes the true development of character – the stalwart, rugged, honest character which overcomes all obstacles" (*Thrift* ii). Not only is practicing thrift *evidence* of good character, but it also helps to *build* such character.

This interest in character building was not limited to Canadians, and in the United States the notion

> that war could be an excellent way to build character at home particularly resonated among educators and government leaders in World War I. This was a crisis; those who wanted to see change in society were determined not to let it go to waste.
>
> (Collins *Children* 34)

In both Britain and North America, many saw the war as a perfect opportunity for improving children's character in ways that aligned with the broader goals of the nation. According to the *Thrift Campaign*, some of the qualities that Canadian children should strive for, and which are presented as fundamental to national identity, include a strong work ethic, loyalty to the nation, sacrifice, generosity, and support for the government.

In encouraging Ontario's children to help strengthen Canada, the author of *The Thrift Campaign* implores the reader to become worthy of the title 'Canadian citizen' and says that children should ask while Canadian soldiers "'were fighting so valiantly [...] what were we doing to help their cause?'" (*Thrift* 55). He states that they will be happy, and their country "blest [...] in her loyal children" if they can say "'We have saved and [...] to our soldiers lent, [...] that's what WE have done" (*Thrift* 59). Designed for use in schools, this booklet reveals some of the ways in which the schoolroom was a politicized space in which children could be indoctrinated with attitudes towards war and nationhood that promoted the objectives of the government. Jonathan Vance notes that from the start, "Canada's schoolchildren had been vital foot soldiers in the crusade against the Kaiser's Germany. No student was too young to be educated in the issues of the war or to take a hand in winning it" (234). There was a general understanding that "the war could provide Canadian schoolchildren with an appealing and potent example of the value of discipline" (Vance 234). *The Thrift Campaign*'s author sees the recent war as an opportunity to teach students about good character and citizenship and observes that young people "require to learn many lessons not contained in the ordinary text-books" (ii).

While *The Thrift Campaign* is focussed on Canada's post-war needs, wartime texts from other nations share its portrayal of the thrifty child as one who can secure the nation's future, including Myrick's *Fifteen Little War Stories*, published in New York by the National Security League in 1918 as part of its Patriotism through Education Series. Founded in 1914, the NSL was the largest and one of the most influential preparedness societies established in the United States.[6] While other works in the league's Patriotism through Education Series are not aimed primarily at young readers, this one is specifically directed at children and adolescents and contains short anecdotes and stories designed to encourage them to help the war effort in different ways. As seen in the following excerpt, children were figured as cheerful, selfless, and happy contributors:

> "What will you do with so much money, bub?" asked the kindly housewife of the little boy, hardly as big as his shovel, when she dropped a quarter into his cold hand for clearing the snow from her sidewalk.
>
> "Buy another thrift stamp and help win the war!" was the cheerful response.
>
> That's patriotism!
>
> (Myrick)

The small size of the child is emphasized as he is a "little" boy "hardly as big as his shovel." Despite his young age and small stature, however, he is pictured as a hardworking citizen who is willing and able to make sacrifices for the good of the American nation.

A similar message is apparent in Edna A. Cooke's aptly titled "Little Patriots," published in the popular American children's periodical *St. Nicholas* (1917–1918). This poem[7] shows that quickly after America joined the war, children were encouraged to contribute financially to the cause:

> The posters on the street all say
> That we must do our share;
> And all around are sailor boys
> And soldiers everywhere.
>
> Our nursie says they'll go away
> Far, far across the sea,
> And on the fields of sunny France
> They'll fight for you and me.
>
> So don't you think that you and I
> Might see what we can do
> Then, even if we're very small,
> We'll know we're helping too.
>
> And if we don't know how to knit
> The mufflers and the socks,
> Still we can save our pennies up
> For the Junior Red Cross box.

For every one can do their bit
  If they but do their best;
And Uncle Sam needs little folk
  As well as all the rest.

(Cooke 121)

Given that the Western Front had become an infamously muddy wasteland by the time of this poem's publication, Cooke's description of "the fields of sunny France" reflects an optimism that is at odds with the reality of the war, but which is in keeping with the confidence of the child narrator. This first-person narration creates the impression that the child's desire to help is not imposed by the adult but comes from within, with children enjoying the reward of knowing "we're helping too." The suggestion that the nation (Uncle Sam) "needs little folk" just as much as it needs adults, further exploits this longing to be of use.

Equally important as giving money was the practice of saving, including conserving food and fuel. Running throughout these works is the message that even the smallest children can help because they possess the qualities of selflessness and patriotism. For example, the short article "Turn Off the Light!" from 1918, teaches young Americans the importance of saving coal and argues that every child "can do his part [...]. You may never see or handle a lump of coal from one year's end to the other, yet you can help save it. And no patriotic service is more important or fundamental than this" (208). For readers who might doubt the impact that one individual can have, the author elaborates on the power of collective effort:

> The efforts of a single individual in the careful, stinting use of electricity and gas may seem to be infinitesimal; but multiply such efforts by millions, and the total is staggering. [...] The little sacrifices and savings will count here heavily, and that is why Dr. Garfield[8] is appealing to the boys and girls of the country to aid his campaign.
>
> ("Turn Off" 208–209)

In this piece, the child is pictured as part of a collective patriotic effort in which the actions of the young are every bit as important as those of adults. Child readers are thus taught that they are not only capable of serving their nation but have an obligation to do so and are not exempt simply by virtue of their young age.

Clearing the Land and Cleaning the Plate: The Child's Role in Food Production and Conservation

The figure of the selfless child encouraged young readers to make contributions like sewing clothes, buying war stamps, and working in war-related industries, but it also promoted patriotism and sacrifice; virtues that adults deemed essential qualities of the wartime citizen. These were also encouraged in accounts of food conservation and production, which were among the most important ways children on both sides of the Atlantic could assist the war effort. Britain's island status made it vulnerable to German blockades and citizens were asked to save food, but the severity of shortages meant that compulsory food rationing was eventually introduced. In North America, the situation was less dire but there was still a clear need to conserve in order to ensure that troops in Europe, as well as the population at home, had sufficient food supplies.

In Canada, regulations to prevent food hoarding and profiteering were introduced and children were encouraged to do their part in saving and producing food, while in the United States a significant food conservation campaign began in 1917 to help supply food to American troops and European civilians. American children were warned of the dangers, and even the sinfulness, of wasting food, and historian Justin Nordstrom observes that the "'doctrine of the [...] clean dinner plate'" that was promoted to children was "sometimes elevated in religious tones as the 'Gospel' of the clean plate" (185). As Nordstrom remarks, childhood "was chiefly a rhetorical category" in wartime efforts to prevent food waste (182), and examples of children's thrift "were designed to both encourage and shame adults into complying with government directives" (184). The message that children should not waste food thus had a twofold effect: it encouraged children to do their part but also reinforced the importance of adult sacrifice.

The message that wasting food was unpatriotic and even wicked appeared in a variety of forms. An issue of *St. Nicholas* from 1917, for example, contains a reproduction of a food-conservation bulletin in which Uncle Sam offers tips on how to help save food, including "how to use meat substitutes," "how to save wheat," and how to save fat, fuel, and use substitutes for sugar ("Uncle" 117). The same issue also contains a copy of a U.S. Food Administration poster that encourages readers to "eat less wheat, meat, sugar and fats to save for the army and our allies" ("Eat" 311).

In addition to advertising campaigns, the message that children had a role to play in these food-saving efforts was conveyed through fiction. For example, a section of *St. Nicholas* from January 1918 that is "Contributed by the U.S. Food Administration" contains a traditional Hindu tale that has been adapted to teach young Americans about the importance of the child in food conservation efforts. In "The Story of Rama's Bridge," the god Rama is building a bridge and is helped by the monkeys, who "carried earth and stones and trees, and piled them up. They moved cliffs and mountains" (211). When a little squirrel that "could not carry much" comes to help, the monkeys laugh to see him as he "rolled himself in the sand and scampered to the bridge and shook the sand from his coat and scampered back again" (211). The monkeys are scornful, but Rama says, "that according to his powers the squirrel was doing as much as any of them" and he "stroked the squirrel kindly, and from that day to this the squirrel has always borne upon his coat the stripes that are the marks of Rama's fingers" (211).

The author explains that the

> old tale has a food-saving point: We are all enlisted as volunteers to build a bridge from war to peace. Part of that bridge must be built of our surplus food materials. This great task enlists the whole nation. [...] even the little child who saves a slice of bread is like the squirrel in the Hindu story, doing his or her utmost according to his or her powers.
>
> (211)

Adapted for the context of America's participation in the First World War, the tale's clear message is that even the smallest person can make a difference, and that these efforts will not go unnoticed.[9]

In addition to conserving food, children on both sides of the Atlantic were urged to grow it. In *The Thrift Campaign*, for instance, the author notes that the province's "Department of Education has made it easy for pupils of the schools to spend a good deal of time at farm work without losing credit for their work in school" (vii). In Ontario and elsewhere, children played an important role in growing food, and Kristine Moruzi notes how the children's section of the *Canadian Grain Grower's Guide* "was the voice of Canadian farming children" and encouraged them "to see themselves as active contributors to the war effort" (Moruzi "Very" 214–215). Farm children were cognizant of the importance of their work and,

> despite their distance from the battlefield, nonetheless saw themselves as important contributors to the First World War. They provided food for women, children, and soldiers; they took on increased responsibilities for farming work; and they raised funds to support the war effort in a myriad of ways.
>
> (Moruzi 214)

For such children, growing food would be a familiar activity, but the outbreak of the war suddenly made their labour of paramount importance.

It was not just farm children who participated in this important undertaking, however, and urban children grew food in their yards, school gardens, and even parks. A 1918 article from *St. Nicholas* celebrates the efforts of the Boy Scouts of Washington who cultivated a large crop of corn on "one hundred acres of undeveloped land in Potomac Park, near the Washington monument" ("Most" 209). The article outlines the difficulties the boys faced, the help they received from Henry Ford in the form of a tractor, and the ultimate success of their efforts, which produced nearly "8500 bushels of cob-corn" (211). Implicit in this account is the message that earlier views of children as relatively weak and helpless have been overturned by the war and replaced by adult appreciation of their abilities. The writer reports that when "visitors saw the enormous stalk growth [...] they could scarcely believe that such corn was being grown by boys having no expert direction" (211), but all doubts are eliminated when the boys successfully produce thousands of bushels of corn and the adults see the significant "sum of money realized from the sale [...] being devoted to various patriotic purposes" (211).

Such food production efforts are echoed in fictional tales like those in the light-hearted but didactic collection *Mother Goose's Garden: The New National Literature for Children*, published in Toronto and copyrighted in the United States ca. 1917. This anthology is a good example of the ways in which fictional child figures taught quite young children that they must be productive and responsible members of society. The emphasis on promoting good citizenship is evident from the title page, which states the collection contains "jolly stories teaching valuable lessons in citizenship, thrift, and production while they delight the rising generation."

One tale, "Patriotic Jack and the Bean Stalk," is an excellent example of how classic texts could be reworked to suit contemporary needs. In this case, the familiar story of Jack the giant-killer becomes a medium through which young readers are inspired to help the war effort by growing food. Like traditional versions of the fairy tale, it can be interpreted as an empowering account of a young hero taking on the role of provider, but rather than caring only for himself and his widowed mother, Jack provides for his entire extended community in this wartime version.

The story's opening makes explicit reference to the original tale popularized by Joseph Jacobs, and this example of intertextuality shows that wartime writers believed children's actions could be inspired by their literature:

> THERE WAS ONCE a very patriotic boy named Jack, who wanted to kill a Giant – if somebody would only tell him where to find one. However, after he had read the story of Jack and the Bean Stalk, in a story book, he formed a plan. He decided to plant beans. By planting beans he would grow bean stalks; and perhaps there might be a Giant lurking somewhere up one of the bean stalks.
>
> ("Patriotic Jack")

The implied hope of this author is that just as Jack's actions are directly inspired by "a story book," readers of this tale will be convinced to help grow food. That the ability and desire to act are already latent in children is suggested by Jack's initial desire "to kill a Giant." Having learned about them from reading fairy tales, he already wants to slay one, and simply needs to know where to find one. In this case, the boy's desire to do battle is innate and needs only to be harnessed and provided with the proper outlet. This desire to "slay the giant" is linked to Jack's patriotism ("patriotic" being the first word used to describe him) and thus serves as a clear metaphor for his eagerness to defeat the nation's enemies.

Recognizing he will need help, Jack enlists other children to plant a garden of bean stalks, hoping that he will then be able to find a Giant to kill: "So he told all the girls and boys at school about his plan, and asked them all to plant beans in the School Garden. [...] All the children worked as they never had worked before" ("Patriotic Jack"). Though still the eponymous hero, Jack is part of a collective effort in this version, and the tale reveals the role of schools in mobilizing children on the home front. The American classroom has been described by historian Branden Little as a "staging ground for students' community and international outreach initiatives" during the First World War (286), and he notes that educators "embraced their primacy in shaping children's activism – the catalyst for action would be located within the schools rather than at home, where parochial concerns were believed to be a limiting factor on this form of service" (286–287). Food-growing efforts were part of the school experience during the war, and engaging schoolchildren in this collective effort was something that took place in both Britain and North America.

In the patriotic tale of Jack, intended for Canadian and American students, schoolchildren are active agents whose efforts are acknowledged by adults as having genuine value. The children's hard work means the beanstalks "grew until [...] our soldiers fighting far across the ocean saw the tall tops, and they cheered, for they knew what they meant" ("Patriotic Jack"). In an inversion of the norm in which children are asked to honour the valiant fighters at the front, here the soldiers celebrate the endeavours of the children back home.

The message that young people can help the troops, as well as other adults, is made even more explicit when the children reach a platform at the top of the bean stalks covered by "a great white mountain of beans" and surrounded by "many large empty bags." Jack points below and says the "men in those factories yonder who are making shells and supplies for our soldiers at the front, depend on us for food." He then asks the other children to look at the homes where "there will be many cupboards as bare as Mother Hubbard's if we do not do all we can to produce food." Next, he points to the "great ships carrying food over the sea to our soldiers" and notes that many are being sunk by German submarines and that the children "will have to work so much harder to beat those under-water boats" because the ships "look to us for this year's cargoes of food." Jack then asks the children to look across the ocean to "where our brave soldiers are fighting for us in France! They need food as much as they need bullets to win the War." Finally, he opens "the great empty bag marked 'FOR OUR SOLDIERS,' and many little fingers flew swiftly to pour the little white beans into the bag. Click! Click! Went the beans into the big bag, clicking like thousands of little white ivory buttons" ("Patriotic Jack"). The effects of the children's work are widespread; not only are they directly helping to fight the enemy by ensuring soldiers have food, but they are also feeding the people at home, including those working in war-related industries.

The giant that Jack and his peers help to slay is "Old Giant Hunger," who threatens soldiers and civilians alike, and this is an excellent example of a classic fairy tale being reworked to teach children how they can contribute to the war. There is a blend of fantasy with reality here, as the tale of the giant and the magic beanstalk incorporates contemporary realities like food shortages and the sinking of supply ships. In keeping with Joseph Jacobs' nineteenth-century version in which the boy hero outsmarts a Giant out for the blood of Englishmen, the fairy tale depicts North American children saving Britain (as well as their own community) by performing the important duty of 'slaying' hunger.

A similar fantasy work from the same collection is "Idle Ike, The Hour Stealer," in which the importance of fulfilling one's duty is highlighted by a prefatory verse:

> Idle Ike, I Dislike,
> He Steals My Hours Away;
> He Won't Work, He Will Shirk
> His Duty Every Day.

The story includes an illustration of a thin figure holding a gun to an anthropomorphized clock while stealing its numbers and stuffing them into a bag labelled "lost time." This "odd-looking man, stealing the hours from the Clock" is "Idle Ike" explains the author, who warns children of the threat Ike poses: "Some day he will ask you to help him; perhaps he may want you to hold the bag; but don't you do it" ("Idle").

Through this story, North American children are taught that it is their duty to work hard, specifically by growing food:

> There is nothing left on the clock now but Dinner Time and Supper Time. IDLE IKE will leave those two hours on the clock, for he always wants to know when to eat. Eating is the only work he ever does.
>
> But what shall we eat if boys and girls are idle and do not grow food in their gardens? Without the children's gardens we might soon

> become as thin as IDLE IKE. This is the year for all children to use all their spare hours in the garden. Work willingly and well. [...] Be busy and you will be healthy and happy.
>
> ("Idle")

This little piece is another example of children's literature that conveys the implicit shame in being idle. Canadian and American children must use their "spare hours" well, and gardening, which might be viewed as a form of child's play during peacetime, becomes a form of war work that is anything but frivolous. The food-growing efforts of children were truly meaningful, and one potato-growing scheme by Ontario schoolchildren resulted in them earning "enough from the potato crop to buy an ambulance for the Red Cross" (Fisher 37).

While gardening was one way for young people to grow food, other works suggest that they can be involved in large-scale food production. *To the High School Boys of Massachusetts: A Call for Patriotic Service* (1918) is designed specifically to recruit for farm labour in America those too young to enlist in the military.[10] Aimed at boys between the ages of sixteen and twenty-one, this pamphlet does not rely on fantasy to capture readers' attention in the way that "Idle Ike" does, but it does show the pervasiveness of shame as a tool for encouraging young people to contribute to the war effort.

This pamphlet promotes enrolment in the Massachusetts Division of the United States Boys' Working Reserve and includes letters from Woodrow Wilson and Theodore Roosevelt. Wilson's letter exhorts boys to

> show themselves worthy of patriotic fathers who have fought for Democracy in the past, sustain their patriotic brothers who are fighting for it today, and command the affectionate pride of the brave mothers who are silently bearing the burdens at home.
>
> (Wilson)

Wilson appeals to ideas of family honour as a means of encouraging participation in farming; boys who do not contribute are deemed unworthy of their father's names, uncaring of their brothers in the trenches, and undeserving of their mothers' affection. Implicit in Wilson's letter is the notion that failure to participate in Farm Service would be so shameful as to negate a boy's claim to his family's love and respect.

In the above example, the adult writer wields the threat of disgrace in order to motivate young readers. However, this pamphlet also reveals that adolescents could shame others into action. For example, in its description of the Farm Service program, the pamphlet states,

> Upon your enrolment you will receive the button of the Reserve bearing the seal of the United States and the Word "Recruit" written across the face [...]. WEAR THE BUTTON AT ALL TIMES AND

> BE A BOOSTER FOR THE RESERVE. EXPLAIN TO YOUR CHUMS JUST WHAT THE RESERVE MEANS AND URGE THEM TO JOIN. Every member thus becomes a recruiting agent for the Reserve.
>
> (Committee)

Not only can boys educate one another about possible ways to support the war effort, but they can also exert peer pressure on each other. The author writes, "No boy wants to be considered a slacker or a quitter. So join the Reserve. Induce your boy friends to join" (Committee). Words like "urge" and "induce" reveal the extent to which such literature pressured young readers to dedicate themselves to the cause.

There is a specific iteration of masculinity in this pamphlet about farming that includes honouring one's family, having a strong work ethic, being tenacious, being a team player, being courageous, making personal sacrifices, and demonstrating loyalty to one's nation. The ultimate shame is portrayed as the failure to fulfil this ideal of masculinity, which is also demonstrated in another piece from this pamphlet titled "Play the Game to Win" by C. B. Fritsche, the Assistant Federal State Director of the Boy's Reserve for Indiana. Utilizing a sports metaphor, Fritsche asks the reader, "Young Man, are you willing to sit on the fence while the game goes on? [...] the team **needs you to win!**" (Fritsche). Fritsche then appropriates the voice of his implied reader and writes,

> Now, they won't let me be a soldier yet, [...] but I have a good, clean, strong body and the determination to do a **man's job**, so Uncle Sam wants me [...] on a farm. I do not care particularly about being a farmer, but **I do** care about being a man, so therefore I am going to make a little sacrifice and **play the game** where Uncle Sam says I can serve him best.
>
> (Fritsche)

According to Fritsche, being a man means doing things that one does not necessarily enjoy, in order to serve others.

Although many children's writers exploited readers' fear of failing to live up to the masculine ideal, boys were not the only ones taught they could help with farming. Myrick, for instance, holds Canadian girls and women up as positive examples for his American readers:

> "How can father run the farm if I enlist?" James asked his mother and two sisters. "We will help him," they replied quietly.
>
> That's the patriotism which enabled Canada to increase by 40 percent, or 12,000,000 acres, the land planted to food staples in the past three years during which almost every able bodied farmer has gone to make up the 480,000 men Canada sent to the front.

In praising Canadian patriotism, this American text misrepresents some of the realities of Canadian farming efforts. While Canada did increase the percentage of land cultivated during the war, this was the result of many factors beyond the contributions of girls and women and was not an unmitigated success, as harvests actually diminished from 1916–1918 (Djebabla 80). The push to increase food production was not without controversy or resistance, and the Minister of Agriculture's advice to use fallow land was "something that went against elementary farming principles" and provoked criticisms from farmers (Djebabla 80). Regardless of these realities, by celebrating the example of Canadian women, Myrick reinforces the idea that every able young man should enlist to fight, and that anyone who cannot fight must take up the war effort on the home front.

Children's writers made it clear that producing food was something that both girls and boys should participate in, and the assistant secretary of agriculture in the United States, Carl Vrooman, contributed a piece to *St. Nicholas* titled "The Boys' and Girls' Food Army" (1917) in which he celebrates these united "patriotic efforts of [....] boys and girls, toiling with an enthusiasm that only an ardent love of country could make possible" (1067). He calls these workers "the Children's Food Army" (1067), and children's efforts to grow food were often described using such militaristic language, with their labour on the home front being compared to the work of soldiers on the front lines. Vrooman goes so far as to describe these important food production efforts as "a modern children's crusade [...] against Kaiserism" (1067–1068).[11]

An example of a rather more light-hearted approach to convincing girls and boys that they had a role to play by growing food is "Don't be a Turtle, Be a Beaver" from the *Mother Goose's Garden* collection. It features a conversation between a beaver and a turtle in which the beaver criticizes the yawning, "lazy old Turtle" and contrasts him with the children who are working hard to grow food for the war effort:

> "Well," said Billy Beaver, looking him over [...], "you're the old slacker who loafs in the sun all day, are you? Why in the world were you ever called 'Snap?' If you had an ounce of snap you would be helping to win the war."
>
> "Why – a – is there a war going on?" inquire[d] Old Snap, rolling his left eye.
>
> "Is there a war going on!" shouted out indignant Billy Beaver. "Why, you snoozing old Shirker. We Beavers are giving our work and our meat. [...] and the sheep are giving gladly their wool and meat too. [...] And you sit out in the sun and loaf all day while your animal friends are giving up their lives for your freedom!"
>
> [...]

"Anyway you're a good lesson for the boys and girls. Turtles would never win the war. Boys and girls will not be turtles. They are working like Beavers in their gardens – growing the food that will win the war."

This amusing little exchange encourages children to be "beavers," that familiar Canadian symbol synonymous with industry and hard work. Though the stories in this collection generally seemed aimed at both American and Canadian readers and the collection was copyrighted in the United States, it was published in Toronto and Canadian children were clearly envisioned as part of its intended readership, with the hard-working beaver encouraging them to be patriotic by growing food to help win the war.

As Billy Beaver's speech to Old Snap suggests, participating in food production was one means by which the child became helpful, rather than helpless. Even those who may otherwise have been considered child victims became empowered figures when shown contributing to these efforts, as seen in the following article published in 1916 in the British periodical *Work and Play*:

> A happy party of Serbian boys and girls has been working in the Cambridgeshire fruit farms this summer, picking raspberries to be made into jam for our navy and army. They have already learned a few words of English from the London scholars working in the same fields, and they are now being properly taught by a teacher from Cambridge. If they prove as ready pupils as some of the Belgian boys and girls who took part in *Work and Play* essay competitions only a few months after their flight to this country, they will certainly give their teacher satisfaction.
>
> ("Serbian" 11)

In the above account, displaced children are portrayed as thriving, having transformed from casualties of war into individuals helping make a difference to the British navy and army.

Another British periodical, *The Children's Friend*, includes a tale from 1918 that drives home the message that even those who have their own challenges to face can contribute meaningfully to food production efforts. "Patriotic Blind Boys" gives an account of the students at the College for the Higher Education of the Blind in Worcester, who are "exceedingly patriotic" and "simply 'boiling over' to do something for their country" ("Patriotic Blind"). The article recounts how the boys "set to work to dig up a large portion of their recreation field for planting purposes" and includes photographs of them hard at work. While this piece again stresses the ability, and need, for every individual to aid the war effort, it also teaches another moral lesson about bearing one's burdens.

The author claims, "these boys are amongst the happiest on the face of the earth" and explains why:

> They view their handicap philosophically, or in other words make the best of a bad job, and in this surely they set an example worthy to be followed by others [...]. Every "bad job" is made worse by grumbling and complaining about it; and the worst misfortune that can happen is made less hard to bear by accepting it in a spirit of submission.
>
> Hundreds of brave men have been blinded in this terrible war; and those who have the privilege of caring for them say that almost without exception they are cheerful and uncomplaining [...].
>
> When men who have lost and suffered so much can be bright and brave, surely we, to whom the blessing of sight remains, ought to accept without murmuring our small trials, and carry without complaint the little burdens we are called upon to bear.
>
> ("Patriotic Blind")

In this story of school-age boys helping to cultivate crops, the author not only celebrates the virtues of patriotism and hard work but also stresses the importance of cultivating a spirit of stoicism, utilizing the boys as positive examples.

As the literature discussed in this chapter shows, readers who were too young to enlist as soldiers or serve as nurses were encouraged to help in other ways. Their assistance could be limited to the domestic sphere, where simply exhibiting good behaviour could lessen the cares and worries of adults, but it could also be more concrete and involve tasks like sewing and knitting, contributing money, practicing thrift, and helping to conserve and grow food. These things were not only ones children could do in their leisure time but were frequently part of official school programs, revealing how the war shaped every aspect of children's daily life. The war work performed by children was genuinely helpful to the cause, but the representations of this activity in children's literature were also designed to foster virtues like hard work, patriotism, and sacrifice. Children were not merely the recipients of messages designed to encourage such values but were also viewed as having the potential to instil these qualities in others. Collectively, these texts reveal that adult writers envisioned children not as far removed from the war and the duties of citizenship, but as deeply invested in the cause and vital to the success of their nations.

Notes

1 I am not the first to lament the difficulty in ascertaining how real children responded to representations of the war. Ross Collins observes that a challenge for those interested in childhood experience during the First World

War is "finding out what the children themselves thought about militarization of their daily lives" (*Children* 253). Collins notes that letters submitted by children to juvenile magazines are one source of evidence, but these are limited and, as Collins remarks, often influenced by adult editors (253).

2 "Gard was a regular contributor of poems and stories to children's books and magazines" like *The Boy's Own* and one of her poems from that publication was infamously plagiarized by Dylan Thomas (Towns 43).

3 Artist Chloë Preston published *The Peek-a-Boos*, the first book in this series, in 1910, which featured her own verses (Hillier 15). Preston collaborated with others on different books in the series, but the majority contained a story written by May Byron and illustrated by Preston (Hillier 26–27).

4 Washington is repeatedly depicted as lazy. Given that his name is so evocative of the United States, it is tempting to read him as a symbol of America's hesitation to join the war. However, the fact that he appears as a character in the *Peek-A-Boos* stories at least as far back as 1911 makes it difficult to conclude that his character is intended as criticism of American neutrality.

5 Efforts to raise money were very successful in Canada and the "1918 campaign raised more than $600 million in just three weeks" (Francis, Daniel 84).

6 The preparedness movement arose in 1914 out of concerns about the inadequacies of the US military, and the National Security League was one of several groups that promoted patriotism and argued for the need for military training.

7 The poem and its accompanying illustration are likely both by artist Edna Abigail Cooke (1889–1975).

8 The US government created a Fuel Administration which was under the direction of Dr Harry A. Garfield.

9 It is interesting that an American government agency opted to rewrite this Sanskrit epic at this moment. This may be a nod to India's contributions to the war, which included more than a million recruits, but its publication in 1918 is noteworthy given the lengthy and sensational Hindu-German Conspiracy trial that took place in San Francisco beginning in November 1917. Seventeen Indians were tried for conspiring with Germany in connection with the *Ghadar* movement and, on the last day of the trial in April, 1918, one of the conspirators "was shot and fell dead in front of the jury box with four pistol bullets in his body" (Dignan 58).

10 The draft age was twenty-one to thirty until August of 1918, when it became eighteen to forty-five (Hickel 752).

11 Given that the original children's crusade of 1212 is generally considered a tragic episode in which thousands of European children left for the Holy Land only to die or be sold into slavery, Vrooman's choice of words is somewhat unfortunate; it is difficult not to see an ironic parallel in the First World War, when so many young people left home to fight, never to return.

5 Young Recruiters and Youthful Recruits

Promoting Enlistment and Other Participation on the Frontlines

The celebration of Allied soldiers in wartime children's literature played a role in fuelling support for the war and underscored the crucial need for men to enlist. Britain and Canada did not bring in conscription until 1916 and 1917, so in the early years of the fighting the need for volunteers was imperative. As Kimberley Reynolds has observed, "a key question for those of us interested in children's literature must be whether writing for the young was implicated in making so many young people [...] desperate to take part in the action" ("Words" 255). It would be naïve to presume that juvenile literature was the sole cause of the enthusiasm to enlist as this was driven by several factors that varied between social classes, nations, and individuals.[1] Yet, as this book has already shown, countless children's authors worked to foster interest in the war and many made a concerted effort to prepare children to contribute near the frontlines, either inspiring boys to sign up while underage, encouraging them to do so as soon as they were old enough,[2] or, in the case of girls, preparing them to work in areas like nursing. In addition, children were encouraged to persuade adult males to enlist, often by reinforcing conventional views on masculinity.

A militaristic conception of manliness existed throughout the nineteenth century in Britain and North America and pervaded childhood culture in the pre-war period. Although there were "voices of dissent" that did not embrace militarism, particularly among the working-class, "dominant ideas and values of manliness and militarism [...] permeated virtually every facet of society" (Moss 6), including children's literature. The militarism of this period shaped children's understandings of what it meant to be male, perhaps explaining – at least in part – why so many young men in Canada and Britain enlisted when war broke out in 1914.

The need for enlistment was widely addressed in juvenile literature and many writers advised young readers to use their activities on the home front to prepare for their future role as soldiers, while some suggested that children could convince older siblings, friends, and others to enlist. Meanwhile, some writers submitted that children themselves could take up arms and did not need to wait. These messages were frequently, but not exclusively, aimed at boys, and girls too read tales that

DOI: 10.4324/9781003191605-6

promoted enlistment. Though women did not have regular combat roles during the First World War, girls are figured as literal soldiers in some texts, while in others their role is to convince boys and men to volunteer. Reading literature was thus one means by which both boys and girls could internalize wartime conceptions of masculinity and femininity, as well as messages about duty, sacrifice, and citizenship.

Marshalling the Toddlers and Rallying the Troops: Encouraging a Spirit of Military Duty and Sacrifice in Young Readers

Utilizing war as a didactic tool, authors conveyed many different lessons about duty and sacrifice in an effort to persuade boys to join the military. In many instances, the adult soldier served as a role model, embodying traits like muscular Christianity. Depictions of the strong adult soldier as a Christ-like figure willing to sacrifice himself for the nation and for a cause purportedly sanctioned by God were part of a discourse that encouraged a spirit of sacrifice and Christian piety in young readers. In some instances, presenting the war as a righteous cause and Allied troops as faithful Christians may have helped to mitigate potential criticism of the attempt to promote enlistment among underage boys.

One such work is Harvie's *The King's Uniform* published in London in 1915. Harvie declares that he must share with his young readers "a story from the battlefield" in order to show them that "Christ [...] is the greatest of the world's heroes" (21), and he tells of an Irish soldier in France who gives up his life in order to warn troops that German soldiers are hiding in the village. The narrator describes him as being willing, "like Jesus Christ" to give his life to save his friends (22). Though not all children's texts shared this focus on Christianity, Harvie's is a good example of how, within an overarching narrative of war that celebrated sacrificing oneself for the nation, the adult male soldier became an idealized embodiment of masculine, Christian virtue for the child to emulate.

One tale depicting how a young boy's eagerness to fight is inspired by the example set by adult soldiers is A. Cochrane's "War and the D.W.O." This appeared in the 1915 *Empire Annual for Boys*, published in London by the Religious Tract Society, but it is set in Canada and described as a "Canadian story" (26). The protagonist, young Jimmie Hapgood, eagerly examines the recruiting posters "lately received from England" and muses "If only he were nineteen years old!" (26). Envious of those old enough to "answer the call" (26), Jimmie expresses his own hope that the war will still be occurring in six years' time and, when asked why he would want the war to last so long, Jimmie replies, "I'll be nineteen then" (27).

Jimmie's disappointment at being too young to fight intensifies after he discovers that his older brother, Bob, has enlisted, and "his own enforced inactivity came creeping into his mind" (29). Bob tries to comfort Jimmie by pointing out that not every man who joins up gets "a shot at the actual scrapping" (31), remarking that "the army couldn't do without" the men who perform the many important duties that do not directly involve combat (32). Bob declares he would like to start "a D.W.O. – Distinguished Waiting Order – for exceptional bravery while waiting behind the scenes. I imagine it takes as much grit to do one's duty while waiting as it does when there's all the excitement of an engagement" (32). In order to be awarded this honour, boys would have to display "an exceptionally thorough doing of whatever duty they have while waiting. That'll be the hardest part, because their duties always seem so insignificant compared to the fellows in action" (32).

This didactic story drives home the message that not everyone will have the opportunity to cover themselves in glory and that what matters most is faithfully performing one's duty in whatever role is required. Yet Cochrane unmistakably draws the reader's attention to Jimmie's desire to be old enough to fight and to his frustration at being left at home. So, while the narrative encourages young readers to be patient and do what they can on the home front, it simultaneously celebrates the desire to enlist and depicts it as an important virtue. In this instance, inspired by the example set by older soldiers, the Canadian boy teaches young readers that while lacking the desire to fight is shameful, so too is being driven solely by a yearning for personal glory; the ideal boy should be motivated primarily by a desire to serve his nation and empire.

The Child Recruiter: The Power of Shame

As I have discussed in relation to *The Peek-A-Boos in War Time*, the child was presented as having the potential to unconsciously embarrass adult men into enlisting, and the use of the child figure as a shaming tactic is clear in one of the war's most recognizable propaganda posters: Savile Lumley's "Daddy, What Did *You* Do in the Great War?" from 1915 (Figure 5.1).

In addition to creating war propaganda, Lumley was an illustrator for children's books and periodicals, which suggests he saw the image of the child as something that could serve multiple rhetorical functions and be shaped in different ways for adult and child readers. His famous poster shows a father with his young daughter on his lap and his son sitting at his feet playing with toy soldiers. Meg Albrinck argues that

> the man's troubled expression suggests that he is distressed by the idea of conflict and that he realizes his noncombatant past will not impress his children. Such appeals emphasized men's duty to [...] their children and insisted that men earn their place in the patriarchal tradition.
>
> (324)

Figure 5.1 Savile Lumley's "Daddy, What Did *You* Do in the Great War?," 1915.

Any tension a man might feel between his duty to his family and his duty to his nation is defused by the poster's implicit argument that to disappoint one, is to disappoint both.

In children's literature from Britain and Anglophone Canada,[3] where enlistment was initially voluntary, there is a recurring message that any male citizen who is of age should enlist. In the United States, calls for American men to join the fight also appeared in pre-1917 literature written by those who hoped for, and anticipated, America's eventual entry into the fray. Such calls to enlist were also common in American literature published after the United States declared war in April 1917, when it was still divided over its participation and few volunteers rushed to join, and when, after the introduction of the Selective Service System in May 1917, hundreds of thousands of men evaded the draft.[4] There were conscientious objectors and pacifists in each of these nations, along with those who simply did not wish to risk life and limb, but, nevertheless, the dominant message in wartime literature was that it was one's duty to enlist, and that to do otherwise was deeply disgraceful.

In *The Thrift Campaign* from 1919, the author states that all over Ontario "students who were of sufficient age enlisted" ("Thrift" v), which obscures the fact that not all Canadians were eager to rush off to war and that requests for exemption were widespread after conscription was introduced. By the end of 1917, for example, "404,395 Canadians had reported; of those, 380,510 had sought exemption, leaving only 24,000 men who had been willing to serve in the army from the outset" (Shaw 41). One story that acknowledges the existence of such reluctance and that wields shame as a recruitment tool, is "Don't be a Turtle, Be a Beaver" (discussed earlier in relation to food production). This was published in Toronto c. 1917 when the contentious national debate about conscription was at its height and the need for soldiers was getting desperate, and it ends on a note that aims to convince children that any respectable male worth his salt will enlist. The turtle is described as "lazy," and Billy Beaver calls him an "old slacker" and a "snoozing old Shirker." After Old Snap hears about the hard work children are doing to grow food, he has a change in attitude and asks the beaver, "Please call Mr. Snail's taxi cab for me. I think I'll ride to the recruiting office and offer myself as an armored tank." This closing line shows that Billy Beaver's clear display of disdain, combined with the example of hard-working children, prompts Old Snap to act. What at first seems simply a humorous account of two anthropomorphized animals is, in fact, a sharp critique of men who are reluctant to fight; one that uses the figure of the industrious child to highlight the shamefulness of adult men hesitating to do their part.

Boys in Khaki: Celebrating the Masculine Ideal

The "nexus linking war, militarism, and masculinities has remained an enduring and consistent feature of societies and their cultures across time" (Higate and Hopton 432), and it was clear throughout the First World War when "belligerent nations lured hesitant young men into military service by appealing to their sense of manhood" (Kuhlman 1). The frequent reliance on conventional models of masculinity to shame boys into enlisting is evident in a tale included in the American anthology *Short Stories of the New America* (1919), which, according to its Preface, is intended to "meet the needs of young people" (Laselle iii). "The Coward," by Arthur Empey (1883–1963), is an excerpt from his 1917 bestseller *Over the Top* and it presents a scathing view of men afraid to enlist. Empey himself was an American who joined the British forces prior to America entering the war and *Over the Top* is based on his experiences.[5]

The central figure in "The Coward" is Englishman Albert Lloyd, who is "what the world terms a coward" or a "slacker" (Empey 181). Albert's "country had been at war nearly eighteen months, and still he was not in khaki. [...] Every time he saw a recruiting sergeant, he'd slink around the corner out of sight, with a terrible fear gnawing at his heart" (181). The pressure to enlist is everywhere, and whenever he passed "the big recruiting posters [...] he would pull down his cap and look the other way, to get away from that awful finger pointing at him, under the caption, 'Your King and Country Need You'; or the boring eyes of Kitchener, which burned into his very soul, causing him to shudder" (181). Unlike Jimmie from the story about the D.W.O., the recruiting posters do not fill Lloyd with a desire to enlist. Instead, the prospect frightens Lloyd who, during the Zeppelin raids, "used to crouch in the corner [...] whimpering like a whipped puppy and calling upon the Lord to protect him" (181). Cowardice is Lloyd's defining trait and once a Conscription Bill is passed and the police demand he report to the recruiting station, he does so "immediately, because he was afraid to disobey" (182), not because he has suddenly developed the urge to fight.

Cowardly Lloyd is "despised" by his landlady (182), and regarded "with contempt" by fellow recruits (183). His cowardice is part of his failure to represent the masculine ideal and he is portrayed in feminizing terms, a common tactic by which those who resist military service are ridiculed. After being selected to go to France, he faints and is "carried to barracks amid the sneers of the rest" where he cries and whimpers in his bunk (Empey 183). Once in France, Lloyd is reassigned and an officer gives him the following advice: "Lloyd, you are going to a new company. No one knows you. Your bed will be as you make it, so for God's sake, brace up and be a man" (185). This exhortation to "be a man" further underscores Lloyd's failure to conform to the masculine ideal, a failure that is made complete when, during his first experience of shells bursting in the trenches, he runs away. He is soon caught and sentenced to "be shot at 3:38 o'clock on the morning of May 18, 1916" for desertion (188).

As Empey's story suggests, nowhere were notions of shame, honour, and masculinity invoked more clearly than in literature designed to inspire enlistment. In his study of British adventure fiction, Joseph Kestner argues that "there is a reciprocity between the masculinity imagined, and imaged, in literary texts and the lived experience of males" (12); or, as Graham Dawson puts, it, masculinities "are fashioned in the imagination" but "lived out in the flesh" (qtd. in Kestner 12). Empey's story can be read as a conscious effort to shape or reinforce ideologies of masculinity at a time when particularly great demands were placed on young men. Not simply a story about a coward, it submits that those who may initially be afraid to fight can redeem themselves and reclaim their masculinity. When Lloyd realizes that he is to be executed, he finally grows calm and utters a heartfelt prayer: "'Oh, good and merciful God, give me strength to die like a man! Deliver me from this coward's death. Give me a chance to die like my mates in the fighting line, to die for my country'" (191). Afterwards, Lloyd feels a "peace" he never felt before and he "cowered no more, but calmly waited the dawn, ready to go to his death. The shells were bursting all around [...] but he hardly noticed them" (191).

Unlike his earlier prayer for God "to protect him," Lloyd now prays for the "strength to die like a man" in service of his country, finally embracing an appropriate form of masculinity. Moments later, a shell smashes open the guardroom and Lloyd realises that he is "free," not to run away again, but "to go 'over the top' with his Company. Free to die like a true Briton fighting for his King and Country" (192). On reaching the trenches, he discovers that his comrades are out of ammunition and about to be destroyed. Seizing a machine gun, he turns it on the Germans, shouting "for joy as their front rank went down. [...] He had saved his Company, he, Lloyd, the coward, had 'done his bit'" (197). At precisely this moment, which was "the time set for his death by the court" (197), a German bullet sings through the air and strikes Lloyd down. His death is no longer clouded in disgrace, however, as his fellow soldiers realize that "'Lloyd the deserter [...] has redeemed himself, died the death of a hero. Died that his mates might live'" (198). Once Lloyd embraces the masculine ideal by overcoming his cowardice and asking for God's help to die "like a man," he is redeemed.

Although this story's protagonist is British, Empey was American, and this excerpt from his book was published in a collection for young American readers. The story could thus inspire British and American readers alike to serve their country, but this anthologized version appeared in 1919, which means that encouraging enlistment could not have been the main reason behind its publication. In the early post-war context, Empey's tale serves a different function, addressing concerns about the United States' initial failure to join the Allied cause. The collection's editor, Mary Laselle, writes that the story "shows the splendid regeneration of a despicable man," and describes Empey as "an American and a soldier" who "fought in the British army before America entered the war" and "did all that a brave man can do for the cause of humanity" (Laselle "Something" xi). She says that cowardice like Lloyd's was seen in a few men in every army but adds that this

> was entirely concealed and atoned for by the splendid bravery of the many, and considerable numbers of men, who, when drafted, might have been designated as cowards, are leaving the army with a record of brave action in times of great danger.
>
> (xi)

Given the United States' hesitation to join the conflict, it is possible to read Laselle's comment that a "record of brave action" outweighs original reluctance as a deflection of the charge that American neutrality was a display of collective cowardice.

Laselle's text is part of an outflow of post-war propaganda for young readers in which the continued celebration of soldiers and the ongoing glorification of battle – including praise for its role in "the splendid regeneration of" men – are at odds with the tenor of cynicism that pervaded so much adult literature from the period. Such material may have helped recruitment for the Second World War when, despite having witnessed the horrors of the Great War in their childhood and adolescence, many men signed up with the same type of enthusiasm seen in 1914.

Inspiring Child Readers to Enlist: Tales of Glory and Adventure

One way that authors sparked an eagerness to enlist was by appealing both to children's desire for glory and to their sense of justice. A typical example is "In the Ranks" by Druid Grayl.[6] This was published in the *Boy's Own Annual* (1914–1915) alongside a drawing of soldiers holding guns, and it is an explicit call for "lads" to enlist:

> Come! Lads from the village, and lads from the town,
> Your Country and King make the call;
> The path that we follow leads on to renown –
> The goal that is envied of all.
> [...]
> So, lads, if you long for a glorious life,
> Join in with our ranks as we come
> To the phil-a-loo-loo of the spiriting fife,
> And the rub-a-dub-dub of the drum.
>
> (Grayl 164)

This poem uses the promise of glory to motivate young men to "join the ranks," but it also presents enlistment as a sign of moral virtue, describing British soldiers as "fighting the cause of the just,/With right and religion in hand" and facing off against the "German invader [who] is ruthless" and a "tyrant of might" (164). Through appealing both to their desire for a "glorious life" and to their sense of moral superiority, Grayl encourages the "lads" who are his readers to become soldiers and join the ranks of the just.

In addition to poetry, fiction also underscored the importance of enlistment by appealing to the reader's desire for adventure. In the "Children's Books" section of *The Bookman*[7] from Christmas 1915, for example, there is a description of Escott Lynn's[8] novel *In Khaki for the*

King as a "story for boys" that "will act as a stirring recruiting appeal to those whose turn has not yet come to fight for their country's honour" ("Rev. of *In Khaki*" 124). This explicitly suggests that fiction can serve as recruitment material for underage readers, and describing them as waiting their "turn" normalizes warfare as part of one's coming-of-age.

The review of Lynn's book states that the setting "is not fiction, but fact, and the adventures of the two youths who are the chief characters are adventures that are happening constantly in Belgium and France" (124). Despite these claims, the reviewer's summary of the plot shows it belongs firmly to the genre of adventure fiction:

> Oliver Hastings [...] happened to be in Frankfort when war broke out [...]. A quarrel with a German officer [...] led to a hasty and risky escape from the land of the Hun; and in company with an old school-fellow, met with by chance, he reached the Belgian frontier after many hair-breadth escapes [...]. Oliver and his friend Vivian are then given commissions in the Belgian army, and are among the first to taste the excitement of war.
>
> ("Rev. of *In Khaki*" 124)

This language shows the "construction of violence as a jolly romp" typical of adventure fiction from the period (Hourihan 99), and the reviewer predicts the novel "will be among the first favourites this Christmas" because boys "like adventure books, and the biggest 'adventure' ever known is taking place now and this is a spirited and breathless account of some considerable part of it" ("Rev. of *In Khaki*" 124).

In discussing Lynn's novel, Dorothea Flothow notes how wartime writers frequently relied on the adventure genre's traditional "narrative strategies, plot structure and metaphors" that had typically been means "by which the dark side of war was played down or suppressed [....], the result being that even the Great War was presented as an exciting adventure, not as the terrible mass slaughter which it undoubtedly was" (Flothow "'Train'" 4–5). Presenting war as a thrilling escapade was one way that authors glossed over its emerging horrors and fostered child support for the important recruitment effort. Yet despite such highly romanticized depictions, there was a "complexity" in wartime novels for children that many scholarly assessments "fail to take account of" (Budgen 28). These works "frequently demonstrated nuanced understandings of the war" (Budgen 28), and even those reliant on familiar adventure tropes to convey excitement and depict heroic exploits did not always ignore the dark realities of the conflict.

With the war's unprecedented number of casualties, "death became a vital element of children's fiction" (Budgen 32), and there was "a need to reconcile these basic traditional narratives with the sense of loss that pervaded society as the war continued" (30). Unlike later post-war "narratives [...] that presented the conflict as wasteful and futile, those novels and stories produced between 1914 and 1918 found some glory in dying for one's country" (Budgen 33). In acknowledging the unparalleled casualties of the First World War, children's authors could impress on young readers the need for soldiers and promote the honour that lay in sacrificing oneself for the morally righteous nation.

Martin Green argues that adventure narratives "reveal themselves to be political documents" that reflect "nations' feelings about their status as nation-states" and their "destinies" (Green 23–24). Nationalism and adventure narratives "have worked reciprocally together" (Green 6), and Green goes as far as to say that "great adventure tales *are* those acts of imagination and narration that constitute the imagined communities called nations" (7). Though often about the individual hero, children's adventure tales can be framed in terms of the community, for not only is the protagonist "sometimes not an individual but a group" (Green 22), but the quest is often for the collective good. In wartime adventure stories for young readers, the willing war hero is the ideal citizen who serves the national community, and tales of individual heroism, coupled with portrayals of the honour that lay in rendering service to the nation, embraced the rhetoric of enlistment campaigns. While presenting war as an opportunity for personal glory and excitement, children's literature underscored that joining the fight was a noble duty that men could perform in service of their nation.

Moral Enforcers and Angels of the House: The Roles of Women and Girls

Though many writers were preoccupied with the masculine ideal, it was not just boys who learned they had a role to play in the war. Some texts contained content aimed exclusively at either boys or girls, and it is unsurprising that the lessons they imparted varied according to the intended readership, but many works from the period were read by both male and female readers, meaning that young girls also consumed tales promoting enlistment and sacrifice. This dual readership may have been particularly true of periodicals like the *Boy's Own Paper* that show evidence of "gender drift", and which were eager to keep themselves afloat by having as broad a readership as possible (Nelson "Mixed" 3). The effect of this could be twofold, with girl readers internalizing literature's celebration of masculinity and voluntary enlistment, and simultaneously internalizing iterations of femininity that promoted virtues like domesticity.

It has been well documented that as the war progressed, the roles of women changed. Most obvious was the fact that increasing numbers of women moved into the public sphere as they took up jobs in war-related industries or positions vacated by men at the front. Messages about the contributions women and girls could make to the war were therefore inconsistent, revealing that it was not simply attitudes towards childhood that were complex and unstable, but also views specifically on girlhood. Some of these views included the notions that a girl's place was in the home, that her role was to convince men to enlist, and even that she could participate in the theatre of war herself.

One popular British periodical that frequently endorsed traditional gender roles was the *Girl's Own Paper and Woman's Magazine*. Whereas magazines for boys tended to be dominated by stories of adventure, the *Girl's Own* included articles about flowers, painting, and pets, alongside recipes, sewing patterns, and lessons on topics like the importance of good posture and the dangers of vanity. Many of the articles envision women's contributions to the war along established gender lines, a good example being "In Time of National Stress" from 1915, which encourages older girls and women to help by being calm and docile:

> Calmness and level-headedness are attributes to cultivate in a time of national stress. [...] It is a time to remain as far as possible at home, and to fulfil the ordinary routine quietly and without fuss. [...] It is a time to avoid extravagances not only in dress but in thought and speech. All who have brothers, fathers, sons in the great struggle have it in their power to lessen or to make heavier the tense weight of the responsibilities under which they set forth to go into action. The sane clear-sighted Englishwoman has had the share, inevitably hers, of the watching and the waiting in the past, and when the worst has been [...], none have accepted the crushing sorrow with a braver or more loyal resignation to the mysteries of the Divine Will.
>
> ("In Time" 8)

Echoing the commonly held nineteenth-century view that a woman's place is in the domestic sphere, this piece suggests that the roles of women are to wait patiently and quietly, to remain at home, to be self-sacrificing and self-effacing, and to lessen the burdens of men. It also, notably, instructs women how to respond to the deaths of loved ones in combat, teaching them that calmness is to be exhibited at all times, even when "the worst has been." Women are asked to accept the deaths of men without complaint, and without questioning this cost, but "Loyal resignation to the mysteries of the Divine Will" can also be read as loyal resignation to the will of the nation. What is being demanded of women is their unquestioning acceptance of the need for the men in their lives to fight and die for their country.

Another piece from the *Girl's Own* that takes up this theme of unquestioning sacrifice is "Women and Patriotism," which also submits that a woman's place is in the home, patriotically following the dictates of the nation. The author remarks that "[w]here patriotism is, women must be. A nation is the home. [...] and the centre of the home is woman" (36). In addition to making a comfortable home for their families, women were also expected to foster men's sense of duty and bravery. The author claims:

> Woman will forgive almost anything in man except cowardice or treason. There she draws the line. [...] Not only is this feeling instinctive but it comes to her through long years of human evolution. [....] With full hearts but tranquil souls women can send forth their sons, their husbands, their sweethearts, their protectors, to danger or to death – to anything save halting or dishonour. A great admiral put it neatly when he said victory was won by the woman behind the man behind the gun.
>
> ("Women and Patriotism" 36)

Patriotic women will proudly send men "to death," claims this writer, but they will not abide a man's hesitation to enlist. Although women themselves cannot fight, they can supposedly exert their influence on "the man behind the gun" by shaming him into enlisting. Both a man's unwillingness to fight, and a woman's agitation at the thought of him being harmed, are framed in this passage as unpatriotic attitudes at odds with deep-rooted "instinct" and millennia of "human evolution."

The role of women and girls in encouraging enlistment was evident in the real-life practice of those "who paraded through city streets distributing white feathers to male bystanders not in uniform" after "white feathers came to symbolize 'effeminate' Canadian, American, and British men who refused to join the armed forces" (Kuhlman 1). Organized in Britain in the summer of 1914, the White Feather Brigade's public shaming tactics often targeted boys not actually old enough to enlist (Rosen *Armies* 65), and in the 1917 novel *Doing His Bit* by Tom Bevan (1868–1938), the protagonist is shamed by a woman who incorrectly assumes he is a shirker. By the time Bevan's novel was published, the White Feather movement had already "gained a negative reputation" (Hammonds et al. 36), and the extent of its influence remains uncertain,[9] but it clearly belonged to "a broader movement [...] in which women, girls, and a variety of [...] institutions joined forces to spur recruitment" (Rosen *Armies* 66). Rosen notes that underage boys were deliberate targets of these shaming efforts and argues that "there was widespread complicity [...] to evade age restrictions" (66).

Positive portrayals of girls and women persuading older boys and men to enlist include "How I came to Enlist: How Ella, after all, Sent a Man to the Front," a fictional tale for young readers published by London's Religious Tract Society in the 1915 *Empire Annual for Girls*. When the narrator meets Miss Ella Firbright, the fiancée of his unathletic friend Andrew Jackson, she is not what he expected:

> She was a tall, sturdy, athletic young person, who talked a good deal about tennis – not the kind of girl I should have expected Jackson to choose. And yet, when I came to think of it, it occurred to me that he was drawn to Ella Firbright just because she *was* so entirely different from himself.
>
> (Watkins 87)

Ella is a physical contrast to her bookish fiancée, Jackson, a "slight" man who "wasn't strong" and whose "eyes had a sort of wistful look in them" (87). The narrator comments, "I think he would have liked to have been a strong man, and have been good at outdoor sports; but it wasn't in him" (87). Jackson's attraction to Ella suggests that she possesses some of the characteristics he wishes he had.

When war breaks out, Ella expresses her own desire to fight by declaring "'I only wish *I* was a man!'" (87). She takes on work as a nurse, one of the few paths open to her as a woman, but decides that she can also contribute by sending her fiancée to fight. She urges him to enlist and says, "'if I can't go to the war myself, I can do the next best thing. [...] I mean to send one man into the ranks'" (87). Jackson is not physically strong, but his desire to grant Ella's wish makes him determined to exercise until he is fit enough to be accepted into the military: "'Ella has got to send out a man to the front. I'm her man; and I'm going'" (88). His exertions result in a fatal case of pneumonia, however, and his dying wish is for his friend to enlist in his place. The narrator recalls that he

> just stammered out, 'yes, yes, of course [...] I'll go, and Ella will have a man at the front.' [...] The Tuesday after that I was nineteen, so [....] off I went, and was accepted. And that is how I came to enlist. [...] Ella Firbright sent a man to the front.
>
> (89–90)

Ella exudes a powerful force over the young men in this tale. A strong individual who longs to serve her country, she leads by example, the implication being that the men around her can do no less. They both show their desire to live up to Ella's expectations and she becomes an example to young readers of how girls and women could perform the important task of persuading men, even ones like the narrator who is still underage, to join the fight.

Although Ella determines to send a man to the front, she clearly longs to fight herself. One article from the *Girl's Own* that captures this desire among women is "Women and the War: Help They Can Render, Follies

They Can Avoid" from 1915. Mary Billington (1862–1925)[10] looks to past conflicts to advise readers on how to be of use in the present one, and begins by acknowledging the helplessness women sometimes feel:

> [...] the consciously loyal woman to whom patriotism is, next to her faith, her deepest sense, has sometimes a curious feeling of impotence in a great national crisis. "How can I help?" she asks. "I am not a trained nurse – her place is clearly marked out. I feel I should only make myself look ridiculous if I tried to use a rifle, and I am inclined to be contemptuous [...] of some of the comic-opera-like efforts that involve [...] a pseudo-military uniform. What am I to do?"
>
> (Billington 34)

Billington reinforces the notion that fighting belongs to men but suggests that girls and women can still be of help to soldiers, provided they avoid the mistakes of the past. In recalling the South African war, she remarks on "some of the depths of futility to which feminine effort descended" (34), and recounts the efforts of women who were a hindrance, rather than a help, when they sent soldiers "grotesque knick-knacks for their tents" (35), and hundreds of decorative cushions "as out of place for a field hospital's use as anything to be imagined" (34). Billington cautions readers against such "follies" and suggests that they focus instead on rendering "a real and practical service" (34), giving the example of using "stitchery, knitting, or crochet" to provide "useful" garments for soldiers (34).

Female Soldiers and Red Cross Heroes: Picturing Girls and Women at the Front

Billington speaks to some of the activities girls and women can participate in on the home front, but the fact that women did not have official combat roles did not stop other writers from depicting them as soldiers, both figuratively and literally.[11] Some children's authors recounted historical examples of women warriors and shared similar anecdotes from the First World War. For example, in *The School of Arms: Stories of Boy Soldiers and Sailors*, published in New York c. 1915, Ascott Hope reports on Russian girls who have joined the fight, saying that

> we hear of girls caught soldiering in disguise: there was one Amazon of eighteen who after winning the cross of St. George by her gallantry under the name of Nicolas Popin, and lying in hospital disabled by a wound, fever and frost-bite, slipped off to re-enlist in another regiment where her sex was unknown.
>
> (326)

Such tales about female combatants convey the message that bravery, including courage in the face of physical danger, is required of both men and women.

Hamilton-Honey notes that the

> advance-and-retreat nature of women's gains in the Great War would spill over into the plots of series fiction on the home front. Whether recreating the adventures of female Red Cross workers or depicting the experiences of female ambulance drivers, series fiction both romanticized war work and disseminated ideas about women's freedom to a wider audience.
>
> (136)

Although Hamilton-Honey is speaking specifically about American series fiction for girls, her statement holds true for much of the literature being written for young female readers on both sides of the Atlantic, much of which reflects the fact that war brought certain responsibilities for girls, as well as new freedoms.

One story that proposes girls need to be brave and active, but which also reinforces traditional constructions of femininity, is "The Heroine of Loos" from *The Jolly Book for Boys and Girls* (c. 1917). Recounting a battle in Loos, France, the author draws a parallel with Britain when stating that the village's landmark "is the headgear of a big colliery, which our soldiers called the Tower Bridge, because at a distance it looks something like the noble structure which spans the Thames" (31). He notes that on September 25, 1915, the village gained "a fame which can never die" when British troops "swept into it and wrestled it from the Germans, who had held it for nearly eleven months" (31). Prompting readers to see a connection between their lives and these events in France, the author remarks,

> I dare say you have relatives who fought in this battle. Perhaps [...] they have told you something of the big fight, though my experience is that soldiers will talk about anything but the battles in which they have taken part.
>
> (31)

This reference to soldiers' reticence is noteworthy and may be an acknowledgement of the trauma caused by war and the troubling reality behind the popular image of the stalwart warrior. The assertion that readers will know someone who participated in the battle also reveals the pervasiveness of war in children's lives. By connecting events in France with the lives of young British readers, this passage works to create a feeling of Allied solidarity and establishes the French "heroine" of the story as a role model for British children.

While the story celebrates the wresting of Loos from the Germans, it is not focussed on British heroism but on the efforts of a "French girl of eighteen named Émilienne Moreau" who is an example of both bravery and femininity (31). Moreau's story was reported widely at the time, and the author declares she "ought never to be forgotten by British boys and girls, for she played a noble part in the fighting at Loos" (31). Moreau's part was twofold. First, she tended to the wounded Scottish troops who "were shot down" while fighting the German enemy (32). Moreau, "who had lived in the village during the months of the German occupation, now found her opportunity of helping her deliverers. She bandaged the British wounded and ministered to them tenderly" (32). These efforts are in keeping with the established roles for women during the war as Moreau "tenderly" helps to ease the soldiers' suffering.

The second way Moreau helps is by taking an active role in the fighting, for when

> she saw Germans attacking wounded Highlanders who were no longer able to defend themselves, she was roused to fury. Seizing a revolver, she shot down several of the inhuman Germans, and afterwards flung grenades at them. Right well does she deserve to be called the Heroine of Loos.
>
> (32)

In this scene, Moreau is pictured as a capable combatant who uses a gun and grenades to kill the enemy. It is her fighting, as much as her tender nursing, that earns her the title of 'heroine.' The author reports how "this gallant girl was summoned to Versailles, and there, before a large admiring crowd, General de Sailly pinned on her breast the Military Cross, as a tribute to her great courage and to her splendid care for the wounded" (32). The General congratulates her, saying, "You do honour to the women of France. You are a fine and inspiring example" (32). His esteem is shared by "the bravest soldiers of France, all of whom were eager to acclaim her as the bravest of them all" (32). The teenage Moreau is recognized as a fellow soldier by the French troops and teaches French and British readers that if the situation requires, girls can serve their nations in ways that go beyond traditional female roles.

Although Moreau kills German soldiers in a daring display of fighting skill, the author is quick to establish her femininity, which is crucial to her function as a role model. In her excellent study of First World War propaganda, Celia Kingsbury describes this type of female character:

> The heroines of popular fiction perform strenuous tasks, even kill, as do their brothers, in the name of the state. These militarized young girls have exceptional talents, but their talents never exceed the boundaries of local society. They may be smart, beautiful, strong,

> and even athletic, but nevertheless, at war's end, each is still very much a young lady in terms of cultural expectations.
>
> (Kingsbury 105)

The fact that Moreau still meets the "cultural expectations" of the time is shown through her tender treatment of the wounded soldiers and through her display of great humility when honoured at Versailles:

> She was very modest, and cast down her eyes when the General addressed her. She hated the thought of taking human life, but when she saw the wounded being attacked in so cowardly a fashion, she could not help springing to their rescue. She lost all fear in the defence of those who were stricken, and she will ever remain an inspiring example, not only to the women of France, but to the women and girls of Britain as well.
>
> ("The Heroine of Loos" 32–33)

At a time when women's roles were in flux, Moreau could inspire girls to be brave participants in the effort to destroy the German enemy, while still providing an example of modesty and compassion for them to follow.

It is worth noting that Moreau was not always figured as a soldier. In one earlier account from the *Empire Annual for Girls*, for instance, published in 1916, she arms herself, but only takes "a revolver for her own protection" (Knowlton 190). The killing of German snipers is not attributed to Moreau, but to the wounded British soldiers she tends to. These men "resolved at any cost to put a stop to the sniping that was going on, and, guided by their heroic nurse, they succeeded in disabling their cowardly foes" (190). Moreau merely "guides" the soldiers in this version of events, and her care of the wounded is emphasized more than her fighting. The different iterations of her tale reveal how Moreau served both as an example of a brave girl soldier coming to the rescue of men, and as a model of traditional feminine virtue.[12]

Other girl characters who actively tackle the enemy are those in a series of novels by American author Martha Trent.[13] Trent's *Marieken De Bruin, Somewhere in Belgium* (1918), for instance, is about a Belgian girl risking her life to help English prisoners escape from the German soldiers who are planning to execute them, while in *Lucia Rudini, Somewhere in Italy* (1918), a young Italian girl warns the army after she discovers Austrian soldiers planning an attack.

While Trent's stories were fiction, the *Girl Guides' Gazette* of October 1914 contains "When Women Went to War: Stories of Women Who Have Actually Been in the Fighting Line," an article about real women who fought in conflicts like the Franco-German War, the Russo-Japanese War, and the First World War.[14] It begins by acknowledging that many women "find it very hard to stay at home idle, as they call it, while their men are out in the fighting line. How gladly they would shut up their homes and follow to the seat of war" ("When Women" 3). Recognizing the desire on the part of girls and women to escape the limitations of their domestic roles by "shutting" their homes and leaving to fight the enemy, this article provides young readers with an example of female heroism through the tale of one girl who went to the Front:

> Early in the present war, a young French girl, heartbroken because all the men of the family had gone off to fight, leaving her at home alone, determined to follow. She wanted to avenge some of the wrongs which the Germans had inflicted upon the poor Belgian women.
>
> Dressing herself in an old uniform belonging to one of her brothers, she presented herself at the regimental headquarters.
>
> Something in her manner, and the slightness of her figure, aroused the suspicions of the officer in charge, and the girl was compelled to confess her identity, being told sympathetically that it was impossible for her to fight.
>
> ("When Women" 3)

The girl is not condemned for her actions, as the officer is sympathetic to her desire to defend other women and avenge those in Belgium.

Given that women could not actually join a fighting corps, the tale does not serve as enlistment propaganda for girls, but it does acknowledge their desire to fight and celebrates their bravery. Such tales reinforce the notion that any respectable man should want to enlist, the unspoken assumption being that if young women have this drive, it is disgraceful for any man not to. By mentioning that the girl's disappointment at being prevented from fighting "was very great, but she was somewhat appeased by being taken on as a probationer at one of the military hospitals" (3), the tale also suggests that while girls cannot be soldiers, they can still participate near the front lines as nurses.

Nursing was one way that women experienced the war first-hand, and girls' literature includes many accounts of young women occupying this realm. The title character of Martha Trent's *Phoebe Marshall Somewhere in Canada* (1919) is a young nurse and the story opens at a hospital for wounded soldiers in Atlantic Canada. Another of Trent's novels, *Alice Blythe, Somewhere in England* (1918), is about an English girl working at an army hospital in France.[15] As Susan Ingalls Lewis describes, these heroines "enjoy incredible adventures while exhibiting terrific derring-do in the face of impossible challenges" (131). Prolific American children's author Margaret Vandercook (1877–1958) penned a similar series with titles such as *The Red Cross Girls in Belgium*, about American girls working in a Belgian hospital, and *The Red Cross Girls with the Russian Army*. These tales of adventure centred on women's activities, providing examples of bravery for girl readers to follow and a chance for them to live vicariously through characters that step outside more confining, traditional gender roles.

Another tale that offers this is Grace E. Craig's "The Ambulance-Girl: A Story of the French Front," published in 1917 in *St. Nicholas*. About an American girl's adventures on the front lines, it captures the feeling of frustration that many young women felt at not being able to fight. It opens with sixteen-year-old Esther lamenting, "I want so much – oh, so much – to do something for France" (784). When her companion points out that Esther has been regularly knitting items for soldiers, Esther declares,

> that is nothing. People at home in New York can knit. We Americans who are here in France should do more than that toward paying the debt we owe the French people. Think of all they did for us at the time of our Revolution! Why, we might never have had our dear, beautiful America but for them.
>
> (784)

Craig's tale, published in 1917, encourages Americans to support the war effort by appealing to a historic bond between France and the United States. Rather than picturing this as a European war far removed from the concerns of the United States, Craig suggests that America owes a debt to France, and her protagonist is frustrated that "there seems to be no work – no work at all – for a girl to do" (784).

Esther's chance to do something significant for the cause arises when her mother learns that her son Leslie's good friend has been badly wounded, and she receives permission to go to his aid and to take Esther with her "to the front" (785). While stopped at an American Ambulance Field Service station, the women are waylaid by a German bombardment and witness a badly wounded soldier being brought in on a stretcher. He needs to be transferred to a hospital, but when the ambulance driver suddenly breaks a wrist and cannot drive, it appears the wounded man will die. At this moment, Esther steps forward bravely and offers her help:

> 'I know all about Ford cars,' she announced. 'I've often driven one. I will take the man to the hospital.'
>
> The surgeon stared.
>
> 'You, Mademoiselle!' he cried.
>
> 'The road is dangerous,' the young officer declared; 'exposed to shell-fire for a good portion of the way.'
>
> 'And a young lady –' the surgeon began.

Esther's blue eyes met her mother's brown ones, and what she saw there made her lift her head confidently.

'I'm not afraid,' she insisted; 'and if I wear Mr. Lee's coat and cap no one will know I'm a girl. Oh, please let me go! Your man will die!' (788)

Esther literally steps into a man's role here, donning the uniform of the male driver to brave the dangers of the front.[16] Her ride is full of peril, "and at one point she was obliged to slow down and drive the ambulance very carefully around a vast smoking crater where one of the great bombs had just burrowed into the road-bed" (788; Figure 5.2).

Esther pushes on, however, successfully delivering the patient to the hospital, where she is reunited with her brother Leslie. While Britain and Canada had been sending women ambulance drivers into combat zones for some time, the American Red Cross did not recruit women drivers for overseas duties until October 1918, and Craig's 1917 story may thus be a form of wish fulfilment for readers eager to see American women helping near the front lines.

"WITH SET TEETH SHE INCREASED HER SPEED AND FLEW ON DOWN THE ROAD." (SEE PAGE 788.)

Figure 5.2 Illustration by Oscar H. Schmidt from "The Ambulance-Girl" from *St. Nicholas*, 1917. [University of North Carolina at Chapel Hill – Digitized by Internet Archive].

Like the tale about Émilienne Moreau, Esther's momentary adoption of a man's role does not signal a lack of femininity. When praised by her brother and called "plucky" she responds with humility:

> 'Oh, no!' Esther demurred. 'I'm not plucky at all, Less. I [...] was scared to death out on that dreadful road.'
>
> 'But you kept on just the same,' Leslie said, 'and that's where the courage came in. You saved that poor chap's life [...] and he [...] sends you his thanks. And the fellows of the corps thank you, too.'
>
> The young men of the field service were gathered at the door [...] but Esther looked shyly away.
>
> 'I didn't think anybody knew, she faltered. 'I didn't intend they should. I just wanted to help – to do my part for France.'
>
> (789)

This scene highlights Esther's demure nature and clarifies that her actions were not motivated by a desire for glory, but by a sense of loyalty to the Allied cause. The men name her "an honorary member of Section Ten, American Ambulance Field Service" and cheer "Hurrah for the ambulance-girl" (789), which reassures young female readers that their desire to participate in war is laudable and that they have the capacity to brave the dangers of the front without compromising their modesty or femininity.[17]

The apparent need to balance traditional feminine qualities with girls' desire to help the cause is in keeping with Hamilton-Honey's observation that the "story of American women in the Great War is one of both progress and frustration" (135). As she notes, "American women found many ways to be a part of the war effort long before the U.S. was officially involved in the fighting" and once the nation was at war "women served in ever-expanding ways" (135). Nevertheless, women's efforts to participate in the war were often hindered by "military bureaucracy" and met with "civilian contempt" (135). A reluctance to see women take on anything approaching military service was evident in the attitudes of government officials like Newton Baker, America's secretary of war, who

> was adamantly against women in the armed forces and made it nearly impossible for women to join the army. He refused to authorize the formation of a women's army unit that would have been analogous to the British Women's Army Auxiliary Corps.
>
> (135)

Congress also refused "to grant army nurses military rank" or to give "benefits to female veterans of the Army Signal Corps" (135).

While antipathy towards women war-workers existed at the highest echelons, there were those who held competing views, and women had

> powerful male allies in Secretary of the Navy Josephus Daniels, who authorized women to be enrolled in the Navy and prompted the Marine Corps to follow suit, and General John J. Pershing, who outright demanded the appointment of bilingual female telephone operators to the Army Signal Corps and American Expeditionary Forces.
>
> (Hamilton-Honey 135–136)

American girls thus faced a competing set of attitudes towards women's participation that emerged in fictional accounts like those by Craig and Trent, which valorize the young female who risks her life to serve, but which also reassure readers that such action does not negate femininity.

Trent's heroines are described "in promotional materials as 'half girl, half boy, and the better half of each'" (Lewis 131), but the narrative structure of these novels, which tend to have the climax near the middle, rather than at the end, re-establishes the heroine's femininity:

> The purpose of this narrative space seems to be to rescue these girls from the logical implications of their bold actions – that is, the implication that they are as well (or better) suited to fight the enemy as male soldiers. After their heroic adventures are complete, some of these girls end up wounded, injured, or in the hospital, at least briefly. [...] At the end of each story, the girl seems glad to put herself in the hands of a male hero who admires her courage yet demonstrates a clear desire to protect her from further danger.
>
> (Lewis 133)

Although there were abundant depictions of girls as resourceful and capable, many limited the extent to which female characters stepped out of their familiar roles and into the position of soldiers. On the one hand, this reinforced patriarchal values, but on the other, it enabled these stories to function subversively; by emphasizing how heroines maintain their femininity, vivid images of girls acting as combatants, or otherwise stepping outside traditional bounds, could fly under the radar.

Despite military rules and prevailing social mores limiting women's actions, some children's literature argued strongly for women to have a greater role in the fighting. *St. Nicholas*, for instance, published nonfiction showing that some movement towards militarizing girls was taking place in the United States. This includes Miriam Hubbard's article "The Soldier-Girls at the National Service School," which tells child readers about a training camp for women held in Maryland in May 1916. Before proceeding to outline the details of the camp, Hubbard remarks that

> women and war have always been widely separated [...]. There have been a few trained women who of late years have done most excellent service in war, but universal training of women is a conception of our own time. Any one of the thousands of visitors who went to visit the camp could not but be impressed by the earnestness and joyous zeal of the girls who were in training there.
>
> (518)

This article predates America's entry into the First World War but indicates that some American women were keen to receive some military training and to play a bigger role in war than their ancestors. Hubbard remarks that "we who attended the first National Service School feel that if a national calamity should come, we shall be better fitted to do our part toward upholding the national honor" (520). Illustrated with photographs of uniformed female participants, this article normalises the idea that women could be soldiers.

Margaret Dadmun's "The Girls in Khaki" from the same issue offers another viewpoint on this training camp, where women wore uniforms of khaki "skirts, flannel blouses, and campaign hats" and participated in drills (520). Unlike the woman from Billington's article who is "contemptuous" of this kind of "pseudo-military" activity (34), Dadmun claims that the women at the American camp felt every bit as accomplished as their male counterparts. She notes, "A sergeant from the marine corps [...] found us very apt pupils. Indeed, in our execution of squad movements we were said to rival our brothers at Plattsburg" (521). Among the skills the women learn at the camp are telegraphing, semaphore, and nursing.

Despite providing a more supportive view of women's militaristic training than Billington, Dadmun remarks,

> it was understood that the duty of actual fighting does not belong to women. There was not a gun at the camp. Should war ever come to this country, we women could [....] go behind the lines as an organized body of nurses' aids; or we could carry on work for the sick and wounded in our own homes and communities.
>
> (522–523)

This somewhat undermines the image of the female soldier, but Hubbard and Dadmun, nevertheless, convey that American girls and women were eager to see themselves as soldiers, to receive some degree of formal training, and to adopt some military practices.

While some writers advocated that a girl's primary role was in the home, others pictured her as having further responsibilities. These included instilling a sense of duty in men, striving to be brave and disciplined in order to engage in work like nursing, and preparing to take up arms should the need arise. The First World War "demanded a new kind of heroine, but the portrayal of women's war work in series fiction was just as uneven as women's real-life experiences" (Hamilton-Honey 167). While girls' books "championed women's patriotic service, exactly what constituted that service and how much of it was appropriate [...] was clearly open to cultural debate. Women had changed – and girl readers and girl heroines were changing with them" (167). These differing portrayals of girls and women give us a glimpse into the ways in which the First World War played a key role in destabilizing traditional gender roles and increasing women's presence in the public sphere.

From depictions of children shaming or encouraging adult men and older adolescent boys into enlisting, to representations of young men and women fighting or working near the front, representations of young people played a role in promoting enlistment and other service to the military. Children's writers instilled the values of duty, patriotism, and sacrifice in young readers, at times employing notions of shame to achieve this, while at others picturing service to one's nation as the route to individual liberty, excitement, and adventure. In the case of young girls, getting close to the action was often represented as a way to achieve freedom from traditional gender roles and the limitations of the domestic sphere. For boys, the promise of adventure, coupled with the emphasis on masculinity and the shame of failing to live up to the masculine ideal, meant that children's literature had the potential to convince underage readers to enlist. As the next chapter will demonstrate, the boy soldier was a common figure in children's literature from the period, but the uses to which this figure was put by children's authors varied, and it served both as a symbol of child agency, and child exploitation.

Notes

1 Kate James observes that while some boys had "grown up on a diet of military adventure through popular literature" (155), there were many reasons people joined the military, including the fact that it "offered a route out of poverty" for some and the chance "to continue the family tradition" for others (155).

2 Conscription "brought a virtual halt to the systematic enlistment of underage soldiers" because it "enabled the mass mobilization of the entire male population and eliminated the need for incentives to recruitment. [...] there simply was no longer any need to recruit young boys" (Rosen *Armies* 63).

3 In Canada, the debate over conscription was largely between Francophone and Anglophone Canada. An in-depth study of how this was addressed in French-Canadian children's literature from this period would be very valuable.

4 David M. Kennedy notes that the precise number of Americans who "willfully dodged the draft" is not known but the "Provost Marshal General estimated that roughly 337,000 men escaped his net during the war, some 12 percent of the men inducted" (165).

5 After his medical discharge in 1916, Empey returned to the United States where he became involved in the propaganda effort and where his book played "a direct role in preparing the public for the recruitment effort" (Kember 49). He went on to write and star in a 1918 film adaptation of it.

6 Druid Grayl (possibly a pseudonym) was a prolific writer of song lyrics, verse, and fiction for children in the late-nineteenth and early twentieth centuries, whose works include *Fairy Tales from Foreign Lands* and *Pillow-Dust Ditties*, both published by Blackwell.

7 *The Bookman* (1891–1934) was a monthly literary magazine published in London by Hodder and Stoughton that also had an American edition. It "profiled popular authors, circulated the latest literary intelligence, and featured [...] chatty discussions on fiction of the day" (Sutherland 72). The Christmas 1915 edition has an extensive section advertising books for children.

8 Escott Lynn was a pseudonym used by Christopher George Holman Laurence (1866–1950) who wrote numerous works for boy readers.

9 There is debate over how widespread the White Feather movement was and some stories pertaining to it have "the air of myth" (Rosen *Armies* 66). References to the movement in children's literature are rare, with Bevan's novel providing one of the few clear examples. For a good discussion of the movement see Hammonds et al.'s "'Tickling Men to War': The White Feather Campaign."

10 Billington was described in her obituary as "the most outstanding figure among women journalists in London" ("Woman Journalist"). A long-time staff member of the *Daily Telegraph*, she authored several books including *The Roll-Call of Serving Women: A Record of Woman's Work for Combatants and Sufferers in the Great War* (1915).

11 Although women served in combat zones, they were not officially present as fighters except in extremely rare instances (for examples see Kate Lindsay's "The She-Soldiers of World War One").

12 Moreau received several honours including the French Croix de Guerre and Britain's Military Medal. She later earned the Cross of the Companion of Liberation for her role in the Resistance during the Second World War.

13 Trent's *Somewhere* series included six novels published by Barse and Hopkins in New York between 1918 and 1919. In Carty's *Dictionary of Literary Pseudonyms*, Martha Trent is noted as a pseudonym for Dorothy Whitehill Smith, identified as a "US writer" born in 1893 (742). The series continued to be published after the war and "lived on into the following decade, no longer useful as propaganda for the war effort, but fulfilling its audiences' desire for adventure and romance in exotic settings" (Lewis 139).

14 It is very difficult to estimate how many women participated in the war because "incomplete, missing, and sometimes inaccurate" records mean "there is no way to completely verify how many women performed war work of some kind" (Hamilton-Honey 168).

15 For a more detailed discussion of Trent's series see Chapter 3 of Kingsbury's book.

16 Women ambulance drivers "often came under direct fire" and "could be the difference between life and death for wounded soldiers and civilians, who depended on the transport and medical supplies they made available" (Hamilton-Honey 156).

17 Intentionally or not, the protagonist's name evokes the biblical Esther, whose efforts to defend her people have provoked debate over her position as either a heroic feminist role model, or a "model of compliance with patriarchy" (McGeough 54).

6 A Babe in Arms

The Conflicted Figure of the Boy Soldier

Literature for the young does not simply reproduce commonly held outlooks on war, but, in fact, participates in "the construction and legitimization of positions within these debates" (Kieran 9). One debate surrounded the wartime role of children, who were frequently portrayed as figurative "warriors" helping on the home front and as future soldiers, but who were also depicted as actual combatants. While some authors portrayed girls and women participating near the front lines, soldiers were, for the most part, pictured as male. The image of the boy soldier was common, but the complexity of wartime views on children and childhood is evidenced by the fact that the use of underage troops was both celebrated and condemned. Where one stood on this issue depended to a degree on whether one viewed young people as exceptionally vulnerable, or uniquely resilient. Some authors embraced notions of childhood innocence and saw boy soldiers as victims, whereas others celebrated them and used them to instil patriotism in the child reader. Diverse representations of the youthful warrior figure reveal the various ways in which authors defined childhood and adolescence, and they help to construct different positions within the debate over the rights and responsibilities of youth.

The adult soldier embodied a masculine ideal predicated on physical strength, military skill, and a strong sense of duty, but war reveals "masculinity as constantly under negotiation" (Kestner 100), and even as familiar notions of it were reiterated through art, literature, and official enlistment requirements, understandings of masculinity were continually in flux. Children's adventure narratives had long suggested that through facing (and overcoming) physical challenges and suffering the hero could prove his prowess and resolve, and many accounts of the Great War reinforced the established view of physical strength as central to the masculine ideal. But "death and dismemberment often confound [conventional] masculinity" (Kestner 100), and the staggering number of fatalities in the First World War, coupled with the visible and permanent physical injuries and psychological damage sustained by so many soldiers, meant that traditional notions of masculinity were inadequate. Manliness had to be reconceptualized in order to provide an ideal that

DOI: 10.4324/9781003191605-7

could withstand the trauma caused by a modern war, and the image of the child soldier allowed for a vision of masculinity that was not reliant on bodily strength. Instead, qualities such as bravery, loyalty, and Christian piety were elevated above the purely physical. This may have allowed both male and female child readers to internalize some of the virtues embodied by the soldier, the most significant being a patriotic willingness to sacrifice oneself for the nation.

Character Training: The Boy Soldier as Exemplar of Faith and Justice

In numerous representations, boy soldiers embody a positive spirit of duty and sacrifice that is often coupled with Christian piety. This can be seen in John Oxenham's poem "What Can a Little Chap Do?" This was published in *Princess Mary's Gift Book* in 1914 with illustrations by Gordon Browne and together, the verse and illustrations clearly equate religious duty with military duty, and the child with the adult soldier (Figure 6.1).

The illustrations depict a young boy in different poses, but the final drawing is of a grown man dressed as a fighter, the implication being that the "little chap" has exchanged his Scout uniform for that of the adult soldier. These illustrations answer the poem's central question, "*What can a little chap do/For his country and for you?*" (112), indicating that one thing "a little chap" can do is fight for his nation. The verse itself, meanwhile, combines military and religious imagery to present young readers with an inspiring example of muscular Christianity; a little chap "can fight like a Knight/For the Truth and the Right" (112), and "can shun all that's mean, He can keep himself clean,/Both without and within" (113).

The image of the boy's spiritual battle continues as the poet says, "His soul he can brace / Against everything base" (113), "He can keep his thought white" (114), and "He can do with his might / What is good in God's sight" (114). The poem's final stanza reaffirms the image of the "little chap" doing his religious duty and states that "in each smallest thing / He can follow [...] Christ, the King" (114). Oxenham's poem and Browne's illustrations present an image of the boy as a righteous follower of Christ who brings his faith to bear in service of his country as both a spiritual fighter and an actual soldier.

Cecil Eby notes that in "the first months of the war students all over England were exposed to" this poem, and he offers a scathing view of Oxenham:

> What, the reader might ask, did John Oxenham do? He went to the front, very late in the war – not as a soldier but as a visiting literary gentleman. [...] He travels in style – at the expense of the Ministry of Information. At a requisitioned chateau [...] there are wide hearths

> with blazing logs, and the bath water arrives early. Outside, placid cows graze in the well-groomed park – a contrast, had Oxenham bothered to note it, with the filthy middens and barnyards inhabited by thousands of British Tommies back from the trenches.
>
> (Eby 248)

Eby is critical of the disingenuous and jingoist tenor of Oxenham's observations on the war and suggests he was in no position to demand

Figure 6.1 Illustration by Gordon Browne from "What Can a Little Chap Do?" in *Princess Mary's Gift Book*, 1914.

sacrifice of schoolboys. His assessment highlights how the figure of the pious Christian fighter was employed by writers, sometimes hypocritically, to persuade boys that it was their duty to enlist.

The practice of presenting the war as morally just was common in the juvenile periodical press, which was "an important provider of moral education and character training" (Olsen 165). The *Boy's Own*, for example, often emphasized the war as a righteous undertaking that every upright citizen should support. In "The Editor's Page" from the 1914–1915 *Annual*, the writer declares, "however terrible and devastating war may be, [...] there does arise a time when it may be considered just, necessary, and unavoidable. In this instance [...] our war with Germany is a just and necessary one" (41). Justifying the war on moral grounds was one way in which writers for children and adults alike sought to ensure support for the war effort and to convince males to join up.

The righteousness of the Allied soldier's cause was framed in terms of Christianity, but it was also connected to arguments about civilization and democracy. The above editorial states that "there are spiritual forces [...] at work in this huge conflict" and elaborates on why the war is deemed necessary:

> Great Britain [...] has a right to regard herself as a civilizing influence; justice and equality follow the flag [...]; the great enemy [...] is Prussian militarism, which stands for brutality, which recognizes no higher law than that of force. [...] I want every "B.O.P." reader to understand the real causes that lie behind the present crisis, and in understanding them he will come to a consciousness of a patriotism that is founded on the highest and purest principles – on reverence, unselfishness and honour.
>
> ("Editor's Page" 41)

This essay represents a paradox at the heart of much writing about the war. On the one hand, readers are told war is horrible and that militarism, equated here with savagery, stands in opposition to the "'machinery of civilization'" (41). On the other, they are taught that military participation is required of the young, patriotic Briton if "justice and equality" are to prevail. By presenting the Allied side as morally just, and its soldiers as honourably upholding the tenets of Christianity, writers taught young readers that those who fought the German enemy, including underage soldiers, followed a righteous path and performed a vital duty.

Fostering a Masculine Ideal: Masculinity, Militarism, and the Ubiquitous Image of the Boy Soldier

While the author of the *Boy's Own* editorial hopes that the future will bring "the end of war as a means of settling international disputes" and will "see arbitration taking the place of conquest by the sword" (41), he, nevertheless, embarks on an extended discussion of how boys can prepare to fight. Rather than proposing how they might ensure that future disputes are resolved peacefully, he instead outlines how boys can ready themselves for battle. Claiming that young correspondents "constantly" ask, "What can boys do to help at the present time?" he observes that "so many boys want to render help in a directly *active* manner" (41), implying that it is not only adults who want to groom the next generation of soldiers, but that it is children themselves who desire to help in a direct way.

The writer suggests that some boys, including Boy Scouts, have already given "valuable assistance" (41), but claims that there are "many hundreds of other boys, who are too young" to do the same,

> burning with the desire to do something, however small, for their country. To these boys I would say, take advantage of the opportunities now afforded you to undergo the training which will help to make men of you in the years to come.
>
> (41)

Boyhood is clearly viewed as a time when those "too young" to enlist should train themselves so that they will be ready to take up arms as soon as possible. Pointing out that there are "cadet corps," "rifle clubs [...] and other athletic bodies" that readers should join, he urges them to "Get all the best physical recreation that you can [...] and strive to make yourself 'fit' in mind and body" (41).

The author writes that in addition to the "physical benefits" this will bring,

> there is the discipline under which you will be brought, and this, to my mind, is an even more valuable schooling. This war will have done one good thing if only it results in a general bracing up of our young manhood; there has been a tendency towards too much pleasure-loving and slackness.
>
> (41)

Despite the author's earlier hope that the world will see an end to "conquest by the sword," this passage does not advise boys on how to train for a future in which peaceful arbitration has replaced war. Instead, it reinforces the notion that military skill and physical strength are fundamental to "manhood" and even suggests that the war is rescuing British masculinity from a state of decline and helping "to make men" of the nation's youth.

In the war's early stages, "recruitment of volunteer soldiers owed much to Victorian ideologies that defined masculinity in terms of strength, courage, determination, and patriotism. In turn, this image of masculinity was reinforced by wartime propaganda that glamorized military culture" (Higate and Hopton 434). The "Editor's Page" from 1914 reflects this "reciprocal relationship between militarism and masculinity" (Higate and Hopton 434), but it also expresses concern that Britain's "manhood" needs "bracing up." Evidence that Britain's men were not living up to the masculine ideal was abundantly clear in official reports on the medical examinations of those conscripted for service, which showed widespread illness and infirmity among the British working classes and revealed how "the ravages of poverty weakened the regimental strength and fighting efficiency of the British Army" (Winter 241).[1]

Anxiety over the decline of British manhood was not limited to concerns about physical health, and in A.C. Freeman's "The Making of a Hero," published in the *Boys' Own Annual* (1914–1915), unease about declining physical and moral character emerges. At the poem's outset, the eponymous hero is a "lazy boy" who is "Clumsy-bodied, dull of brain" (484). The poet elaborates:

> At work, each of his fingers a thumb;
> At home a boor, in company dumb;
> Tired of himself, moody and glum –
> John Jones, hobbledehoy.

John Jones does not live up to the masculine ideal until he enlists, which has a transformative effect:

> Who is he? – In khaki clad,
> Bright of eye, straight of limb –
> John Jones, soldier-lad.
> Proud of his calling, keen at his work;
> Never been known any duty to shirk;
> Ready for German, Austrian, Turk –

The soldier-lad's progress continues until he become "John Jones, V.C." for his bravery under fire and his ability to single-handedly capture a trench (484). Enlistment produces a positive change in the "lazy boy," who escapes the disgrace of being a useless shirker by proving himself a dutiful soldier who embodies the masculine ideal.

The idea that the war could positively transform the child is neatly expressed by one writer who observes that it "is remarkable how the occasion brings forth the man" ("A Young French" 484). According to such views, not only does war require a firm moral character and strong masculine identity, but it also helps create these. As Higate and Hopton note, "maintaining strong ideological links between militarism and masculinity" preserved the state's ability "to manipulate public support for its right to use violence to pursue its policies [...] and to encourage young men to join the armed forces" (435). While not official state

Figure 6.2 Add for Fry's Cocoa from *Work and Play*, 1916.

propaganda, the above examples of children's literature, nevertheless, reinforce the idea that young boys should actively prepare to eventually take up arms. Other works, meanwhile, such as an advertisement for Fry's cocoa published in the British children's periodical *Work and Play* (1916), imply that children do not even have to wait until they come of age to be "soldiers" (Figure 6.2).

This advertisement contains a picture of a small boy cheerfully holding a rifle and the caption reads: "One of Britain's Future Hopes lies in a virile, dominant manhood. '*We are what we assimilate,*' and growing boys and girls [...] will find that a Pure Cocoa (like FRY'S) is ALL GOODNESS" (Fry's). This image shows how pervasive the figure of the child-in-arms was and how it furthered the narrative that strengthening the young, masculine citizen was critical to maintaining Britain's military power and securing the nation's future.

A similar image appears in a 1915 advertisement for Cassell's Tablets titled "The Nerve of a Soldier," which ran in the British publication *Girls' Mirror*. It includes a photograph of a very small boy sporting a uniform and holding a rifle. Together with a caption that reads "Who said Germans?" the picture implies that the child is ready and willing to combat the enemy. The advertisement itself claims:

> Steady nerves, energy and endurance – these are the qualities which make the British soldier invincible against every foe. [...] This little boy [...] was cured of weakness and nervousness by Dr. Cassell's Tablets and now his mother [...] writes: -

> My little boy [....] is bright, full of life, can eat and sleep well, and is a big bonny lad. His father, who is at the front has sent to me for some Dr. Cassell's Tablets for his own use in the fighting line, and I have sent him a supply.
>
> (Cassell's 45)

In this instance, the image of the child-as-soldier accompanies the propagandist claim that the British soldier is "invincible" against any enemy; a claim belied by the unprecedented casualties suffered by British forces. The emphasis on "steady nerves" and endurance is particularly ironic given that many of the casualties of war were shell shock victims, and that the First World War was the first major war "in which mental breakdown played a significant role" (Showalter 62).

The advertisement's dubious assertions that Cassell's Tablets cure everything from back pain to paralysis find their parallel in the declarations about the masculine fortitude of British troops, and in the laudatory representations of the boy soldier, found in the pages of children's literature. In the same way the image of the armed child could be exploited to sell cocoa and medical cures, it could also be used to 'sell' boy readers on the idea that they had a duty to fight for their country. These images foster a militaristic masculine image, normalizing war as an element of boyhood and the boy soldier as an element of modern war.

The Tantalizing Prospect of Adventure: Living Vicariously through Tales of Boys in Action

Literature for the young "can have a part to play either in confirming acceptance of violence as an integral and unavoidable ingredient of modern life or as something we must strive to eradicate" (Whitehead 213). Images of boys eager to go to war certainly tend towards the former by normalizing violence and making it appear an inevitable and acceptable part of childhood. Many works naturalize the image of the boy soldier, situating the desire to fight in the hearts of young people impatient to play their part. One British work that suggests boys could act on their longing to fight is Jeanne Chappell's "How a Small Boy Helped to Win a Battle," published in 1918 in *The Children's Friend*. Chappell begins by calling this "a true story," and even though the lack of detail about setting and character suggests it is likely a work of fiction, this claim of authenticity frames the actions of Stannie, the boy protagonist, as ones that readers too could execute. Stannie's parents have emigrated to America, leaving him in Europe in the care of a neighbour until "they should be able to send for him" (158). After war breaks out, the neighbour says she can no longer afford to keep the boy and he must "turn out and earn his own living" (158). He finds work on a farm and, free from the parental constraints that might keep readers within the domestic sphere, he exercises his independence by leaving the fields one day to join a line of passing soldiers.

One soldier takes the boy under his wing, making sure he is fed and has a warm place to sleep. The following day, Stannie is wakened suddenly "by the sound of firing" and finds himself caught in a battle:

> It was like ten thousand of the biggest crackers all going off at once. Stannie thought it grand. The soldiers all jumped up [...] and they all got their guns ready, for they knew that the enemy was coming upon them. A lot of the men began digging trenches as fast as ever they could. When Stannie's big soldier got into a trench, he let Stannie get in beside him and hide.
>
> (158)

Though the boy hides in the trench, he is not fearful, but actually thinks it is thrilling. He proves himself resilient and capable and, when the trench becomes very hot, he runs with the soldiers' water cans to a nearby pond. Stannie's work is difficult and dangerous, but he does it without complaint for hundreds of soldiers "all through that long, blazing afternoon" (159). The child contributes directly to the battle and many "brave soldiers were able to fight better that day because of the water Stannie fetched" (159).

Stannie's task is full of risk, with "bullets flying all round," but the selfless boy is "so glad to get drink for the thirsty soldiers that he never thought about being hit himself" (159). He is discovered in the middle of the night by the edge of the pond, "moaning with the pain of a bullet wound in his chest, but still clutching tightly in his hand the last can he had tried to fill. [...] It was only when they put him to bed that Stannie would give up that last can" (159).

In recognition of his work, the wounded child receives a visit in hospital from "a very grand old gentleman" who "came and pinned on the front of Stannie's nightgown a beautiful cross that is only given to grown-up soldiers who have done the bravest deeds of all" (159). Beyond this honour, which equates the boy with the "grown-up" soldier, what makes him truly happy is learning that he will be allowed to remain "with the regiment he had helped in the battle, and ride with them wherever they went, on a fine brown horse of his very own" (159). This ending, in which the child is literally rewarded with a pony, sees the solitary boy find a new surrogate family with the regiment. In allowing the reader to live vicariously through Stannie, Chappell manipulates the young reader's simultaneous desire for a sense of belonging and family, and for adventure and empowerment.

While Stannie is a young and "small boy" who is "made no end of a fuss of" by adults while in hospital (159), many authors depict older boys caught up in the fighting, as in Mrs Belloc Lowndes's account of two English teenagers embroiled in action in Europe:

> I think most of you will envy the two Eton boys who were on a bicycle tour in France when the war broke out, and who [...] suddenly found themselves in the fighting zone! By luck more than anything else they stumbled on to the French General Staff, and there came across an English officer. Both implored him to help them to get into the French Army, and, amazing to tell, they were both made honorary sub-lieutenants.
>
> (146)

Lowndes presents underage participation in war as something that makes these older schoolboys enviable. Like Chappell, she frames this account as a true story, suggesting that the excitement of war enjoyed by these Eton boys is something that her readers could potentially experience too.

Countless wartime novels and works of series fiction offered more extended narratives about adventure on the front lines. Some series started before 1914 and simply used the war as another source of adventure for their protagonists. For example, the "Dave Porter Series" by Edward Stratemeyer[2] (1862–1930) began in 1905 with the protagonist as a fifteen-year-old schoolboy, and the fourteenth volume was published in 1918 as *Dave Porter Under Fire: Or, A Young Army Engineer in France*. Though Dave Porter is no longer at school in this novel, it is still aimed at adolescent readers and the synopsis in the Preface explains that "the great World War is on" and Dave Porter "joins Uncle Sam's forces, to [...] do his duty on the battlefields of war-scarred France. The young army engineer faces many grave perils, but does his duty unflinchingly" (vi).

In this volume in Stratemeyer's series, which had been running for more than a decade, the former adolescent protagonist is now a "young" man, and his escapades are set against the backdrop of war, but the series was still "in the price range of every child with a paper route or an allowance" and it permitted young people to read about a familiar character's new wartime adventures (Hamilton-Honey 96). While Hamilton-Honey argues that Stratemeyer's books "gave young men and women a chance to make choices about [...] what they wanted to do with their lives, outside the confines of adult authority" (96), the emphasis on Dave Porter's "unflinching" performance of duty shows that however free from adult authority fictional *characters* may have been, writers still sought to influence the choices made by young readers.

Numerous American series depict characters younger than Dave Porter who find themselves caught up in the action, even though they are not old enough to enlist. An example is Herbert Carter's "The Boy Scouts Series," which started before the war. Most of the novels tell of boys' adventures in various parts of the United States, but in 1916 Carter[3] published *The Boy Scouts on War Trails in Belgium: Or Caught Between Hostile Armies*, in which three American Boy Scouts on holiday in Europe are trapped in Germany when war begins and must make their way to Belgium. While the boys encounter their share of adventure, the novel's fairly impartial account of the war echoes America's position of neutrality at the time.

Another series featuring American protagonists is Clair Wallace Hayes's "Boy Allies" series, which also began before the United States entered the war.[4] However, unlike the *Dave Porter* series or the *Boy Scouts* series, this one began with a novel about the Great War. *The Boy Allies at Liege: Or Through Lines of Steel* was published in 1915 and is about seventeen-year-old Hal Paine and his younger friend Chester Crawford who are in Berlin with Hal's mother when war breaks out. This novel and the ones that follow (which include titles like *The Boy Allies on the Somme* and *The Boy Allies in the Balkan Campaign*) recount the perils and adventures encountered by the boys as they find themselves participating in battle, despite their young age.

In works of wartime fiction, children often performed adult responsibilities "and had voices and opinions that were often ignored in real life" (Hamilton-Honey 96). War novels about boys getting close to the action thus appealed to the reader's desire to experience adventure and be taken seriously by adults, but the celebration of underage youths taking up the mantle of adult men can also be understood as a form of manipulation. If wartime children's literature is considered in relation to the "humanitarian narrative" that proclaims, "children are recruited and conscripted as child soldiers because they are vulnerable and can be easily manipulated" (Rosen *Armies* 16), then stories celebrating child soldiers can be considered recruitment tools through which adult writers manipulate children into fighting. But as Rosen notes, the view that "child soldiers are simply vulnerable individuals exploited by adults who use them as [...] weapons of war" is oversimplified (Rosen *Armies* 132). He correctly points out that various aspects of history and culture "shape the lives of children and youth during peace and war, creating many different kinds of childhood and many different kinds of child soldiers" (132). In both literature and real life, therefore, we find a range of responses to the child soldier. In some cases, this figure represents the adult manipulation of children's desires, while in others we may see genuine examples of child agency and empowerment. During the First World War, the literary representation of boy soldiers suggested to young readers that age was not necessarily an impediment to serving the nation, and that children were not powerless.

Representing the "Real" Boy Soldier: The Promise of Reward and Glory

Boy soldiers were not simply artistic or literary creations. Historian Tim Cook notes that "as many as 20,000" underage soldiers served overseas in the Canadian forces ("He Was Determined" 41), a striking number, especially given that Canada's population was less than eight million. In Britain's armed forces, conservative estimates put the number of underage soldiers around 250,000 "and about 55 percent of these were killed or wounded during the war" (Rosen *Child Soldiers* 64).[5] Underage Americans also saw combat, the youngest reportedly being just thirteen when he enlisted (Stover 24). Some of the artistic and literary representations discussed here were undoubtedly inspired by these real-life examples, and while many people were troubled by the use of child soldiers (evidenced by the existence of a minimum age of enlistment, even if it was poorly enforced), many works of non-fiction celebrated them.

The 1914–1915 *Boy's Own Annual* contains numerous articles praising the participation of real boys in combat. One is the anonymous "Boy Heroes of the War," which begins by noting that the war

> abounds in instances of young boys who are serving with the colours, or who otherwise find opportunity for the display of their patriotic ardour. Especially in France and Belgium is this the case; [...] one reads of peasant lads who have shouldered a rifle and stood by the side of their fathers and brothers in the attempt to check the hordes of Germans.
>
> (228)

This article depicts young boys contributing alongside adult fighters and praises them for facing the same risks.

Examples of boys from Allied nations like France and Belgium seem designed to encourage active service in the British and colonial readers of the *Boy's Own*. For example, the same article refers to a twelve-year-old Serbian "fighting side by side with the soldiers in the rifle-pits" (228). Similarly, it discusses how "the Belgian Boy Scouts have demonstrated their usefulness" around Liege where "those plucky youngsters were engaged in serving food and drink to the soldiers in the firing line. It was a veritable baptism of fire for them as they were exposed to the bullets and shells of the enemy" (228). Also cited is the "plucky [...] deed performed by a French peasant boy during the fighting on the Aisne" who (228), using a wheelbarrow, "successfully carried off several wounded soldiers from the firing-line, taking them to a place of safety where they could be attended to by the Red Cross" (228).

In inspiring readers with these examples of initiative and patriotism, the author suggests that such brave actions will bring honour to the child, and he reports on those who have been celebrated by their nations, including a Russian "boy of sixteen, named Nicholas Orloff" who was awarded "the Cross of St. George, the equivalent of our V.C." (228). He notes that Orloff was in the Fourth Form when he left school

> to join the army. In an action near Lvoff his company was surrounded [...] and it became necessary to send for reinforcements. At the call for a volunteer young Orloff stepped from the ranks, and, under fire, made his way to the Russian lines.
>
> (228)

Similar works from the 1914–1915 *Boy's Own* include "A Young French Hero" about Gustave Chatain, a fifteen-year-old French boy who, while out farming, suddenly "threw down his hoe, ran out into the road and joined the line" of a passing regiment (483). He was later "nominated for the French Military Medal" (484), an honour bestowed on him "despite his youth" (484). Likewise, "France's Youngest Soldier" is about a thirteen-year-old who joins a passing regiment because he is "full of martial ardour." The author celebrates the boy's brave defence of his nation and observes that "Robert Baden-Powell has reminded us that when we were fighting the Boers we found that a boy could be just as efficient as a man for the defence of his country" ("France's"). Such examples of foreign child soldiers suggest to *Boy's Own* readers that they are fully capable of performing a man's role in defence of their nation and empire, and that this is not new or uncommon.

These examples are all pictured as cause for celebration, and the author of "Boy Heroes in the War" says that Britain too can take pride in the efforts of its young fighters, noting that in "our ranks there are many youths, some of them little more than boys, who have valiantly borne a man's part in the fighting" (228). One example is Private Preston of the Manchester Regiment, who lead a charge against the enemy. In relating the story of their battalion being surrounded by Germans and being left without an officer in command, a comrade of Preston's notes,

> "While we were wondering what to do, Private Preston, a lad of eighteen, known as 'the baby of the company,' threw up his cap and with a ringing cheer yelled, 'Fix your bayonets lads!' we did so and charged [...]." Preston himself bayonetted a German [...] and bore himself gallantly in the close hand-to-hand struggle. He was recommended for distinction.
>
> (228)

Although Preston is eighteen, the use of the word "baby," like the author's earlier description of youths who are "little more than boys," seemingly endorses Britain's use of young combatants. Through such accounts, the *Boy's Own* reads like an instrument of wartime propaganda, seeking to inspire in readers a desire to fight and a willingness to embrace death. Such action, young readers are told, will be rewarded through the bestowing of medals, and through the sense of satisfaction that comes of helping to defend the nation.

The contributions of underage soldiers are further celebrated by W. Augustus Steward in a piece published in the *Boy's Own Annual* (1914–1915). Steward begins "War Medals Won by Boys" by quoting from the "Killed in Action" column of the *Times* and he notes several examples of "little heroes" killed at sea (327). These are teenaged fighters, aged fifteen and sixteen, listed in the *Times*' Roll of Honour, and Steward describes them as "embryo Nelsons or Fishers going down to that glorious grave of Britishers – the deep blue sea –" (327). Steward clearly celebrates the boys' service "to King and Country" (327), noting that the

> mothers of Britain are asked to give their sons, and the boys and young men of Britain are nobly responding to the call of the Motherland; some account, therefore of the medallic recompenses gained by boys, in conflict against the foe, will be of more than passing interest.
>
> (327)

Absent from Steward's article is any concern about the early deaths of these "embryo" soldiers. Instead, he situates them within a long history of British boys being honoured for participating in war, enumerating previous instances from "the days of Queen Anne" to the more recent wars in South Africa (327), and describing these young soldiers as individuals who "covered themselves with undying glory while they calmly awaited death" (328).

Steward's accounts make the participation of young soldiers seem a long-standing British tradition, and the same is true of *The School of Arms: Stories of Boy Soldiers and Sailors* [c.1915] by Scottish-born writer A. R. Hope.[6] Published in New York, Hope's book includes many stories about young soldiers from a variety of historical battles. Steward's and Hope's accounts suggest that young boys around the globe have participated in warfare for millennia, presenting this as a fundamental part of a boy's coming of age, and drawing a direct connection between boy soldiers of the past and those engaged in recent battles. Steward writes, for instance, that "First-class Boy C.B. Jones [...] was taking a man's part in the China War of 1900, as the lads are doing now in the long North Sea vigil which ensures the safety of our Islands" (328). Here, he argues that a "boy" can do "a man's" job and fight to ensure Britain's safety.

When they point to a long history of "brave little lads" who have fought throughout British history (Steward 328), writers like Steward and Hope suggest that British boys have inherited a noble willingness to sacrifice themselves for their nation. In addition to this attention to British national character, however, they cite examples from elsewhere in the empire. For instance, Steward writes that "another who was proud to fight for Britain was a black boy, Tommy Zizer, of West African Regiment, who was awarded the West Africa medal with bar for Sierra Leone, 1898–99" (330). He adds that in the present war,

> black lads of the Nigerian regiments are fighting the battles for 'King George' in the Cameroons, and, be they white or black, the lads who fight under the Union Jack know that they battle not for vain glory, not to satisfy ambition, but for all that is good and sweet and noble in life.
>
> (330)

Steward is clearly aiming to encourage loyalty to the empire by expanding his examples beyond young soldiers from the British Isles.

Although Steward claims that boys are not motivated by a desire for "glory," he, nevertheless, cites the recent awarding of medals to young fighters, including two British drummer-boys who he hopes will "live long to wear these records showing they were among the bravest of the brave" (330). Drummer-boys were some of the youngest participants on the battlefield, but their role in the First World War was limited. Steward's piece was published in April 1915, but Britain's War Office had decided in February of that year to formally end the tradition of drummers and buglers going to war, setting the minimum combat age at eighteen (James 162). The drummer boys Steward celebrates are therefore anomalous, but they are well-suited to his purpose, which is to persuade young readers that there is value in them participating in combat and that such work will be formally celebrated.

A similar account of young soldiers being honoured is given in "How Lieut. Smyth Won the V.C.: A Desperate Deed of Courage" from *Young Canada: An Illustrated Magazine for Boys* (1916). The author writes that several "of the very bravest acts in the present great war have been performed by those who, in age, are 'little more than boy'" (24), and he outlines how Lieut. Smyth, who had "scarcely reached [...] majority," won the Victoria Cross while fighting as part of the Indian Army Corps (24). One officer describes Smythe as "a boy" and as a "smiling officer lad" who "seemed quite out of place there. He was altogether too cherubic, innocent, and happy. He glanced up smiling at the passing shells exactly as if he had never heard them before, and did not know what they were" (24). Lieutenant Smyth is, in fact, twenty-one, but this description of him conjures up an image of someone much younger and suggests it is wrong to assume youth and innocence are "out of place" in war. Instead, the article implies that the young and "cherubic" should not be discounted and can make valuable contributions on the battlefield. Smyth is explicitly described as "a young officer who, in spite of his years [...] had already been brought to notice for his gallantry" (24). In detailing the events that led to Smyth receiving the Victoria Cross, the writer repeatedly emphasizes the soldier's young age, along with his great bravery, in a clear effort to encourage young male readers to join the fight.

The suggestion that boys and men alike can bear the responsibility of fighting is found in works published in Britain, Canada, and the United States. These texts appear to dismantle the traditional hierarchy between adult and child, presenting the war as an equalizer. This is evident in the American text *Fifteen Little War Stories*, in which Myrick emphasizes the ultimate sacrifice made by youth from all walks of life: "The flower of youth – rich and poor, learned and ignorant, high and low – of America, Britain, France, Russia, Italy, the English colonies – are giving their lives to the war of right over might. That's blood patriotism!" (Myrick).

Throughout the war, writers argued that young fighters could be the equals of their adult counterparts, and when Lowndes describes the torpedoing of the Cressy, for example, she quotes one survivor who remarks, the

> best thing I saw was the coolness of a little cadet. Not more than fourteen he looked. [...] I never saw anything so calm as that lad! [...] 'Well,' he says, 'we've got to carry on like this, and if we die we shall die game'.
>
> (46–47)

Lowndes suggests that children are particularly resilient, and in the same account she writes that one

> little drummer-boy [...], who was only fifteen, had a great adventure, for he kept himself afloat in the water for about four hours with the aid of an empty rum cask. And when he got back to his father, [...] he was just as rosy-cheeked as when he went away! So he did not suffer much from his long bath.
>
> (47–48)

In describing the boy's survival of one of the war's most infamous naval disasters[7] as a "great adventure" and a "long bath," she clearly glosses over the trauma and employs the language of adventure fiction to present such real-life experiences as thrilling escapades.

Too Young to Fight? Representing the German Boy Soldier

Like other texts, Lowndes's seems intended to inspire enlistment. She remarks that boys "have played a splendid part in the war" and gives many examples of them serving their nation (209). These include the case of twelve-year-old French boy André, who she presumes her readers "will envy" for running off to join the army because he is "ready to defend his dear country to the last drop of his blood" (149). After recounting another story about a Frenchman with six sons at the front, she says

> the great outstanding fact about France [...]is that every one of her sons is, will be, or has been, a soldier! [...] it is a splendid, inspiring thought that the whole manhood of a nation is in arms to defend her. No need of recruiting there – no need to remind the young men that their country needs them.
>
> (217)

Ignoring the fact that France had "no need" to recruit because men were conscripted, and that compulsory service meant that these men were not necessarily happy to serve, Lowndes calls this family "inspiring" and implicitly criticizes those in Britain who have to be reminded that their country needs them.

These types of accounts portray young fighters from the Allied nations as heroic examples of bravery, rather than as victims, but the depiction of boy soldiers was inconsistent, particularly where their use by Germany was concerned. Lowndes, for instance, remarks that the British felt surprise

> when it was heard that quite young German boys were in the firing line, but in the great American Civil War there were lads as young as thirteen and fourteen, fighting. [...] let me break off to tell you that German boys have not been backward in helping their beloved country.
>
> (209–210)

The "surprise" Lowndes mentions is in keeping with the widespread view of children as requiring protection and the assumption that children should not be engaged in warfare, but it is also at odds with her own celebration of child soldiers. This includes her praise of German boys for not being "backward" when it comes to fighting. Perceptions of childhood can undergo dramatic and rapid change during war, but as Lowndes's uneven account of young fighters shows, the First World War did not result in a simple transition from the image of the carefree or helpless child to that of the valiant child soldier; rather, the figure of the child combatant remained contradictory.

Although Lowndes makes some positive comments about Germany's boy soldiers, many writers pointed to them as evidence of German brutality and barbarism, even as they celebrated Allied boy soldiers. In such works, the German enemy's use of child soldiers is criticized, and protecting children is held up as a hallmark of civilized society. The victimization of young German fighters was even seen as justification for Allied involvement in the war; it was not only Allied children who needed saving from the enemy, it was argued, but German children themselves. Though one could argue that tales about boy soldiers empower child readers, many writers negatively portray their use by the enemy. Often, these competing views appear within the same work of literature, revealing hypocrisy on the part of authors who only see the child soldier as a victim when his "exploitation" is at the hands of the Germans, and who celebrate the same figure as a sign of bravery and patriotism when he supports the Allied cause (Figure 6.3).

An example of this conflicted representation can be found in Hope's work, in which he suggests that the British have made progress when it comes to protecting children, stating "we no longer send to war twelve-year-old middies and ensigns hardly in their teens" (320). This seemingly reflects the developments in children's legal rights that transpired throughout the nineteenth and early twentieth centuries, and it appears to anticipate today's humanitarian view that "something is clearly and profoundly wrong when children are soldiers" (Rosen *Armies* 1).

Figure 6.3 "Les dernier soldats du Kaiser" French postcard, c.1914–1918.

As discussed earlier, however, Hope's work contains many examples of young boys contributing meaningfully to the Allied cause and he proudly states that "many who have [...] shown themselves worthy sons of Britain are not beyond schooldays" (320). Conversely, though, Hope also suggests that the "precocious courage" exhibited by young German fighters is misguided and results from naivety (327), observing that these "brave youngsters have the excuse of ignorance for their patriotism, since in Germany newspapers are not allowed to tell the truth" (327).

The notion that British papers tell only "the truth" of the war is, of course, problematic, as is Hope's comparison between the use of children by the Germans, and by the British. In speaking of the efforts of Boy Scouts, for instance, he reproaches Germany for allowing children to gather scrap metal to "be used up for ammunition" and contrasts this with Britain, declaring "our boy-scouts go tramping [...] about from farm to farm, on the more gracious duty of gathering eggs for the wounded" (Hope 329). German children are thus directly implicated in the deaths of Allied soldiers, whereas British children are depicted as performing a more "gracious" and innocent duty.

The inconsistency of Hope's views on the use of children in the war, which are cast in a negative light when they involve Germans but lauded when they involve British youth, is made even more apparent when he praises British Scouts for "taking the places of men gone to the front" (328). He elides the difference between the child Scout and the adult soldier, seeing this ability of children to step into the roles of men as a commendable achievement. Despite his claim that Britain no longer endorses the use of boy soldiers, the bulk of Hope's narrative reveals his tacit approval of them as he celebrates the bravery and tender age of British fighters.

Like many writers, Hope presents the child figure as both a helpless victim and a responsible citizen, depending on which image best serves his needs. For example, in his reference to boys who acted as lookouts along England's coastline, he talks about their "baptism of fire" when, in 1914, "German ships of war made a dash across the seas, hurled deadly missiles into quiet towns, then made off in haste to triumph over this exploit of 'baby-killing'" (Hope 330). The term "baby-killing" to describe the deaths of young Britons creates an image of the German enemy as decidedly vicious and immoral, ready and willing to kill those who cannot defend themselves. Yet this image of child vulnerability gives way to Hope's declaration that these events "show what war is and how young hearts have steeled themselves against its dangers and hardships. So long as men are what they are [...] nations must be ready to defend themselves against aggression" (335–336). Even as Hope condemns Germany's killing of children and suggests the use of boy soldiers is a sign of a retrograde civilization, he, nevertheless, presents war as an inescapable outcome of human nature and perpetuates the view that childhood is a necessary training ground for military duty.

A similar paradox is found in in A. Tegnier's 1916 article "Boy Heroes of the Present War" from *Young Canada.* Like Hope, Tegnier attempts to distinguish between German and Allied treatment of child soldiers. He acknowledges the widely-held view that their use is wrong when he states that within "the German and Austrian troops several youths have been promoted to lieutenantships at the ages of sixteen and seventeen [...]. But with the British, youngsters in the actual fighting front are sternly discouraged and kept back." Tegnier undermines this apparent distinction, however, when he elsewhere lauds the contributions of young Allied fighters and writes, "when the tremendous conflict in Europe is ended, and its history is written, some of the most stirring and appealing chapters will be those dealing with the heroic deeds of boy soldiers" (327). Like Hope, Tegnier is being disingenuous by stating on the one hand that the British are better than the Germans because they discourage young boys from fighting, while on the other giving examples of teenage British soldiers who have been "heroic" in the war.

The sheer volume of literature from the First World War that praises the use of child soldiers supports Rosen's claim that "the child soldier as an abused and exploited victim of war is a radically new concept" (*Armies* 6). Rather than describing such figures as victims, these early twentieth-century authors celebrated them. At the same time, however, some presented the figure of the child soldier as an example of child suffering and victimization, particularly when it came to Germany, considering it evidence of German barbarity and decline. Such contrasting images are a clear indication of the extent to which notions of what constitutes "the child" or "childhood" were malleable and transient during the First World War.

As discussed earlier in this book, images of child war victims were very much in keeping with the notion of childhood as a period of vulnerability. However, the countless literary examples of children supporting the war effort in one form or another show that during this time of crisis, when the need for military recruits was extreme, images of passive and innocent children were accompanied by those of youngsters happily sacrificing themselves for their nation. Indeed, the frequency with which young people were depicted as being deeply entangled in the war around them supports the contention that even before the war, authors conceived of children "as socially saturated beings, profoundly shaped by the culture, manners, and morals of their time, precisely in order to explore the vexed issue of the child's agency" (Gubar 4). Kate James observes that a lack of distinction between adult men and boys "was more pertinent during war" and that "in some circumstances the military, notably the navy, saw boys as a necessary pool of manpower for wartime roles. Thus, the distinction between boyhood and manhood was often negated through military policy in order to meet wartime requirements" (James 153). Wartime children's literature, which alternately presents images of child simplicity and child resourcefulness, was part of an ongoing negotiation of the child's position in relation to the adult.

Some wartime writers see the child soldier as an empowering figure for young readers, while others see him as an emblem of the child in crisis, and these attitudes are often present within the same piece of literature. Hope writes, for instance, that the more the

> atrocities of this warfare came to be known, the readier was our youth to encounter such fell foes. Every bomb killing women and children in their sleep brought recruits eager to punish so futile attacks. Every day we have heard of boys who should be at school trying to pass for older that they might enlist in the army or navy. (326)

As in his account of German bombing raids along the coast of England, Hope is simultaneously horrified by the deaths of innocent children, and eager to celebrate the many underage British boys who have rushed to enlist.

Many children's writers, while outwardly criticizing the use of child soldiers, nevertheless celebrate their contributions and these "sentiments reveal a deliberate blurring of the constructed boundary between adults and children, as boys are not presented as innocents deserving of protection, but as citizens with the full responsibilities and capabilities of adults" (Galway "Competing" 302). Tegnier, for instance, praises the "heroic and impressive [...] way in which youths, who can truthfully be termed schoolboys yet, have played the part of men in their nation's hour of need" and have accepted "all that modern warfare offers just as grandly as the men." This statement ignores the fact that these children did not have the same rights as those adult citizens, revealing that there existed in the early years of the twentieth century "an ambiguity over children's natural rights" (Cockburn 107). Children "were considered citizens in the making, rather than citizens now" (107), and children's literature, which leaned towards discussing one's duties, rather than one's rights, had a role to play in fashioning these future citizens, with the figure of the boy soldier providing an excellent role model. Ironically, Germany's own use of boy soldiers was highly criticized in many portrayals of the enemy, which form the subject of the next chapter.

Notes

1 During their time in training, many recruits actually gained significant weight, grew taller, and saw their general health improve as they experienced a healthier diet, better living conditions, and improved medical care (De Groot 163).

2 In 1906 Stratemeyer formed the Stratemeyer Literary Syndicate, which published approximately 1,500 books, including the popular *Nancy Drew* and *Hardy Boys* novels. Many of these relied on ghostwriters but there is evidence that Stratemeyer wrote the volumes printed under his own name, such as the *Dave Porter* series (Hamilton-Honey 90).

3 Herbert Carter was one of several pseudonyms used by prolific American children's author St. George Henry Rathborne (1854–1938). This novel was followed in 1917 by *The Boy Scouts Afoot in France: Or With the Red Cross at the Marne* that continued the account of the American boys' adventures.

4 Hayes (b.1887) was the author of numerous children's adventure stories, including those published under the name "Ensign Robert L. Drake" (Pavlik 200).

5 Rosen observes that

> underage enlistment was at its highest in the beginning of the war, representing between 10 and 15 percent of recruits. Young people could enlist without providing any documentation of age, so boys between the ages of fourteen and eighteen joined the steady stream into the ranks [...]. Ultimately, conscription substantially reduced the flow of those under eighteen into the army.
>
> (*Child Soldiers* 64–65)

6 Ascott R. Hope was the pen name of Robert Hope Moncrieff (1846–1927), a prolific author of works for adults and children and a frequent contributor to the *Boy's Own*.

7 On September 22, 1914, the threat of the German submarine became painfully apparent when the Germans successfully destroyed the *Cressy*, the *Hogue*, and the *Aboukir*, three British warships, off the Dutch coast. "The dead numbered 1,459" and "barely a third of the men aboard the three cruisers survived to be rescued by Dutch steamers and fishing boats" (Sondhaus 2).

7 "Why We Fought the Hun"

Portraying the German Enemy to Child Readers

Children's literature shared certain things in common with official First World War propaganda, including negative representations of the enemy. Variously referred to as Germans, Huns, Boches, and "Fritz," the enemy was portrayed as possessing undesirable qualities at odds with those supposedly embodied by the Allies, and child figures often helped highlight differences between the opposing sides. For instance, an alleged willingness to commit atrocities against children was often held up as proof of German cruelty, whereas coming to the rescue of the weak signalled the moral superiority of the Allies. Images of aggressive, bullying, and depraved Germans culminated in a popular narrative that figured "the Hun" as something "other." In children's literature, the German became a monster to be feared and a dragon to be slain; an opponent against which North American and British children could prove their bravery and loyalty.

In response to a growing perception of Germany as a military threat with increasing imperial ambitions, negative portrayals of Germany became common in British children's literature between the end of the Boer War in 1902, which "provided the catalyst for [...] the rise of Anglo-German antagonism" (Francis "Willingly"), and the start of the First World War. Nevertheless, wartime writers did not entirely forgo sympathetic portrayals of Germans. Some avoided negatively characterizing the entire population, instead picturing the average German as a victim of the nation's rulers and highlighting the common humanity of those on both sides of the conflict. Herbert Strang,[1] for example, observes that "it would be wrong to condemn the whole nation indiscriminately" and, by attributing blame to German leaders, writers could argue that the Allies were motivated by a desire to overthrow tyranny and liberate the victims of an unjust state, including Germans themselves.

Unsurprisingly, overtly negative representations of Germany seem to be less common in pre-1917 American texts than in those written after the United States entered the war, but throughout the conflict, literature on both sides of the Atlantic contained mixed representations of the enemy. These included negative, humorous, and even favourable ones, and these differing portrayals reveal much about how the war was justified to the public, how national identities were constructed during the war, and how children played a part in these processes.

DOI: 10.4324/9781003191605-8

Trouble at Home: Germans as Victimizers of German Children

Writing in 1918, American Herbert Myrick describes the war as a "struggle for the survival of the fittest," claiming it "is the inevitable step in Evolution. Victory over Kultur means the coming of a new civilization." Myrick's framing of the war in social evolutionary terms is part of a narrative in which the Allied nations represented progress, and Germany signified decline. Some saw the militarization of the young as a manifestation of Germany's apparent degeneration[2] or failure to progress and, as discussed in the preceding chapter, there was a hypocritical tendency to point to its use of underage combatants as a reason why the enemy must be destroyed.

In his article "The German Schoolboy," Ernest C. Pulbrook[3] (1873–1936) explores the notion that children's involvement in military service is proof of a flawed civilization. First published in 1906 in *The Boy's Own*, it was reprinted in *Young Canada* in 1916 and shows that wartime critiques of German society were neither new, nor consistent. Pulbrook focusses on school-aged boys, inevitably drawing young English readers' attention to the things they have in common with German youth, but he also points out ways in which their childhoods are dissimilar. He observes that "Germany is so busy calling on every available man that even senior schoolboys have been ordered to undergo a course of musketry and military drill, and many have already been taken prisoners" (15). The word "even" suggests that training schoolboys to be soldiers is non-normative, an idea echoed by American writer Herbert Carter in his novel about Boy Scouts in Belgium. When a small German child is spotted waving "his hand in a real soldierly fashion" one American boy remarks, "Even the kids over here have got the military spirit born in 'em'" (34). Such comments imply that the militarization of youth is unusual, and many considered it a consequence of increasing strains on the army following German unification in 1871.

Somewhat inconsistently, while Pulbrook suggests the militarization of the young is unprecedented, he simultaneously argues that it has long roots in German culture and observes that

> almost from his birth the iron hand of the military system seizes the German boy, and as soon as he reaches school age he becomes acquainted with some of those rules and regulations which order his daily doings from the cradle to the grave.
>
> (15)

In his discussion of militarism and imperialism in British schools in the decades preceding the war, Alan Penn notes that in the eyes of the British, "'militarism' was particularly associated with Germany" (165), a view evident in Pulbrook's account of life for the average German boy. Pulbrook notes that "military service overshadows most of his school life" and claims that every boy strives to perform well enough in school "to reach the class which will allow him to serve only one year with the colours" (15). The idea that German pupils shun military service[4] supports the view that it is inappropriate for schoolboys to serve, and that a hunger for war has made the nation violate a natural barrier between adulthood and childhood. German youth are no longer protected by the state but are exploited by it, their childhood overshadowed by a thirst for warfare.

When Pulbrook originally wrote this piece, Britain did not have compulsory military service which, "though deemed by some to be necessary, was seen as contrary to Liberal principle" (Penn 165). Ironically, Pulbrook's article was reprinted in *Young Canada* in the same year Britain introduced conscription laws and Canadians were fiercely debating doing the same. Those ironies were apparently lost on whoever chose to republish this work for children at a moment when required service could no longer be pointed to as something that distinguished Germany from its opponents.

As part of his implicit critique of required military service, Pulbrook presents German society as rigid, contrasting it with the supposed freedom of British life. He notes that on entering school, each German boy receives a booklet outlining the rules that "regulate his goings out and comings in [...], the age at which he is allowed to smoke and the places in which this is allowed, [...] and the general order of his daily life" (15). Pulbrook further states that "German school life is one long round of work" (16), remarking that despite "what is so frequently said, German education is really no better than our own" (15). Although it is not clear whether it is the Germans or the British who "frequently" claim German education is superior, he evidently sees a need to defend England's reputation by asserting that longer hours and more homework, which to some might signal academic rigour, are merely evidence of the German boy's lack of freedom and subjugation by the state.

Similar claims that German society is heavily regulated appear repeatedly in Allied literature, with Strang writing, for example, that because of "the usual easy-going British way we have underrated the enemy" whose "virtues of patience and method have been devoted to the building up of an immense war machine." Similarly, in describing Germany's monopoly on toy-making, Frenchman Frédéric Masson calls it "the terrible, methodical organiser next door" (16). This supposed discipline is often regarded as contrary to the freedom many considered integral to childhood, and Pulbrook's account of German schoolboys differs from the typical British boarding-school tale in which independence and rule-breaking are celebrated components of the British boy's educational experience.

Unacknowledged in Pulbrook's critique is the fact that children's behaviour was also controlled in Britain, and what he points to as overregulation could also signal a German desire to protect children from harm, not unlike aged-based laws elsewhere. Similarly, despite militarism being "ostensibly frowned upon" in Britain (Penn 164), there was a successful and "active lobby in favour of [...] military drill within the school curriculum" long before the First World War (160). The narrative that German children are harmed by their own society is not only inconsistent, therefore, but also fails to address similarities between German, British, and North American childhoods. Nevertheless, these inconsistencies did not stop wartime writers from portraying the German child as a victim whose suffering underscored the justness of the Allied cause.

The Beastly Boches: Germans as Victimizers of Allied Children

While Pulbrook focusses on German youth, many wartime authors depict Germany's impact on Allied children, and these representations are not unlike the official propaganda posters that used child imagery (including illustrations of babies being bayonetted) to convey German brutality. For example, Ellsworth Young's ominous propaganda poster "Remember Belgium" (c.1918) shows a young Belgian girl, silhouetted against a burning village, being dragged away by a German soldier (Figure 7.1).

Figure 7.1 "Remember Belgium" by Ellsworth Young, 1918. [Library of Congress, Prints & Photographs Division].

Similar scenes appear in *Told in Gallant Deeds*, with Lowndes writing of how the Germans "wreaked their vengeance on the innocent inhabitants of the villages and small towns through which they were retreating" (146–147), including women and children.

Such callousness also appears in Lowndes's account of the treatment of "two innocent little boys" in an occupied French village after the German commander notices that the church clock has stopped and demands that it be fixed (147). After the village curé and two young choir boys wind the clock and it begins to strike, the

> commander, in a great fright, decided that this was a dodge invented by the curé to warn the French that a number of weary Germans were in his village. At once he had him arrested, and the two little boys as well. Without more ado all three were sentenced to be shot the next morning.
>
> (Lowndes 147)

Unlike the "worthy" French priest (147), who is distraught that the boys will have "their young lives cut short" and who wants the Germans to "spare the two lads" (148), the cruel commander thinks nothing of killing "two little boys," but his fright at the striking of the clock also renders him ridiculous. This cowardice ultimately saves the children, for the Germans rush "out of the village, forgetting all about their captives" after hearing the French forces are closing in (148).

The contrast between the noble Allies and the cowardly, child-killing Germans is replicated when Lowndes describes the British bombing of a Zeppelin shed at Düsseldorf and notes that the "gallant" aviators "were most careful to do no harm to private or public buildings [...]. In fact, they could have destroyed another Zeppelin shed had they not thought it wrong to run the risk of injuring innocent women and children" (172–173). She then remarks, "I cannot help contrasting this behaviour with the conduct of German airmen, who killed or mutilated with their bombs numbers of women and children" (173). Here, a main point of contrast is the treatment of children, with the British going out of their way to protect young lives and the Germans showing a blatant disregard for them.

Similar accusations are found in "Boy Heroes of the War," published in Britain's *Boy's Own Annual* (1914–1915). A French boy doing "valuable scouting work" falls "into the hands of a German patrol" and his young age does nothing to spare him from the Germans who,

> after futile efforts to make him betray the French regiment [...] tied him to a tree. Then they pointed their revolvers at him and threatened him with instant death [...]. The brave boy held out against

> them in spite of this, and paid the penalty with his life, his secret unrevealed.
>
> ("Boy Heroes")

The French boy is a praiseworthy example of a child sacrificing himself for his country, but the image of the murdered child also serves to highlight German barbarity. The child figure, be it the German boy at the mercy of a highly organized, militaristic society, or the Allied child threatened by German soldiers, thus plays a role in constructing the enemy as a loathsome figure whose values oppose those of Britain and its allies.

"Enemy of the Human Race": Germany as a Cowardly Bully and Abusive Imperial Ruler

The ill treatment of children was one manifestation of an abuse of power frequently portrayed as central to German national character. One post-war example appeared in the May 1920 issue of Vancouver's *School Days: A Magazine Published Monthly for the Pupils of the Public Schools.*[5] "Why We Fought the Hun" by Canadian educator R. S. Sherman[6] (1865–1941) seeks to explain why the Allies went to war in "the slaughter-house of the Huns" in the first place:

> 'Twas neither for gold nor glory;
> Nor yet for revenge, nor pride;
> Neither for land, nor largesse,
> Nor lust of the homicide;
> No hymn of hate to inspire us,
> No tyrant hand to compel;
> We were cheered by a voice from heaven,
> Not cowed by a voice from hell.
>
> (Sherman)

Perhaps written in response to the widespread sense of disillusionment that followed the war, Sherman's poem pushes back against post-war cynicism to reaffirm for child readers the necessity of the conflict, claiming that the Allies "fought for a world-wide freedom."

Sherman's effort to convince young Canadians of the war's necessity relies on establishing a dichotomy between the two sides, and the "hymn of hate" he refers to is the popular "Haßgesang gegen England" ("Hymn of Hate against England"), published in 1914, which "for a time supplanted the national anthem" and for which Ernst Lissauer was awarded the Iron Cross (Marquis 490).[7] In citing this, Sherman depicts hatred as motivating Germany, whereas the Allies are inspired by "courage, to fight for the weak" and respect for the "right for each nation to rule" itself. He declares that along with those in other nations, the "Bavarian [...] will enjoy the blessings/Bought by the blood" of the Allies. Bavaria had a strong nationalist movement but was officially part of Germany, so this verse suggests that Germany's hunger for war came at the expense of its own citizens who needed rescuing from the tyranny of the state.

Writing in 1914, Lowndes observes that the German nation was completely sacrificed "to the awful, sinister War god" (218), even as she celebrates the martial spirit displayed in France, where "every man over eighteen and under fifty is a soldier" (218). The Allies, however, "only arm [...] for defence" (218), whereas Germany is an aggressor. Similarly, in a chapter titled "Germany – Enemy of the Human Race," Strang writes that for a quarter of a century "Germany has been organising herself for the conquest of the mastery of the world. [...] 'World power or downfall' has been her motto." Likewise, in explaining the outbreak of the war for child readers in simple prose, Englishman Robert Harvie personifies Germany as a bully and leads the child reader to identify with the small, aggrieved nation of Belgium. Establishing the foe as abusive and dishonourable, he writes that Germany declared it "would never let a wretched treaty keep her from doing just as she liked" (14). Depictions of Germans as bullies extended from its political leaders to its soldiers, who were frequently described as "un-sportsmanlike" and whose "tactics were regarded as underhand" (Kennedy *Children's* 74). In contrast, writers like Harvie presented Britain as "determined to do right" (Harvie 14), which meant protecting those "weaker than Germany" (14), much as adults might feel obligated to protect children.

Representations of Germany as abusive and Britain as a protective parental figure extended to discussions of empire. For example, in "Our Widened Empire: A Few Facts Concerning the Former German Colonies," published c.1920 in *The Wonder Book of Empire for Boys and Girls*, the author describes Germany as a terrible imperial power and justifies Britain taking control of its colonies. Quoting Lloyd George's statement that this is part of the "already gigantic charge which now rests upon the shoulders of the Empire" (x), the author depicts Britain as a conscientious imperial leader that considers the governance of these territories "a very sacred trust" (xii).

While Britain is presented as mature and responsible, Germany is described as "a newcomer among Colonial Powers" (x), and the article encapsulates British resentment of "Germany as an upstart nation" at a time when many were "equating the rise of German power with the decline of British" power and were hoping for "the containment of Britain's most threatening competitor" (Peppis 105). The author of "Our Widened Empire" presents Germany's colonies as children in need of protection, declaring that the so-called "dependent races look to us with trust and reverence, for they are aware that Britain is true to her word, and generous in her attitude" (xii). By contrast, he claims, Germany "ruled almost entirely by fear [...] and virtually adopted what one of her leading men called a 'splendid' system of slavery" (xii). Remarking that "better times are in store for the peoples who have passed under the sway of the British Empire, which, whatever its faults, is founded upon the bed-rock principles of justice, humanity and freedom" (xii), the author draws a clear contrast between the two nations. This assessment justifies the war on the grounds that it eased the suffering of the German colonies, for rather than protecting its children and its colonial subjects, Germany exploited and victimized them.

Given the extent to which bravery was extolled in wartime children's literature, it is no surprise that depictions of German abusiveness were coupled with portrayals of German cowardice. In "Pluck and Peril Among the Bombers," for example, published in 1916 in *Young Canada*, the author describes bomb-throwing as a dangerous practice in which "the British soldier has developed an expertness" and recounts an incident in which the British welcomed an opportunity to fight "as a pleasant change from the monotony of trench life" (194). In contrast, the Germans showed "little desire for hand-to-hand fighting, as they quitted the post they had occupied the moment" the British bombers advanced (194). Like the Germans in Lowndes's tale who flee in terror at the striking of a clock, the reluctance to engage in close combat is a sign of cowardice that contrasts the "pluck" of the British soldiers.

In his discussion of the tone of the articles published in *Young Canada*, Stephen Dale observes there is a sharp distinction between glorified accounts of heroic fighting like the one in "Pluck and Peril," and those found in the letters and memoirs written by soldiers themselves. Dale argues that the recurring narrative of soldiers facing death "with joyous hearts and cheerful outlooks" is "the one force powerful enough to neutralize the continual, dispiriting news about casualties" that children heard (70). While some young readers may have accepted positive tales like the one about joyful bomb-throwers as accurate accounts of Allied success, others may have consciously suspended their disbelief as they sought reprieve from war's grim truths. Giving child readers "hope" that the British side would eventually win was considered key to maintaining support for the war effort, but writers faced a dilemma: they had to avoid implying that the Germans could not be beaten, but also had to resist depicting them merely as cowards, for there was little honour in fighting such an opponent.

Some writers tried to preserve readers' hope in victory while still presenting the Germans as challenging adversaries. In "A Great Battleship in a Gale" from 1916, for instance, also published in *Young Canada*, a British sailor remarks that the Germans "may be very good sailors, but when you see our guns and the way they are handled I would not give much for their chance" (196). The point here is not that the Germans are fainthearted or inept, but that the British are even better. Strang goes further in his praise, writing that Germany's soldiers "were brave, well-trained, and thoroughly confident. Her organisation was as near perfection as is possible to mortal men." He observes that the Germans have not become complacent but "have the will to win, and are backing their will by the sternest determination. In these respects they show a notable example to the world."

For Strang and others, the shortcomings of the Germans did not lie in cowardice or incompetence but were instead moral failings. In the same paragraph in which he praises their determination, Strang states "their ambitions are unworthy and would bring disaster on mankind" and says their determination "to win at all costs" has crowned the nation "with eternal infamy." Citing the use of poison gas, he declares that a society "that can stoop to such barbarous methods as these has proclaimed itself the Enemy of the Human Race, and deserves extinction." This description establishes the Germans as something other, their barbarity and dishonour rendering them less than human.

The Enemy Within the Gates: Germans on the Home Front

In addition to portraying the enemy on the battlefield, authors grappled with widespread antipathy towards Allied citizens of German ancestry, and children became implicated in these discussions. Groves's 1917 Canadian school play *The Wooing of Miss Canada* exposes existing hostility, including the fear that German-Canadians posed a threat from within. At the time of the war almost half a million Canadians had German ancestry and "many Anglo-Canadians distrusted naturalized Germans" (Thompson 5). Some envisioned the possibility of "a large-scale invasion of Canada from the United States" comprising "anti-British elements" living in North America (Kitchen 248), fears evidenced by the introduction of an internment system in October 1914 that imprisoned more than a 1,000 German "enemy aliens" and nearly 6,000 Austro-Hungarians (Thompson 7).

Despite such concerns, Groves's play shows that the threat Germany poses is not always a military one. Miss Canada's German suitor is not a soldier but a scholar, costumed in a "Cap and Gown with a huge book under his arm" (27). When he says he had a difficult time getting to Canada Miss Canada replies, "to be perfectly frank with you, Germans are not wanted here" (27). This sentiment points to the widespread rejection of German thought and culture during the war, but comes as a surprise to arrogant Germany: "Not wanted? What nonsense! Why, we are the most wonderful people in the civilized world – look at our efficiency, our inventions in the realms of art and science, and then our kultur" (27). This dialogue reveals that Germany was seen as more than a military threat, its conceit manifest in its goal of cultural imperialism.

Claudia Siebrecht asserts that, in Germany, the conflict was "understood to have been caused by the jealousy and resentment of Germany's neighbours" and German victory was considered "proof of the superiority of German culture" (42). Scathing discussions of Germany's *kultur* are recurrent in children's literature, and Groves's decision to garb Germany in the costume of a scholar may be a nod to the infamous "Manifesto of the 93" that was framed as an "Appeal to the World of Culture" and signed in October 1914 by 93 intellectuals, writers, and artists "in defence of Germany's war aims and denying the charge of German atrocities" (Siebrecht 44). The Manifesto helped solidify the view that German academics had embraced militarism with complete and unwavering enthusiasm and aligned themselves "with the war aims of the Kaiser" (MacLeod 61). It is significant, therefore, that in Groves's play for schoolchildren, the enemy is not presented as a soldier, but as a scholar.

Demonizing academics might seem like an odd choice for a school play, but it serves an important function: by focussing less on the enemy as a military threat, Groves turns children's attention to the risk posed by Germany on the home front. During the war, German language, literature, and cultural traditions were presented as threats that could linger even after Allied military victory might be achieved. The child actor playing the part of Germany thus embodies this potential menace to Canada's future, for it is not just the adult soldier that is to be feared, but the future "offspring" of Germany's continuing cultural influence.

When Germany tries to explain to Miss Canada the advantages of a union between the two, the fear that its cultural influences could reshape Canada is revealed:

> I have come to tell you of the advantages that will be yours once you ally yourself with Germany. [...] everything will be taken in hand by efficient leaders – every inch of ground will be made to produce, there will be no waste anywhere, and Canada will see a prosperity [...] she has never dreamed of. [...] In Germany the rulers rule by divine right and you will share in the grandeur and greatness of an empire that will dazzle you.
>
> (27–28)

While Germany believes that Canada will benefit from being "under German rule," Miss Canada firmly rejects his proposal and his claims about German culture: "Efficiency – How we hate the word! Kultur – we know too well what it stands for. Civilization – Germany does not know the meaning of it" (27). Miss Canada's disdain reflects a critique of German arrogance and anti-democratic tendencies, one that was widespread in Allied children's literature.

Unlike Uncle Sam, who respectfully accepts Miss Canada's rejection, Germany is determined to seize her by force and grabs her by the arm, demonstrating how "the actual victimization of women" during the war "was transformed into a representation of a violated, but innocent, female nation resisting the assaults of a brutal male assailant"[8] (Harris 170). The stage directions indicate that "Canada utters a cry and Jack Canuck dressed in khaki rushes on" (29). By having the young boy playing Jack Canuck wear khaki, Groves puts a physical incarnation of the boy soldier onstage and presents Canadian masculinity as a protective force that contrasts the belligerent masculinity of Germany.

In her Epilogue, Groves cautions Canadians to "be ever on the alert to guard well" the nation's interests (32), "to watch the immigration and see that undesirables do not enter and to ever remember our watchword, 'Canada for Canadians'" (32). The implicit hostility towards naturalized German citizens expressed here was not unique to Canada and often extended to the German language itself. Some place names were anglicized in Britain and North America (Berlin, Ontario changed its name to Kitchener in 1916, for instance), and in 1917 King George replaced the royal family's Germanic surname with "Windsor," reflecting the pervasiveness of anti-German sentiment. The article "German in Our Schools" by Edward N. Teall[9] (1880–1947), published in a 1918 issue of *St. Nicholas*, provides an example of how American children were exposed to this rhetoric. Teall says that a

> phase of the perfectly natural, though perhaps not morally justifiable, inclination to refuse to have anything to do with Germany after she is defeated by the free nations is the agitation against continuing to teach the German language and literature in our schools.

Teall is not referring simply to wartime measures that might weaken Germany but is anticipating post-war actions following an Allied victory. This rejection of "anything to do with Germany" is about more than winning the war; it reveals a deep-rooted antipathy to German culture and a fear that military defeat alone will not stop Germany's rising global dominance.

Although Teall acknowledges that this is "perhaps not morally justifiable," he also describes it as "natural" and says the main reason to ban German from American schools is that

> the nation led astray by insane rulers has made use of every contact with the rest of the world for propaganda. The farther the German

> language travels, the more wide-spread is the baneful influence of the German philosophy of life, with its contempt for everything that the civilized nations hold dear – peace, and honor and justice.

Teall establishes Germany not as a temporary military adversary, but as an ongoing and insidious threat to civilization, and his article shows how schoolchildren were conscripted in this continuing fight.

The familiar theme of children's self-sacrifice emerges when, after noting that banning German means some students would lose credits towards their diplomas, Teall questions "how many American boys and girls" would want to earn these given that the language is a tool for spreading German propaganda. Although he says that Americans "must not let prejudice sway our reason," he also says there exist "excellent reasons" to "shun the German language and the literature that embodies the old, bad German kultur!" (Teall). American pupils, he argues, have the power to stem the flow of German influence and should be willing to sacrifice a credit if it means protecting the world. According to Teall's reasoning, child ignorance becomes a positive trait that can stop German propaganda in its tracks.

While Teall advocates for limiting children's learning, in other texts a knowledge of German is presented as advantageous, and antipathy towards German culture is even ridiculed. For instance, in the humorous "How We Caught the Spy" by Edward Shirley, a group of British schoolboys falsely accuse a man of being a German infiltrator, largely because they are scornful of learning German and mistake his copy of Faust for something sinister. The children's humiliation on discovering he is really a distinguished British general makes them appear ridiculous, not heroic, and the young narrator remarks, "we did feel asses – every one of us. We had mistaken one of the bravest generals that ever wore the King's uniform for a German spy, and had mauled him and trussed him up as if he had been a burglar!" (29). Shirley appears to be critiquing the more zealous anti-German attitudes of the day, as well as satirizing the popular genre of espionage fiction in which child figures were frequently portrayed as successful spy-catchers.

Shirley's tale shows that a stubborn rejection of all things German is problematic, and a similar view is expressed in a British Board of Education circular from 1914. It stresses that students should learn German history and "that use should be made of the children's foreign language skills, encouraging teachers to use French and German texts on the Napoleonic Wars as well as the English ones" (Kennedy *Children's* 131). Despite approaches that aimed "not to 'encourage national animosities'" (131), however, efforts to keep German language and culture out of Allied classrooms continued. In Berlin (later Kitchener), Ontario, for example, which had a sizeable population of German ancestry, the school board decided in 1915 to remove German from the curriculum and reasoned that to produce good citizens, "schools needed to force their students to abandon their German ethnicity and become like their Anglo-Canadian neighbours" (Coschi 326).

Such efforts did not cease with the war's end. Schools and universities throughout the United States stopped teaching German and a handful of "zealous states actually prohibited German foreign language instruction through primary school" (Collins *World* 160). Similar measures in various Allied nations resulted in "the destruction of bilingual education in many countries" because laws banning German "were not immediately rescinded in 1919, and [...] the language they barred was not always reinstated" (Proctor "Patriotic" 232). By 1948, "only 0.8% of American students were studying German in high school" (Baron), showing that the impact of anti-German rhetoric on young people extended well beyond the conclusion of the First World War. Wartime children's literature and education may have helped to sow the seeds of anti-German sentiment that persisted through the interwar years, continuing to shape children's attitudes throughout the lead up to the Second World War.

Laughing at the Enemy: The German as a Childish and Humorous Figure

While many writers posited the dangers of German "kultur" or told stories of German cruelty, others sought to diminish the enemy by making the German a figure of fun at whom child readers were invited to laugh. Sometimes this was achieved by drawing comparisons between Germans and children themselves. For example, in *At War!* (discussed in Chapter 3), Charlotte Schaller depicts Bobby, her young French protagonist, demonstrating greater self-control than the Germans in a section titled "Boche Gluttony":

> Bobby returns from attacking the trenches with a tremendous appetite. But, as a well-brought-up little French boy, he does not copy the Boches, who want to devour everything: the French tart, the English plum-pudding, the Belgian cake, the Charlotte russe, and the Japanese rice blanc-mange ...! and who will finish by eating nothing at all.
>
> (Schaller 24)

This gluttony is clearly a metaphor for German military aggression, and Bobby demonstrates greater moderation and maturity than the imagined enemy, whose impulse to "devour" every dessert is typically associated with young children (Figure 7.2).

Figure 7.2 "Boche Gluttony" from Charlotte Schaller's *At War!*, c. 1916. [BnF].

Ironically, it is precisely because of the Germans' seeming childishness that the child reader is invited to look down on them and feel superior. Asking child readers to scorn "the Boches" for this reason complicates the ways in which childhood was presented to young readers. In this instance, the positive portrayal of the boy protagonist coincides with the suggestion that so-called childlike behaviour constitutes the enemy's flaws. While this wartime tale centres on a child at play, it also encourages children to display maturity by shouldering some of the same responsibilities as adults and exhibiting some of the same restraint required of the adult citizen.

The attempt to diminish Germans by equating them with children is seen too in *Swollen-Headed William: Painful Stories and Funny Pictures After the German!* Published in London in 1914, this book by prolific humourist E.V. Lucas (1868–1938) is a satirical reworking of Heinrich Hoffmann's well-known German children's book *Struwwelpeter.* Lucas's work was not published explicitly for children, but it likely had its share of young readers given that it parodies Hoffmann's famous children's text. In many of its poems and illustrations, Kaiser Wilhelm is represented as "naughty, restless" (16), and wilful. Termed in one instance "Fidgety Will" who "wouldn't sit still" (15), he is depicted as a foolish child whose immaturity and selfishness lead to the suffering of many. "Lucas transfers all the mischief done by Hoffman's child characters and their consequent punishments to Kaiser Wilhelm, that naughty boy who has brought upon himself and Europe all the troubles of the war" (Fisher 112–113).

Susan Fisher argues that the book is "a cautionary tale" that is "ruthless but reassuring: just as bad little children are punished for their sins, so too bad rulers will get their just deserts [sic]" (114). I question however, just how reassured child readers might be by seeing "bad little children" punished when they themselves are at the mercy of adult authority and discipline. The supposition that child readers are comforted by seeing childlike characters castigated rests on the assumption that readers embrace the parameters set by adults and offer no resistance to the hegemonic forces that constrain them. Associating a childish trait like being fidgety with the infamous Kaiser Wilhelm renders children themselves as adversaries; to avoid being viewed as akin to the German enemy, the child must moderate and transform his own "childish" behaviour.

By presenting the Kaiser as childlike, Lucas does not aim to make him sympathetic, but rather ridiculous. While this denigrates children, there may be something comforting for young readers in being on the same footing as the fearful German enemy. By appearing as a tempestuous child, Wilhelm is transformed into a more manageable foe that children and adults alike could help defeat. Such depictions could play a role in maintaining hope for Allied victory, but they also leave open the possibility of redemption; just as the "naughty" child might one day be disciplined, educated, and brought into the fold, so too may Germany be redeemed.

One piece that suggests humour may have been used to diminish children's anxieties and maintain optimism is a remarkable collection of letters written in 1918 by Frank Edgar Evans (1876–1941), an American lieutenant-colonel posted in France who wrote to his young son in America. These illustrated letters from "Daddy Pat," published in 1919 in *St. Nicholas,* present the child with a detailed but humorous report of what soldiers were experiencing. Evans recalls learning "to lick the old Germans with their square heads" (368), and later describes a "German captain and old square-head, with spectacles, and a fat, red-nosed German wife and six square-head kids – all mean little imps – at home" (464). This unflattering depiction is accompanied by a comical drawing of the square-headed German family (Figure 7.3). By making the foe appear ludicrous, Evans attempts to alleviate his son's fears about his father's safety. In some letters, Evans imagines his son is with him, even including a drawing of them walking through the mud with the boy dressed as a soldier but being led by the hand by his father (Figure 7.4).

Figure 7.3 "The German Captain's Family" by Frank Evans from *St. Nicholas*, 1919. [University of North Carolina at Chapel Hill – Digitized by Internet Archive].

Figure 7.4 "You and Daddy in the Mud" by Frank Evans from *St. Nicholas*, 1919. [University of North Carolina at Chapel Hill – Digitized by Internet Archive].

Though often amusing, the letters reveal the dangers of the front, including the risk of gas attacks (Figure 7.5), and one touchingly concludes,

> good-by, little soul, and take awful good care of Mother; and when you hug her tight, think of all the millions Daddy would give to be there; and don't hurt when you hug. [...]. With whole battles of love to you and Pretty Mother, Daddy Pat.
>
> (373)

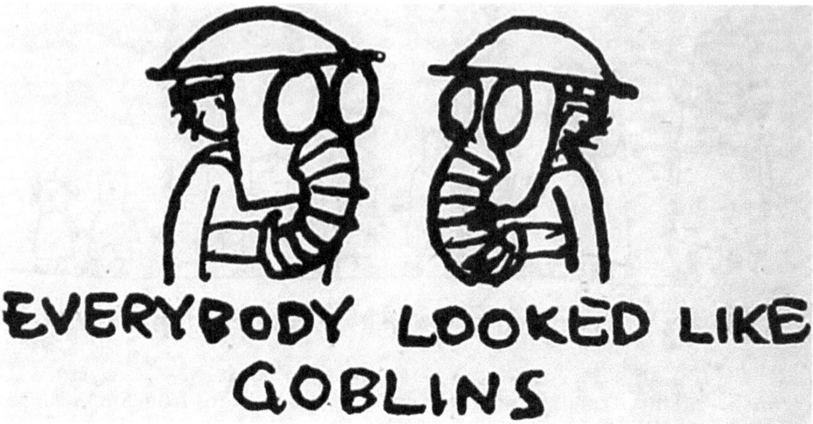

Figure 7.5 "Everybody Looked Like Goblins" by Frank Evans from *St. Nicholas*, 1919. [University of North Carolina at Chapel Hill – Digitized by Internet Archive].

Evans's son is an example of a child reader whose exposure to accounts of the First World War may have affected his own understanding of armed conflict. He grew up to fight in the Second World War and was awarded the Bronze Star in 1945 ("Townsend" 35), and his father's letters are a remarkable example of how adults used humour to instil hope in children whose loved ones were in the fight.

Humanizing the Hun: Neutral and Positive Portrayals of the German Foe

Over the past century, claims that the First World War was unavoidable have come under scrutiny, and even at the time many questioned whether war was necessary. The very fact that the United States was slow to join reveals this, and even some stridently pro-war literature inadvertently acknowledges people's doubts, for propaganda that tries to convince inevitably betrays the *need* to persuade. In her discussion of Albert A. Cock's *A Syllabus in War Geography and History* (published in London in 1916), Rosie Kennedy cites Cock's observation that thoughtful students may raise the question of "the morality of 'crushing Germany'" and outlines what she calls his "more sophisticated view on the causes of the war" than those found in other works for children (Kennedy *Children's* 132). When Cock was writing in 1916, it was clear the war would be a long affair and he likely recognized that a "simplistic appeal to children's sense of right and wrong" would not suffice as war dragged on and some students began to question "the validity of their earlier belief in the justification for war" (Kennedy *Children's*

132). Cock's text shows that there were different understandings of how young readers might view the war and that writers thus took different approaches to portraying the enemy.

Some representations reflected the view that anti-German rhetoric was inappropriate for children and that there could be long-term consequences of repeatedly exposing children to it, including the risk of glorifying war and sparking another conflict down the road. In some instances, writers express concern that too much negativity might fundamentally damage the spirit of future generations. Similarly, some more positive portrayals are rooted in the belief that it is anti-Christian to view fellow human beings with hatred and to see them as unredeemable. Both Canada and the United States were particularly attuned to the long-term problems that might result from anti-German rhetoric because so many of their citizens were of German ancestry. Anthony Pavlik remarks that in the United States, the "public facade of neutrality" of the Wilson administration may have been partly due to the fact that there were many immigrants that had "divided loyalties" and that some ethnic groups opposed to American involvement in the war were sizeable and influential (187). The presence of a substantial population of German origin was likely a factor in how Germans were portrayed in some Allied literature, with some writers demonstrating concern that anti-German sentiment would only lead to a harbouring of animosity that would harm national unity in the long run.

In works in which the German enemy is portrayed more sympathetically, the child (either as a character within literature, or as a reader outside the text) is often figured as being in a position to help achieve the healing necessary for the world to move towards lasting peace. British writer Robert Harvie, for example, acknowledges Germany as an aggressor but also provides anecdotes of German decency. Writing circa 1915, he suggests that the actions of the state do not necessarily reflect the spirit of the individuals within, as illustrated by the following story:

> Two of our soldiers, badly wounded, lay beside a dying German. "What would I not give for a drink," said one Briton to the other. The German understood, for our word "drink" is very like theirs - only they spell it with a "t." The soldier who told the story said, "The German kept saying 'here' - pointing to his side." Our men thought he wanted lifting up, so after a while one of them managed to raise himself and give him a pull. Then he discovered that the man was lying on his water-bottle, and this he held to the dying man's lips. But the German refused it, saying, "No, not me - I die - you drink." He did die, and our men gave him a proper burial. They put up a sort of headstone, and they fastened to it a piece of paper on which was written the inscription "A1."
>
> (75–76)

Harvie underscores the similarities between the British and the Germans who not only face the same hardships and have the same basic human needs, but whose similar languages reveal close cultural ties. Furthermore, the soldiers all show compassion, with the British initially offering the German water from his bottle, and him refusing it so that they can drink instead.

The narrator explains "it is good for us to remember incidents like this, which prove that there is another side even to war [...] in which brave men of all nations rival each other in sympathy and courtesy and generosity" (Harvie 76). In explaining the soldiers' inscription, Harvie also reminds readers of Christ's instruction "to be gentle and kind and thoughtful for others. [...] The [...] German's act was Christ-like. For that he stands, with Christ, in Class A1" (76–77). Harvie's underlying concern is that basic Christian principles are at risk from an unrelentingly negative portrayal of the German enemy. Showing the foe's "Christ-like" actions may be a step towards preventing a descent into brutality on the part of the Allies, who presumably want to model behaviour that is as good as, if not superior to, that of their adversaries.

Such concerns may help explain why stories of mutual respect among warring soldiers did appear in very pro-British children's literature like the *Boy's Own*. In a section titled "For Humanity's Sake" from the 1914–1915 annual, the author portrays the Germans and British sharing traits like bravery that if "coupled with humanity will always extort admiration" (229). He then cites an incident at Ypres when a badly wounded German soldier was left on the field as his comrades fell back:

> A British officer ran out quickly, picked up the fallen man and carried him toward the German trenches. Before he could accomplish his mission, a bullet laid him low, but the same enemy that sought his life could pay a tribute to his self-denying humanity. When his own men brought him in wounded it was seen that an Iron Cross had been pinned to his breast.
>
> ("For Humanity's Sake")

Pinning the German medal of honour on a British soldier is the German soldiers' way of showing they respect his empathy and bravery, but this act also erodes the barrier between the warring factions and presents both in a favourable light.

Another children's tale in which Germans appear favourably is Franchot's *War Babies* (discussed in Chapter 1). The escape of orphaned French siblings Jacque and Jacqueline to the United States is made possible by the assistance of German pilots who transport them across Europe. One German airman takes the young orphans home for the night where Jacqueline witnesses his affection for his own children:

> she heard a footstep, and peeping over the covers she saw [...] him stoop and kiss each little face and whisper something [...], then he

> tiptoed quietly down the stairs and [...] Jacqueline said, 'Our bird-man must be father to these little German boys,' and she guessed right, as little girls usually do at such times, where mother and father love is concerned.
>
> (39–40)

In this instance, both the French orphans and the pilot's children play a role in softening the portrayal of the enemy and humanizing him. The fact that Jacqueline recognizes the pilot's display of "father love" makes parental affection appear universal and something the German has in common with those he fights against.

Franchot is not alone in allowing young readers to see that German soldiers are similar to Allied ones. The *Boy's Own Annual* (1914–1915) contains a tale called "The Song in the Trenches" that reveals the humanity of German soldiers and contrasts the negative portrayals found elsewhere in the periodical. Reportedly a news correspondent's account of an incident in Flanders, it details a spontaneous truce one wet night when a Welsh soldier sang a cheerful ballad, and the Germans called from their trench demanding more, at which point,

> it dawned on both sides that the singer had created a truce, for while he sang not a shot was fired. A bargain was struck on the German proposition that if the soldier with the 'beautiful voice' would sing again they would agree to fire no more until daylight.
>
> ("Song")

While the story speaks for itself, the author, nevertheless, underscores its moral:

> The grim business of war must wait now and then while humanity asserts itself; and men whose hands only a moment ago were at each other's throats accept a pause in the firing to stroll across from trench to trench to exchange tobacco and chocolate! This is no fancy picture of mine; we have seen recorded numerous instances of such little courtesies of the field of war. Even the un-Christian teaching of a General Bernhardi cannot stifle all the gentler feelings in a German soldier's breast.

The observation that human decency must be allowed to assert itself now and then suggests that humanity itself is under threat.

The distinction the author makes between German troops and the "un-Christian" General who leads them is echoed by Herbert Strang who, despite calling Germany an "enemy of the human race," observes that human nature is "much the same all the world over." He suggests that the German people have been "deluded by their Emperor, their military class, their sycophant professors and philosophers" and "fed with lies." He provides an anecdote about an interaction between a German officer and a British soldier, describing both as "easy-going and good natured" and asking, "Who will say they were very much unlike each other?" Similarly, he remarks, "we cannot with any reason say we see much difference between French and German soldiers." Strang says the Germans "have in the past displayed many admirable qualities" and now suffer because of "the vices of their rulers" and he predicts that "a new Germany will arise, purged and humbled, prepared to take her place worthily with others in the work of the world." Though Strang is deeply critical throughout his work, his account of the German people being misled by their leaders offers hope for a future in which Germany will work together with other nations for the good of the world.

Some children's authors were clearly concerned with the impact that relentlessly negative depictions of the foe and continual exposure to the horrors of war might have on young readers. Lowndes observes:

> There are thousands and thousands of little children who will look back all their lives to this war as their first important recollection, the first impact on their minds of the great world of realities lying outside all childish things. It will not be possible to keep from them the knowledge of many horrors and savage brutalities, and it is therefore the more necessary that there should be shown to them as soon as possible the other and glorious side of the shield. It is the more necessary that for our children, through the long years that lie before them, the memory of the Great War should be touched to noble issues – that it should be, first and foremost, a memory of deeds as gallant as any that have ever been inscribed in Christendom's long roll of honour.
>
> (Lowndes ix–x)

While many of Lowndes's tales are about British gallantry, she does not limit herself to these and writes that the

> Happy Warrior is to be found in all ranks and in all armies, and it is an inspiring thought that, for every brave deed the record of which has leapt to light, there must be ten others of which the stirring story will never be known.
>
> (x)

While Lowndes encourages her readers to be proud of Britain, she is not without praise for the Germans. She gives an account of the fighting in Liege that she calls "a fine little incident, and one to the credit of the enemy" (10), during which the Germans are "touched" by the "splendid courage" of the Belgian soldiers who persevere as their garrison is destroyed (11). Lowndes writes that "the Germans, instead of attacking, flung aside their weapons and ran to the help of the brave Belgian soldiers" who were injured (11). This graciousness is mirrored in the actions of their Commander. When General Leman was brought before him and "tendered his sword [...] the German general handed it back to him, and, bowing courteously, congratulated General Leman very warmly on the splendid way in which he had conducted the defence" (11). This "example of German magnanimity" stands in contrast to the depictions of dishonourable German fighters found throughout children's literature (11), including elsewhere in Lowndes's own text.

Lowndes's writing typifies the contradictory portrayal of the enemy that young readers encountered, and the above depiction of the noble German warrior is quickly undercut when she writes, "As they marched through the lovely, peaceful villages [...], which all other invaders had spared even in the so-called dark ages, the Germans burnt, blew up, and destroyed far and wide, killing even women and children in their ruthlessness" (13–14). Lowndes presents the killing of children as evidence of German degeneracy, but she alternates between tales of German brutality and tales of German mercy, and later gives an account of a German doctor who performed "an exceptionally kind and delicate-minded action" when an elderly French man (167), too ill to be moved, lay in a town captured by the enemy. The German doctor took pains to disguise himself as "a captured English doctor, in order to go and see the sick man" and Lowndes remarks that this is "all the kinder, inasmuch as, being an Army doctor, he was, of course, under no obligation to treat people in the town" (168).

Shortly after this account, Lowndes provides another anecdote that further complicates her portrait of the enemy. She tells of a German soldier refusing a wounded Scottish artilleryman's request for water and writes that in a later battle this Scottish soldier "recognised the same German among a party of wounded whose cries for water couldn't be attended to quickly enough" (170). The German

> stopped his moaning, thinking he was sure to be paid back in his own coin. But the Highlander took out his water-bottle and handed it to the German without a word. According to one who was there, the German had the grace to look very shamefaced indeed.
>
> (170–171)

With this sketch, Lowndes creates a complex portrait of the German enemy, initially portraying him as heartless, but subsequently acknowledging that he was not a monster but a flawed human with enough "grace" to feel shame, implying there is hope for his redemption.

In an interesting counterpart to this tale, Lowndes writes about two wounded and thirsty soldiers, one French and one German. They spend a frigid night "with only the dead about them" and when dawn breaks and they begin to talk, the Frenchman shares his water with the German, who kisses "the hand of the man who had been his enemy" and declares, "There will be no war in Heaven" (Lowndes 209). Lowndes's book contains its share of negative portrayals of the Germans, but she also seems to recognize that for the sake of future peace and the child reader's own faith in humanity, a different view of Germans needed to be presented. She softens her image of the German as a victimizer of children, for instance, when she recounts the story of sixteen-year-old Londoner Freddy Ascher who is attending school in Belgium when war begins. While riding his bicycle, he encounters German soldiers who question him about the whereabouts of some British troops. Determined to "never give away the English" (84), he denies all knowledge, but the Germans persist and threaten to shoot him if he runs away. However, unlike the Germans in the tale "Boy Heroes" who murder a French boy for refusing to give up information, these Germans do not follow through on their threat, eventually returning Freddy's bicycle and sending him on his way.

While mustering the spirit to portray the enemy in a positive light may have been more difficult for writers as the war dragged on, and Allied casualties mounted, favourable portrayals of Germans appeared throughout the conflict and became particularly important towards its end. Writing in 1918, George Bedborough[10] (c. 1868–1940) anticipates the war's conclusion and the need for children to have a more nuanced understanding of the German people if a sense of common humanity is to survive. In the Preface to his collection *Not Only Men*, Bedborough writes that his book is

> aimed at helping parents and those who have the charge of children, to find topics for their entertainment [...] and generally to suggest ways of helping the coming generation to be a kinder, more humane, more loving race than our own.
>
> (7)

One way he tries to achieve these goals is by sharing stories that show compassion on the part of the German foe, and Bedborough recognizes that children of different ages may require different messages. He observes that parents of young people "of military age [...] may find it necessary to explain, with a breaking heart and through tears, that their duty is to enter the fray and fight in wars which never ought to be" (7). For younger children, however, he says another approach is needed:

> But what will you say to the very young, to those who have to live with their neighbours after the war is ended? The [...] young who

> cannot help in the fight might at this time learn some truths which will make wars less frequent when they are men and women. The seed sown now, watered indeed with many tears, may yet save mankind when the harvest of ideas ripens.
>
> (7–8)

According to Bedborough, literature for young children may help to "save mankind" by instilling the important lesson that the enemy is not a monster but a fellow human. "Every time you see good in an enemy, every time you weep for a friend and foe in their common suffering, you sow seeds which will one day abolish all wars" writes Bedborough (9). While acknowledging that killing the enemy might be one's duty, he demands that adults "kill also the lust of hate [...] and above all keep things that make for war outside the realm of childhood. There you must sow the seed of the harvest you wish the world to reap in the years to come" (9).

Bedborough presents a vision of childhood as a different "realm" from adulthood, but he does not simply argue that children should be sheltered. Instead, he suggests they should be given the tools that will make them resilient, the underlying assumption being that their emotional and psychological health will profit society. Bedborough's thinking reflects the understanding that there are different "dimensions of resilience" that "include the concepts of hope, dignity, respect for human life, sense of agency and sense of purpose" (Karadzhov 10). Believing in the importance of fostering hope and respect for human life, Bedborough suggests that one way to "sow the seeds" of peace is to give children "stories of noble deeds in this war" and he writes that "German, Russian, Austrian and British have all contributed fine human acts from their rank and file. This is the aspect of the war we can bring home to the youngest of our circle" (9). Bedborough concludes his Preface by stating "[t]here is never a time when love and mercy and kindness are out of place" (10).

Tales in Bedborough's collection use animals to reveal the humanity of the German foe and include "The Dog of an Enemy" and "The Wounded Dog." The first is about a dog who crossed the battlefield and ended up in the British trenches. The narrator remarks that the men named it "Bist" and that the dog responded particularly well to a fellow soldier named Conway who spoke some German (25). The narrator comments that the dog "had displayed wonderful courage in 'deserting' (as it seemed), for it required real bravery to plunge into what was almost certain to be sudden death" (25). Conway eventually guesses that Bist crossed over the line in the hopes of finding his master who had been taken prisoner, and in an expression of empathy, the narrator remarks that the soldiers "always felt sorry for men who were prisoners, as we might ourselves be one day" (26). When Conway learns that Bist's owner is injured, he takes the dog to the hospital where the two are reunited:

> Bist knew him at once, lying helpless there, covered with bandages, and only his face visible, his face, which was now suffused with a pathetic smile of love for his 'Hanschen.' There was no mistake about it. Our enemy's dog had not deserted, but had come through our fire to find his master.
>
> (27–28)

In this tale, the love of a pet highlights the common humanity of the British and the Germans, providing hope to young readers that a day will come when the two will no longer be foes. The narrator declares that once

> war is over, Conway and Williams and Hamilton and I are going to put up a stone over the grave where Bist's master is buried. We think he must have been a kind master to make Bist so fond of him. At any rate, we are so fond of Bist that we cannot resist a tear for his dead master - our late enemy.
>
> (28)

The affection the dog feels for both his German and British masters, as well as their mutual love for the animal, create a bond that underscores the humanity of the men on both sides of the conflict.

"The Wounded Dog: A Soldier's Story" functions in a similar manner and begins with an account of fighting in the trenches. Even as Bedborough draws attention to the intensity of the fight, he points out how similar the two sides are by saying the men

> could almost read our neighbour-enemy's thoughts, and of course they could equally well read ours. [...] Some of us sang songs, and we often caught the refrain of our enemies' songs borne to us on the slightest breeze. We told stories, too, and I am sure the German soldiers listened to similar stories on their side.
>
> (11–12)

Bedborough emphasizes the men's shared values, and once again it is a dog that serves as the vehicle for his message. When one comes bounding out of the German trench, an Allied soldier shoots it before realizing it is an animal, and then is quickly shot and killed himself when he leaves the trench to help the wounded dog. The narrator's lack of animosity towards the German enemy is evident when he states there was not any "special wickedness about that shot. It was probably fired more by instinct than from a deliberate desire to murder the rescuer of the dog" (12). This remark is another means by which the author neutralizes his portrayal of the German enemy, for the killing is a simple reality of war, not evidence of a moral defect.

The conclusion of the story further demonstrates the common values of the men on both sides. Committed to saving the dog, the narrator crawls on his stomach towards the injured animal after nightfall and is surprised by what he encounters:

> There was a human being bandaging the wound in the dog's shoulder. [...]. One of our enemies had crawled out of his trench as I had crawled from mine, and here we met, mortal foes he and I, sworn to destroy each other, but rivals in our desire to show our love for a poor brute who needed it.
>
> German soldier, I never learnt your name, I never spoke to you, and if I met you on the field of battle I should kill you, if you did not kill me first. But at that moment you and I shook hands in the silence of the dark night between our trenches of war. You and I saw into each other's hearts for a few seconds. You and I were brothers for a moment. An eternity of hate could not make me forget that moment of mutual love and understanding.
>
> (Bedborough 14)

The narrator's description of the German soldier as a "human being" and "brother" further humanizes the enemy, presenting child readers with a striking alternative to the image of the German as an inhumane beast.

In his concern that a steady diet of hate-filled propaganda will harm young readers and impede the progress of peace, Bedborough presents a different view of the enemy, even as he acknowledges that overcoming negative attitudes will be difficult:

> I left the German soldier with his dog, while I crawled back to my comrades [...]. I told them everything ... but they had not felt the magic touch of an enemy's hands bandaging a wounded dog in the dark.
>
> (Bedborough 14)

This statement, with its significant ellipses, suggests that without their own personal interactions with German people it will be difficult for soldiers (and, by extension, young readers) to overcome the view of Germans as inhuman, shaped as it was by countless wartime narratives.

Frequently violent, often disparaging, sometimes humorous, and occasionally sympathetic, differing portrayals of the German enemy in First World War children's texts reflect a variety of attitudes towards war, masculinity, national identity, and childhood. Children's literature does not offer "a monochrome presentation of a wholly despotic enemy or completely reliable allies" and this "suggests that a more subtle awareness of the complexity of war was required even among the juvenile reading public" (Cowman 113). Representations of the enemy were about far more than justifying the war and they reveal different views on "civilization," on what constituted childhood, on how peace was to be achieved, and on the risks that the devastating conflict posed to the emotional and physical well-being of children. Depictions of the German enemy spurred enlistment and fuelled patriotism among the Allies, but they were also entwined with discussions of how to achieve post-war reconciliation between nations and what the role of the child was in this vital process.

Notes

1 Herbert Strang was the pseudonym under which the work of writing team George Herbert Ely (1866–1958) and Charles James L'Estrange (1867–1947) was published. Both men were staff members in the Juvenile Department of Oxford University Press (Clute).

2 Invoking a narrative of evolutionary social progress, Myrick suggests Germany must be defeated so that the highest form of civilization can emerge. He pictures this as a democratic society "based upon the Fatherhood of God and the world-parliament of man," reflecting the efforts to achieve lasting international peace that culminated in the League of Nations.

3 Pulbrook was an author and editor whose published works also included *The English Countryside* (1915) and *English Country Life and Work* (1922) ("Notable").

4 Prior to the First World War, active military service was required of all eligible German men for two or three years, depending on the branch of the military. The single year of service to which Pulbrook refers was an option only for a special class who "had to meet stringent requirements of education and character, as well as pay for their own uniforms, equipment, quarters, and rations" (Keller).

5 *School Days* ran for eleven years and its content "was almost entirely provided by British Columbia authors and schoolchildren. It was intended for younger students, and sold for ten cents" (Sim "School").

6 Born in Ohio, Ruiter Stinson Sherman moved to Canada as a child and worked as a teacher and Principal in British Columbia, publishing more than 125 stories in *School Days* between 1919 and 1930 (Sim "Ruiter").

7 The "Hymn of Hate" was criticized by diverse groups, including both German-Jews and anti-Semites, who saw it as "un-German" (Aronsfeld 49). Lissauer, who was Jewish, came to regret the poem and "did not want the young to read it and he refused to have it printed in school books" (49).

8 Ruth Harris identifies another manifestation of the child figure, "the so-called *enfants du barbare*, the hordes of 'mongrel' children anticipated as the products of German rape" and discusses how commentators expressed "sometimes phantasmagoric fears about the threat these infants posed" (170).

9 Teall was a member of the editorial staff for several periodicals, including the *New York Sun*, where he worked from 1903–1917 ("Author").

10 George Bedborough was a writer and editor of *The Children's Realm* who supported several progressive causes, including vegetarianism (Gregory 149). He was a secularist, publishing his long poem *The Atheist* in 1919, and advocated for the legalizing of illegitimate children through his involvement with the Legitimation League (Wallace 123). *Not Only Men* reflects his interests in both child welfare and animal rights.

Conclusion

The Child as the Embodiment of Hope

As the First World War drew to a close, children's authors faced a new challenge. After four years of writing about armed conflict and readying children for their part in it, how were authors to address what came next? As some of the texts I have discussed have shown, even in the midst of the war some writers were anticipating this question and doing their part to prepare children for a time when Germany would no longer be a loathsome enemy, when schoolboys would no longer have to think about enlisting as soldiers, and when the costs of the war would have to be met and a damaged world rebuilt. As the long lens of history has shown us, the effects of the war did not cease in November, 1918 but reverberated throughout the following century. Just as wartime writers felt a need to address the conflict and help young readers make sense of it while it was happening, so too did they feel the need to prepare them for their role in the world that would emerge in war's aftermath.

One of my goals in writing this book has been to look beyond the propagandistic and nationalistic elements of children's literature from the Great War in order to explore some of the complexities within, particularly the different representations of children and childhood. While most of the texts I have discussed are in some sense pro-war (as opposed to pacifist), they are nevertheless diverse in their treatment of child figures. The nuances of how children and childhood were understood, and of how these categories were actively constructed during this moment of unprecedented social upheaval, can open our eyes to ways in which literature for young people can both uphold and challenge dominant ideologies in times of armed conflict.

I have explored some of the ways in which authors employed notions of childhood innocence, but as this book has shown, children were deeply embroiled in the war and in questions of empire and nationhood, and their status as "innocents" did not mean that they were peripheral to questions of citizenship, patriotism, militarism, and national identity. Some children's writers proposed a post-war role for children that extended beyond serving the nation to playing a part in reshaping global relationships, and the child came to represent hope for a better future at home and around the globe.

DOI: 10.4324/9781003191605-9

The child is sometimes imagined as "a vessel that adults fill with their cultural values, with skills, thoughts, and emotions that will create a better future, as though the vessel was neutral or empty until filled in this way" (Kokkola 2). This is a view perpetuated by many First World War authors who employed child figures in an attempt to recruit young readers to the cause of creating "a better future." While for some writers that meant fostering values and skills that could help achieve military victory, for others it meant trying to inspire optimism within children in a bid to ensure future peace. For others still, hope was seen as naturally occurring in the young and authors sought to harness this latent power. Readers whose childhoods had been shaped by one of the darkest chapters in human history were thus served a vision of the child as both the incarnation of future promise, and as an agent who needed to actively cultivate a spirit of positivity and deploy it for the betterment of society.

One article that situates the child as both a natural symbol of hope, and as a vessel in which optimism needs to be cultivated, is "The One Hope for the World," which was published on March 22, 1919 in the inaugural issue of *The Children's Newspaper.* This paper ran for forty-six years, half of those under the editorship of Arthur Mee (1875–1943), who was filled with the "drive to educate the children of the masses" ("History"). The paper was one of Britain's "most successful magazines for children" with weekly sales of 500,000 copies ("History"), and thus held great potential to shape children's attitudes throughout the interwar period. The author of this particular article puts a positive spin on the recent war, observing that nobody

> could have dreamed of the wonders that have come to pass. The thrones of the kings who held Europe in terror have gone toppling down [...]. The great free nations are represented in a single room in Paris, where their statesmen, with not a king among them, are writing new laws for the world.
>
> ("One Hope")

The Paris peace conference is framed here as the dawn of a new world based on "new laws," democracy, and diplomacy, and not on the tyranny and might of monarchies.

Seeing great promise in the new League of Nations, the author says its ability to create peace and make "a better world for all [...] depends upon the children." The centrality of children to the League's success is repeatedly emphasized in the article, which states that "the children of these nations will have it in their power to make it work, or else to ruin it." The author suggests that the new *Children's Newspaper* "is appearing at this time because there is nothing more important now than that boys and girls should understand the world they are growing up in" and goes on to declare "that the whole fate of the world, the success of the League of Nations, and the welfare of sixteen hundred million people, is in the hands of the children." Rather than envisioning the end of the war marking a return to a carefree and innocent childhood, the author places the burden of responsibility for achieving peace on young people in a manner reminiscent of the common wartime emphasis on the child's "duty."

There is an interesting contradiction of sorts in this article, which perpetuates a wartime depiction of the child as an agent deeply enmeshed in the affairs of the state, while at the same time suggesting that there is great value in preserving some type of childhood innocence and distancing the child from the concerns of adulthood. Echoing worries of wartime writers like Bedborough, who urged adults to "remind our young ones that to love one another and to be kind are still the laws by which men must live" (10), the author of the article in *The Children's Newspaper* argues that in order for children to achieve their potential as the bringers of future peace, efforts need to be made when they are very young to lay the necessary foundations.

Looking back to the childhood of those who fought in the First World War, he sees it as the ground in which the seeds of the war were sown:

> For fifty years they grew up thinking of war, reading of war, seeing pictures of war, singing songs of war. They began with little toy soldiers and little toy guns, and they grew up dreaming of the day when no nation should be stronger than theirs, and when perhaps they would pay the children of another nation out for something their father had done. And so they prepared for war, often without knowing what they did, and when they cried for peace it was too late. The seed had borne fruit.

Knowing as we do that the readers of this first issue of *The Children's Newspaper* would grow up to experience the Second World War, this passage is eerily prescient, and again raises the question of whether the kinds of wartime literature that I have discussed throughout this book helped influence views on that later conflict. In this article from 1919, the author blames childhood culture from a half-century earlier for creating the spirit of militarism that led to the war, but he could just as easily offer the same critique of the toys, literature, and lessons given to children from 1914 to 1918. His words acknowledge the potential for children's literature and culture to foster sentiments that could continue well beyond the war's cessation.

What this writer shares in common with others I have discussed in my study is the belief that the games, lessons, and stories of childhood have the power to influence young readers and shape the views they will hold as adults. For many wartime writers this meant working to secure children's support for the war in order to help achieve Allied victory, but the author of this article presents childhood as the time for teaching lessons that would prevent war altogether. He observes that to create peace "you must begin at fifteen or sixteen, at twelve or thirteen, at nine or ten. You must grow up loving peace and hating war. You must fill your heart and head with the great idea of a united world" ("The One Hope"). These observations blend notions of children's agency with notions of innocence, simultaneously implying that children have a duty to help ensure a peaceful future, but also suggesting that children's true power lies in their blamelessness. The author writes:

> Think of the children of the world at this moment. Who hates them? What harm have they done to anyone? Why should the day come when suddenly you will turn against them? It need not come. It never can come if all who have the power will use it now to bring the boys and girls of every country into a mighty ring of peace, a Children's League of Nations. That is the hope of the world; it is the greatest hope the world has.
>
> ("The One Hope")

Here, children are viewed as innately loveable and innocent, and it is these inherent qualities that hold the key to preventing war, and which make youth "the greatest hope the world has."

This emphasis on the blamelessness of children echoes some of the wartime representations I have discussed in this book and reasserts the view that children and childhood belong outside matters of war. It holds up children's innocence as the very thing that shows peace is possible and brings to mind the wartime text *Josephine and Her Dolls* (1916) by British children's author H. C. Cradock (1863–1941), in which a little girl tires of incessant war play. The doll who plays the part of King George declares, "don't let's have any more war; it's not nice" (Cradock 46), and this caption accompanies an illustration of young Josephine gravely contemplating her toys (Figure 8.1).

The only real power the girl has is that which she can exercise over her inanimate dolls, but Josephine's simple declaration that she and her toys "are all tired of the war, so we are going to have peace" (46), can also be seen as an expression of hope that children's loathing of armed conflict will result in a non-violent future. Rather than war play with her dolls strengthening a spirit of militarism in young Josephine, it instead results in her rejection of discord. She says to her dolls: "'Now, children, [...] let this war be a lesson to you all. No more quarrelling'" (48), and the simplicity of this statement suggests that children living through the First World War long for its end, and that their desire for peace may prevent future wars. Cradock's work, the first in a series of *Josephine* books, was published in Britain but also in the United States, where its image of the child longing for peace had the potential to strengthen support for American neutrality in the war's early years.

Figure 8.1 Illustration by Honor C. Appleton from *Josephine and Her Dolls*, c. 1916. [University of Delaware].

While many writers see childhood innocence as potentially powerful, the author of the article in *The Children's Newspaper* believes that it must be purposefully harnessed by adults. He writes of the need for children of all nations to be bound

> in a mighty League of Peace, with all the machinery of government and education and literature and art and science enlisted for peace, with all the schools and pulpits and papers and kinemas building up and pressing on the true and deep and fervent love of peace in which no hate can grow and no seed of enmity can ever find a root.
>
> ("The One Hope")

Just as wartime writers recognized the potential for school, play, and literature to harness children's support for the war, this writer envisions the "machinery" of childhood culture serving more peaceful ends when war is over. Writers from Britain, Canada, and the United States shared this view of the child as the great hope for the future, and the responsibility of the child thus shifted from helping to win the war, to building a world in which war could be avoided altogether.

For adults, the post-war years produced mixed reactions to the long period of death and destruction they had endured. For some, war remained a beacon for ideals like civic duty, sacrifice, bravery, and perseverance. Writing of Canada in 1919, for example, J. O. Miller remarks:

> No nation ever yet became great whose citizens made self-interest the supreme aim in life. Before the war, this was the great danger that threatened the Canadian people [...]. But we were awakened to other thoughts and nobler ideals [...]. The future will show that Canada's entry into the war, which involved the willing sacrifice of over fifty thousand of her best sons, saved the nation from greater perils that threatened her from within.
>
> (Miller 84–85)

According to Miller, the people of Canada "learnt through suffering the supreme lesson of service to the nation" (85), which is one he clearly wants to teach his child readers.

For Miller, the war provided valuable lessons about the importance of sacrificing for the nation, but for others the war epitomized imperial greed and collective madness, breeding widespread disillusionment and resentment towards an older generation that had sacrificed its young. In the century that has passed since the war's end, we have seen both attitudes manifest themselves in commemorations of the conflict. People today may look back with a mixture of gratitude and reverence for those who "did their bit," incredulity at the scale of the war and its terrible costs, and anger and dismay that it did not prove to be "the war to end all wars." Such mixed sentiments are not unlike what children of the time would have felt.

Even as it was happening, the war was already being mythologized for children, but it was also their lived reality. The trauma inflicted by the war was undeniable and for four years it was part of the basic fabric of children's lives, influencing their play, shaping their school experiences, and transforming family life. Writing at the time, Lowndes remarks on the "new and disturbing sense of personal loss" experienced by children and observes that there is hardly

> one British child whose little world of personal affections and interests has not been roughly disturbed by the war. Many have seen their fathers and brothers going off to fight, and to many those dear fathers and brothers will never come back.
>
> (x)

Although many literary studies have focussed on how the personal losses and collective sacrifices of the war were addressed in literature for adults, these things were also experienced by children, and this book has tried to draw attention to how their literature conditioned young readers to respond to loss in particular ways. The various incarnations of child figures in wartime literature demonstrate that young readers encountered a range of views on what constituted childhood and, more specifically, what it meant to be a child in a time of war. While we cannot know with certainty how readers responded to these representations, they do tell us something about how adults perceived children, and how they utilized them to achieve certain ends. From being invested in notions of childhood innocence, to seeing childhood as the time to create the next generation of battle-ready adults, to viewing the child as the best hope for achieving an end to all war, adult authors showed the malleability of the concept of 'the child.'

The ability of the adult to manipulate the figure of the child – for consumption by the child – is no less relevant today than it was a century ago. Although children are *not* empty vessels and respond to and critique what they read in many different ways, it nevertheless behoves us to continue to examine critically their representation by adults. As I write this conclusion, we are experiencing a pandemic unlike anything seen since 1918, and we can see children being invoked in different ways as societies navigate their responses to this new global crisis. Narratives of presumed child resilience or, conversely, child vulnerability, are shaping debates over vaccine requirements, school safety, and more. Such discussions are not grounded solely in concerns about children's well-being, but in the fact that children directly impact the economy and the basic functioning of society. Such historical moments throw into relief the ways in which notions of children as innocent victims in need of protection, or as helpful agents who can "do their bit" to help the nation, vary according to the adult needs and ideologies of the day. For those who were children during the First World War, those adult needs included everything from requiring young people's practical help with war work, to maintaining optimism and believing that the world would eventually be at peace. For many, the child served as proof that this hopeful future would eventually be realized. Let us hope that they will one day be proven right.

Works Cited

Primary Sources

A Boy Worker. "The Boy Munitioner: A Real Story of Life in a Great War Factory." *The Best of Chums*. Ed. Philip Warner. London: Cassell, 1978: 73.

"A Canadian Soldier's Story: An Extraordinary Career." *Young Canada: An Illustrated Magazine for Boys throughout the English-Speaking World*. London: Pilgrim Press, 1916: 290.

"A Deadly Blow." *The Kiddies' Magazine*. London: J. Alfred Sharp (May 1918): N. pag.

"A Great Battleship in a Gale." *Young Canada: An Illustrated Magazine for Boys*. London/Toronto: The Pilgrim Press/William Briggs, 1916: 196.

"A Guide We Are Proud Of." *Girl Guides' Gazette* 9 (September 1914): 11.

A.T.M. "How They Honoured the Captain." *The British Story-Book: Tales of Adventure in Canada, Australia, Africa, India, &c.* London: Blackie, 1916: N. pag.

"A Young French Hero." *The Boy's Own Annual* 37 (1914–1915): 483–484.

Baden-Powell, Agnes. "Miss Baden-Powell's Letter." *Girl Guides' Gazette* 8 (August 1914): 1–2.

Bedborough, George. *Not Only Men*. Illus. J.P. Munro. Letchworth: Garden City Press Limited, 1918.

Bevan, Tom. *Doing His "Bit": A Story of the Present War*. London: Nelson, 1917.

Billington, Mary Frances. "Women and the War: Help They Can Render, Follies They Can Avoid." *The Girl's Own Paper and Woman's Magazine* 36.1 (1915): 34–36.

"Boy Heroes of the War." *The Boy's Own Annual* 37 (1914–1915): 228.

"The Boys' Social League. The President's Weekly Chat. What B.S.L. Members Can Do in Time of War." *The Boys' Journal*. Special War Issue 52.3 (September 12, 1914): 27.

Burgess, Frederick William. "The 'Boy's Own' Stamp-Collector. Some New War Issues and Overprints." *The Boy's Own Annual* 38 (1915–1916): 707–708.

Bury, Hailey. "How the War Came to Fountainbury: A Complete School Story." *The Boy's Own Annual* 38 (1915–1916): 595–598.

Butler, Ellis Parker. "An Amateur Censor." Illus. Reginald Birch. *St. Nicholas* 45.1 (November 1917): 32–36.

Byron, May. *The Peek-A-Boos in War Time*. Illus. Chloë Preston. London: Henry Frowde and Hodder & Stoughton, [c.1916].

"The Canadian Troops." *The Youth's Companion* 89.28 (July 15, 1915): 356.

Carter, Herbert. *The Boy Scouts on War Trails in Belgium: Or Caught Between Hostile Armies.* New York: A.L. Burt, 1916.

Cassell's. "The Nerve of a Soldier: Dr. Cassell's Tablets." *The Girls' Mirror.* London: Shurey's Publications. No. 1 (November 29, 1915): 45.

Chappell, Jeanne. "How a Small Boy Helped to Win a Battle." *The Children's Friend: For Boys and Girls at Home and at School.* 1918 Annual. Ed. C.D. Michael. London: S. W. Partridge, 1918: 158–159.

Chapple, Bennett. "A Twentieth Century Paul Revere." *Patriotic Selections for Supplementary Reading.* Ed. Edwin Dubois Shurter. New York: Lloyd Adams Noble, 1918: 155–156.

"The Children of the Flag." *The Boy's Own Annual* 37 (1914–1915): 406.

Children's Painting Book: Paint Your Own Picture Post Cards. Little Patriots Series. London: H. Stevenson & Co., [c.1917].

Cochrane, Augustus Robert. "War and the D.W.O." *The Empire Annual for Boys.* Ed. Augustus Robert Buckland. London: RTS, 1915: 26–34.

Committee on Schoolboys for Farm Service and the United States Boys' Working Reserve, Massachusetts Division. *To the High School Boys of Massachusetts: A Call for Patriotic Service.* Boston: Committee on Public Safety, 1918.

Cooke, Edna A. "Little Patriots." *St. Nicholas* 45.1 (December 1917): 121.

Cornish, Phyllis. Illus. "The Martial Spirit." *Collins' Children's Annual.* London: Collins, 1915: 131.

Cornish, Phyllis. Illus. "The War Game in the Nursery: Germania Objects to Her Part." *Collins' Children's Annual.* London: Collins, 1915: 127.

Cornish, Phyllis. Illus. "The War in the Nursery: 'Charge'!!" *Collins' Children's Annual.* London: Collins, 1915: 127.

Cradock, Mrs. Henry Cowper. *Josephine and Her Dolls.* Illus. Honor C. Appleton. New York: Frederick A. Stokes, [c. 1916].

Craig, Grace E. "The Ambulance-Girl: A Story of the French Front." Illus. Oscar H. Schmidt. *St. Nicholas* 44.2 (July 1917): 784–789.

Dadmun, Margaret. "The Girls in Khaki." *St. Nicholas* 44.1 (April 1917): 520–522.

Defenders of the Empire: A Postcard Painting Book. Great Britain: Father Tuck's Patriotic Series, c.1914.

"Don't Be a Turtle, Be a Beaver." *Mother Goose's Garden: The New National Literature for Children.* Originated by Carroll F. Smythe. Toronto: F. & H. McLean Publishers, [c.1917]. N. pag.

"The Dream of Boy Scout Bliss." Illus. Mary Roberts. *Mother Goose's Garden: The New National Literature for Children.* Ed. Carroll F. Smythe. Toronto: E & H. McLean, [c. 1917]. N. pag.

Drew, Eustace. "Rough Luck! The Story of a Boy Scout and a Spy." *The Boy's Own Annual* 38 (1915–1916): 337–340.

"Eat More...." A U.S. Food Administration Poster. *St. Nicholas* 45.1 (February 1918): 311.

"The Editor's Page." *The Boy's Own Annual* 37 (1914–1915): 41.

Ellis, Frank. "The Next Man In!" *The Boy's Own Annual* 38 (1915–1916): 227.

Empey, Arthur Guy. "The Coward." *Short Stories of the New America.* Ed. Mary A. Laselle. New York: Henry Holt, 1919: 181–198.

Evans, Frank E. "'Daddy Pat's' Letters from the Front to His Little Son." *St. Nicholas* 46.4 (February 1919): 368–373.

Evans, Frank E. "'Daddy Pat's' Letters from the Front to His Little Son." *St. Nicholas* 46.5 (March 1919): 462–469.

F.M.G. "Doing His Bit." *Collins' Children's Annual.* London: Collins, 1916: 88.

"For Humanity's Sake." *The Boy's Own Annual* 37 (1914–1915): 229.

"France's Youngest Soldier." 1914–1915. *The Boy's Own Annual* 37 (1914–1915): 254.

Franchot, Annie Wood. *War Babies.* Illus. Mary Louise Davis. New York: William R. Jenkins Company, 1914.

Freeman, A.C. "The Making of a Hero." *The Boy's Own Annual* 37 (1914–1915): 484.

Freeman, Annie F. "The Old Eleven." *The Boy's Own Annual* 38 (1915–1916): 174.

Fritsche, Carl B. "Play the Game to Win." *To the High School Boys of Massachusetts: A Call for Patriotic Service.* Boston, MA: Committee on Public Safety, [c.1918]: N.pag.

Front Page. *Work and Play: The Scholars' Own Magazine* 11.123 (November 1916): 33.

Fry's. "One of Britain's Future Hopes." *Work and Play: The Scholars' Own Magazine* 10.114 (February 1916): 112.

Gard, Lillian. "The Lad Who Was Left Behind." *The Boy's Own Annual* 38 (1915–1916): 340.

Gilson, Charles. "On the Other Side of the Wall: A War-Time Adventure in an Old Castle." *The Boy's Own Annual* 38 (1915–1916): 449–452.

Golding, Harry. "Dad's Soldier Boy." Illus. Charles Robinson. *Wonder Book: A Picture Annual for Boys and Girls.* Ed. Harry Golding. London: Ward Lock & Co., 1918: 9–21.

Golding, Harry, ed. *The Wonder Book of Empire for Boys and Girls.* 5th ed. London: Ward, Lock and Co., [c.1920].

Graham, E. Maxtone. *The Sword of Peace: A Play for Children.* Edinburgh: Robert Grant & Son, [1918].

Grayl, Druid. "In the Ranks." *The Boy's Own Annual* 37 (1914–1915): 164.

Groves, Edith Lelean. *The Wooing of Miss Canada.* Toronto: McClelland, Goodchild & Stewart, 1917.

Guides of Greater Vancouver British Columbia, comp. *Girl Guide Cook Book.* Vancouver: Guides, [c. 1932]: N.pag.

Hagedorn, Hermann. *You Are the Hope of the World! An Appeal to the Girls and Boys of America.* New York: Macmillan, 1917.

Hankins, Maude M. "A Little Red Cross Helper." *St. Nicholas* 45.1 (February 1918): 373.

Harvie, Robert (the rev.). *The King's Uniform: Eighteen Addresses to Children.* London: H.R. Allenson Limited, 1915.

Hausgen, Mattie Lee. "Doing Her Bit." Illus. Decie C. Merwin. *St. Nicholas* 45.2 (July 1918): 852.

Hausgen, Mattie Lee. "Her Sacrifice." Illus. Decie C. Merwin. *St. Nicholas* 45.2 (July 1918): 852.

Hayes, Clair W. *The Boy Allies at Liège: Or Through Lines of Steel.* New York: A.L. Burt Company, 1915.

Hellé, André, illus. *French Toys.* Paris: L'Avenir Féminin, 1915.

"The Heroine of Loos." *The Jolly Book for Boys and Girls.* Ed. Edward Shirley. London: Thomas Nelson, [c. 1917]: 31–33.

Hogben, John. *The Highway of Hades.* Edinburgh: Oliver and Boyd, 1919.

Hogben, John. "Jack in Khaki." *The Boy's Own Annual* 38 (1915–1916): 452.

Hope, Ascott R. *The School of Arms: Stories of Boy Soldiers and Sailors*. New York: E.P Dutton, [c.1915].

"How Lieut. Smyth Won the V.C.: A Desperate Deed of Courage." *Young Canada: An Illustrated Magazine for Boys*. London/Toronto: The Pilgrim Press/ William Briggs, 1916: 24–25.

"How to Make War Models from Matches and Match-boxes." *Work and Play: The Scholars' Own Magazine* 9.99 (November 1914): 50.

Hubbard, Miriam Warren. "The Soldier-Girls at the National Service School." *St. Nicholas* 44.1 (April 1917): 518–520.

"Idle Ike, the Hour Stealer." *Mother Goose's Garden: The New National Literature for Children*. Ed. Carroll F. Smythe. Toronto: E. & H. McLean, [c.1917]: N. pag.

"Important Notice to Our Readers." *Work and Play: The Scholars' Own Magazine* 11.128 (April 1917): 118.

"In Time of National Stress." *The Girl's Own Paper and Woman's Magazine* 36.1 (1915): 8.

"The Junior Red Cross." *St. Nicholas* 45.1 (November 1917): 24–26.

Kerr, Orpheus C. "Picciola." *The Palace Beautiful, and Other Poems*. New York: Carleton, 1864: 75–78.

Knowlton, J. B. "Heroines of the War." *The Empire Annual for Girls*. Ed. A.R. Buckland. London: RTS, 1916: 186–193.

Laselle, Mary A. "Preface." *Short Stories of the New America*. Ed. Mary A. Laselle. New York: Henry Holt, 1919: iii.

Laselle, Mary A. "Something About the Authors and the Stories." *Short Stories of the New America*. Ed. Mary A. Laselle. New York: Henry Holt, 1919: vii–xii.

Lea, John. "The Drum." *The Boy's Own Annual* 37 (1914–1915): 315.

Leigh, Felix. "Warranted to Wear: Or, The Serial Boy Hero." *The Boy's Own Annual* 38 (1915–1916): 557.

"Lord Kitchener and the Indian Princes." *The Jolly Book for Boys and Girls*. Ed. Edward Shirley. 7th year. London: Thomas Nelson, (c. 1918): 194–197.

Lowndes, Mrs. Belloc. *Told in Gallant Deeds: A Child's History of the War*. London: Nisbet & Co. Limited, 1914.

"Loyalty!" *The Boy's Own Annual* 37 (1914–1915): 287.

Lucas, Edward Verrall. *Swollen-Headed William: Painful Stories and Funny Pictures After the German!* Illus. Geo. Morrow. 4th ed. London/Toronto: Methuen & Co. Ltd./Musson Book Company Limited, 1914.

Lumley, Savile. *Daddy, What Did You Do in the Great War?* London: Parliamentary Recruiting Committee, 1915.

Macgregor, Angusine. *Mrs. Bunny's Refugee*. London: Blackie and Son Limited, [c. 1918].

Margery, Aunt. "Thrift." *Work and Play: The Scholars' Own Magazine* 11.121 (September 1916): 14.

Masson, Frédéric. "The Leipsic Soldiers: Beware of the 'Made in Germany' 'of Bimbocherie'." *French Toys*. Paris: L'Avenir Féminin, 1915: 10–16.

Mille, Pierre. "The Wonderful Adventure." *French Toys*. Paris: L'Avenir Féminin, 1915: 37–45.

Miller, John Ormsby. *The Young Canadian Citizen: Studies in Ethics, Civics and Economics*. Toronto: J.M. Dent & Sons, 1919.

"The Most Famous Corn-Field." *St. Nicholas* 45.1 (January 1918): 209–211.

Myrick, Herbert. *Fifteen Little War Stories*. Patriotism Through Education Series, No. 28. New York: National Security League, 1918: N. pag.

Newell, Robert Henry. "The Sergeant and the Child." *The Third Golden Rule Book*. Toronto: Macmillan, 1918: 141–143.

Old One. "Thinking Imperially." *The Boy's Own Annual* 37 (1914–1915): 265.

"THE ONE HOPE FOR THE WORLD: Unless the Children Support the League They Labour in Vain Who Build It. HAS THE PEACE CONFERENCE FORGOTTEN BOYS AND GIRLS?" *The Children's Newspaper: The Story of the World Today for the Men and Women of Tomorrow* (March 22, 1919): 5.

Orton, George W. *Bob Hunt in Canada*. Racine: Whitman Publishing Co., 1916.

"Our Widened Empire: A Few Facts Concerning the Former German Colonies." *The Wonder Book of Empire for Boys and Girls*. Ed. Harry Golding. 5th ed. London: Ward, Lock and Co., [c.1920]: ix–xxxii.

Oxenham, John. "What Can a Little Chap Do?" Illus. Gordon Browne. *Princess Mary's Gift Book*. Toronto: Hodder and Stoughton, 1914: 112–114.

"Patriotic Blind Boys." *The Children's Friend: For Boys and Girls at Home and at School*. Ed. C.D. Michael. London: S.W. Partridge & Co. Ltd., 1918: 113.

"Patriotic Jack and the Bean Stalk." *Mother Goose's Garden: The New National Literature for Children*. Ed. Carroll F. Smythe. Toronto: E. & H. McLean, [c.1917]: N. pag.

"Pluck and Peril Among the Bombers." Illus. John F. Campbell. *Young Canada: An Illustrated Magazine for Boys*. London: The Pilgrim Press, 1916. Toronto: William Briggs, 1916: 194–196.

Price, Edith Ballinger. "The Littlest One." *St. Nicholas* 45.2 (July 1918): 851.

Pulbrook, Ernest C. "The German Schoolboy." *Young Canada: An Illustrated Magazine for Boys*. London/Toronto: The Pilgrim Press/William Briggs, 1916: 15–16.

"Review of *In Khaki for the King* by Escott Lynn." *The Bookman*. London: Hodder and Stoughton, 1915: 124.

Robertson, the Rev. Stuart. *The Red Flowers: Sermons from the Front to the Children at Home*. London: Religious Tract Society, 1919.

Schaller, Charlotte. *At War!* Edinburgh and London: Dobson, Molle & Co. Ltd. [c.1916].

"Serbian Children as Fruit-Pickers." *Work and Play: The Scholars' Own Magazine* 11.121 (September 1916): 11.

Sherman, R. S. "Why We Fought the Hun." *School Days: A Magazine Published Monthly for the Pupils of the Public Schools* [Vancouver] 1:9 (May 1920): 25.

Shirley, Edward. "The Boys Scouts in War-Time." *The Jolly Book for Boys and Girls*. Ed. Edward Shirley. London: Thomas Nelson, [c. 1916]: 230–231.

Shirley, Edward. "How We Caught the Spy." *The Jolly Book for Boys and Girls*. Ed. Edward Shirley. London: Thomas Nelson, [c. 1916]: 9–13; 25–29.

Smythe, Carroll F., ed. *Mother Goose's Garden: The New National Literature for Children*. Toronto: F. & H. McLean [c.1917]: N. pag.

"The Song in the Trenches." *The Boy's Own Annual* 37 (1914–1915): 355.

Steward, W. Augustus. "War Medals Won by Boys." *The Boy's Own Annual* 37 (1914–1915): 327–330.

"The Story of Rama's Bridge." *St. Nicholas* 45.1 (January 1918): 211.
Strang, Herbert (ed.). "Germany – Enemy of the Human Race." *The Red Book of the War*. London: Henry Frowde Hodder & Stoughton, 1915: N. pag.
Stratemeyer, Edward. *Dave Porter Under Fire: Or, A Young Army Engineer in France*. Boston: Lothrop, Lee and Shepard, 1918.
Sullivan, Archibald. "The Plaint of the Children." *Canadian Poems of the Great War*. Ed. John W. Garvin. Toronto: McClelland and Stewart, 1918: 238.
Teall, Edward N. "German in Our Schools." *St. Nicholas* 45.2 (August 1918): 940.
Tegnier, A. "Boy Heroes of the Present War." *Young Canada: An Illustrated Magazine for Boys*. London/Toronto: Pilgrim Press/William Briggs, 1916: 327.
The Thrift Campaign of the Schools of Ontario, with a Brief Sketch of What Ontario Has Done in the War. Toronto: Department of Education of Ontario, 1919.
Trent, Martha. *Alice Blythe, Somewhere in England*. Illus. Charles L. Wrenn. New York: Barse and Hopkins, 1918.
Trent, Martha. *Lucia Rudini, Somewhere in Italy*. Illus. Charles L. Wrenn. New York: Barse and Hopkins, 1918.
Trent, Martha. *Marieken De Bruin, Somewhere in Belgium*. Illus. Charles L. Wrenn. New York: Barse & Hopkins, 1918.
Trent, Martha. *Phoebe Marshall Somewhere in Canada*. Illus. Charles L. Wrenn. New York: Barse & Hopkins, 1919.
"Turn Off the Light!" *St. Nicholas* 45.1 (January 1918): 208–209.
"Uncle Sam Offers with His Compliments these Helps to Food Conservation." A Food-Conservation Bulletin. *St. Nicholas* 45.1 (December 1917): 117.
Vandercook, Margaret. *The Red Cross Girls in Belgium*. Philadelphia: John C. Winston, 1916.
Vandercook, Margaret. *The Red Cross Girls with the Russian Army*. Illus. Philadelphia: John C. Winston, 1916.
Vrooman, Carl. "The Boys' and Girls' Food Army." *St. Nicholas* 44.2 (October 1917): 1067–1069.
Waterford, Guy. "Last Days at Gallipoli." *Young Canada: An Illustrated Magazine for Boys*. London: Pilgrim Press, 1916: 233–235.
Watkins, Watkin. "How I Came to Enlist: How Ella, After All, Sent a Man to the Front." *The Empire Annual for Girls*. Ed. Augustus Robert Buckland. London: RTS, 1915: 86–90.
Weaver, Emily P. *A Canadian History for Boys and Girls*. Toronto: Copp Clark, 1919.
"When Women Went to War: Stories of Women Who Have Actually Been in the Fighting Line." *Girl Guides' Gazette* 10 (October 1914): 3.
Whitworth, Geoffrey. *The Child's ABC of the War*. Illus. Stanley North. London: George Allen & Unwin Ltd., 1914.
Wilson, Woodrow. "My Dear Mr. Secretary." *To the High School Boys of Massachusetts: A Call for Patriotic Service*. Boston: Committee on Public Safety, [c.1918]: N. pag.
"Women and Patriotism." *The Girl's Own Paper and Woman's Magazine* 36:1 (1915): 36.
Young, Ellsworth, artist. "Remember Belgium—Buy bonds—Fourth Liberty Loan." New York: United States Prtg. & Lith. Co., [c. 1918].

Secondary Sources

Albrinck, Meg. "Humanitarians and He-Men: Recruitment Posters and the Masculine Ideal." *Picture This: World War I Posters and Visual Culture*. Ed. Pearl James. Lincoln/London: U of Nebraska P, 2009: 312–339.

Alexander, Kristine. "Similarity and Difference at Girl Guide Camps in England, Canada, and India." *Scouting Frontiers: Youth and the Scout Movement's First Century*. Eds. Nelson R. Block and Tammy M. Proctor. Newcastle: Cambridge Scholars, 2009: 106–120.

Andrews, Irene Osgood and Margaret A. Hobbs. *Economic Effects of the War upon Women and Children in Great Britain*. 2nd ed. New York: Oxford UP, 1918/1921.

Aronsfeld, Caesar Casper. "Ernst Lissauer and the Hymn of Hate." *History Today* 37.12 (December 1, 1987): 48–50.

Audoin-Rouzeau, Stéphane. "Children and the Primary Schools of France, 1914–1918." *State, Society, and Mobilization in Europe during the First World War*. Ed. John Horne. Cambridge: Cambridge UP, 1997: 39–52.

"Author and Editor Dies of Heart Attack." *Matawan Journal* (February 20, 1947): 1.

Baughan, Emily. "'Every Citizen of Empire Implored to Save the Children!' Empire, Internationalism and the Save the Children Fund in Inter-war Britain." *Historical Research* 86.231 (February 2013): 116–137.

Bothwell, Robert, Ian Drummond, and John English. *Canada, 1900–1945*. Toronto: U of T Press, 1987.

Brotons Capó, M. Magdalena. "Broken Toys: Childhood and War in French Cinema (1908–1916)." Translated by María Magdalena Vázquez Amer. *L'Atalante* 21 (January–June 2016): 59–69.

Budgen, David. *British Children's Literature and the First World War: Representations Since 1914*. London: Bloomsbury, 2018.

Carty, Terence John., ed. "SMITH, Dorothy Whitehill." *A Dictionary of Literary Pseudonyms in the English Language*. 2nd ed. New York: Routledge, 2014: 742.

Caswell, Edward S. *Canadian Singers and Their Songs: A Collection of Portraits, Autograph Poems, and Brief Biographies*. 2nd ed. Toronto: McClelland & Stewart, 1925.

Clute, John and Peter Nicholls. "Strang, Herbert." *The Encyclopedia of Science Fiction*. Eds. John Clute, David Langford, Peter Nicholls, and Graham Sleight. Gollancz, 12 Aug. 2018. <http://www.sf-encyclopedia.com/entry/strang_herbert>.

Cockburn, Tom. *Rethinking Children's Citizenship*. Studies in Childhood and Youth. New York: Palgrave Macmillan, 2013.

Collins, Ross F. *Children, War and Propaganda*. New York: Peter Lang, 2011.

Collins, Ross F. *World War I: Primary Documents on Events from 1914– 1919*. Westport/ London: Greenwood Press, 2008.

Cook, Daniel Thomas and John Wall. "Introduction: Broadening the Conversation." *Children and Armed Conflict: Cross-Disciplinary Investigations*. Eds. Daniel Thomas Cook and John Wall. New York: Palgrave Macmillan, 2011: 1–4.

Cook, Tim. *At the Sharp End: Canadians Fighting the Great War, 1914–1916*. Volume One. Toronto: Penguin, 2007.

Cook, Tim. "'He Was Determined to Go': Underage Soldiers in the Canadian Expeditionary Force." *Histoire Sociale/Social History* 41.81 (May 2008): 41–74.

Coschi, Mario Nathan. "'Be British or be d-d': Primary Education in Berlin-Kitchener, Ontario, During the First World War." *Histoire Sociale/Social History* 47.94 (June 2014): 311–332.

Cowman, Krista. "'There Are Kind Germans as Well as Brutal Ones': The Foreigner in Children's Literature of the First World War." *The Lion and the Unicorn* 31.2 (April 2007): 103–115.

Cross, Gary. "Playing at War: Modern Historical Trends and Debates." *Children and Armed Conflict: Cross-Disciplinary Investigations.* Eds. Daniel Thomas Cook and John Wall. New York: Palgrave Macmillan, 2011: 39–53.

Crotty, Martin. "Scouts Down Under: Scouting, Militarism and 'Manliness' in Australia, 1908–1920." *Scouting Frontiers: Youth and the Scout Movement's First Century.* Eds. Nelson R. Block and Tammy M. Proctor. Newcastle: Cambridge Scholars, 2009: 74–88.

Cunningham, Hugh. *The Invention of Childhood.* London: BBC Books, 2006.

Dale, Stephen. *Noble Illusions: Young Canada Goes to War.* Halifax & Winnipeg: Fernwood Publishing, 2014.

De Groot, Gerald J. *Blighty: British Society in the Era of the Great War.* London: Longman, 1996.

Delaney, Douglas E. "Mentoring the Canadian Corps: Imperial Officers and the Canadian Expeditionary Force, 1914–1918." *Journal of Military History* 77.3 (July 2013): 931–953.

Dignan, Don K. "The Hindu Conspiracy in Anglo-American Relations during World War I." *Pacific Historical Review* 40.1 (February 1971): 57–76.

Djebabla, Mourad. "'Fight the Huns with Food': Mobilizing Canadian Civilians for the Food War Effort During the Great War, 1914–1918." *World War I and Propaganda.* Ed. Troy R.E. Paddock. Leiden: Brill, 2014: 65–88.

Eby, Cecil D. *The Road to Armageddon: The Martial Spirit in English Popular Literature 1870–1914.* Durham: Duke, 1988.

"Edith Lelean Groves." *Canada's Early Women Writers.* <https://cwrc.ca/islandora/ object/ ceww%3Ac8b66bcf-d663–4a85-bd78-8e18e7e87b05>.

"Ellis Parker Butler." Americanliterature.com <https://americanliterature.com/author/ellis- parker-butler>.

Enever, Alison. "'How the Modern Girl Attains Strength and Grace': The *Girl's Own Paper*, Sport and the Discipline of the Female Body, 1914–1956." *Women's History Review* 24.5 (2015): 662–680.

Fahs, Alice. *The Imagined Civil War: Popular Literature of the North & South, 1861–1865.* Chapel Hill: U of North Carolina P, 2001.

Fisher, Susan R. *Boys and Girls in No Man's Land: English-Canadian Children and the First World War.* Toronto: U of Toronto P, 2011.

Flothow, Dorothea. "Coming to Terms with the War: War, Propaganda and the German Enemy in British Children's Novels, 1900–1916." *Writings of Persuasion and Dissonance in the Great War: That Better Whiles May Follow Worse.* Eds. David Owen and Cristina Pividori. Boston: Brill-Rodopi, 2016: 223–236.

Flothow, Dorothea. "'Train Yourselves to Defend Your Country': British Children's Novels in the First World War." *War, Virtual War, and Society: The Challenge to Communities*. Eds. Andrew R. Wilson and Mark L. Perry. Amsterdam/New York: Rodopi, 2008: 3–20.

Fox, Geoff. "News from the Front: The Great War (1914–18) in Literature for Young Readers." *New Review of Children's Literature and Librarianship* 11.2 (2005): 175–188.

Francis, Andrew. "'The Meanest Devil of the Pit': British Representations of the German Character in Edwardian Juvenile Spy Fiction, 1900–14." *The Foreign in International Crime Fiction: Transcultural Representations*. Eds. Jean Anderson, Carolina Miranda, and Barbara Pezzotti. London: Continuum, 2012: 153–64.

Francis, Andrew. *Willingly to War: British and Imperial Boys' Story Papers, 1905–1914*. Wellington: Friends of the Dorothy Neal White Collection, 2007. <http://www.dnwfriends.nzl.org/index.php/2015/05/28/nba10-3/>.

Francis, Daniel. *Selling Canada: Three Propaganda Campaigns that Shaped the Nation*. Vancouver: Stanton Atkins & Dosil Publishers, 2011.

Fussell, Paul. *The Great War and Modern Memory*. Oxford: Oxford UP, 1975/2000.

Galway, Elizabeth A. "Competing Representations of Boy Soldiers in First World War Children's Literature." *Children in Armed Conflicts*. Spec. issue of *Peace Review: A Journal of Social Justice* 24.3 (September 2012): 298–304.

Galway, Elizabeth A. "Border Crossings: Depictions of Canadian-American Relations in First World War Children's Literature." *The Lion and the Unicorn* 39.2 (January 2015): 100–115.

Galway, Elizabeth A. *From Nursery Rhymes to Nationhood: Children's Literature and the Construction of Canadian Identity*. New York: Routledge, 2008.

Galway, Elizabeth A. "The Hope of the World? The Figure of the Child in WWI Children's Literature." *Politics and Ideology in Children's Literature*. Studies in Children's Literature. Eds. Áine McGillicuddy and Marian Keyes. Dublin: Four Courts Press, 2014: 104–114.

Galway, Elizabeth A. "What Shall We Tell the Children? Narratives of War in First World War Children's Literature." *Writings of Persuasion and Dissonance in the Great War: That Better Whiles May Follow Worse*. Eds. David Owen and Cristina Pividori. Leiden: Rodopi-Brill, 2016: 237–251.

Gelber, Steven M. "Free Market Metaphor: The Historical Dynamics of Stamp Collecting." *Comparative Studies in Society and History* 34.4 (October 1992): 742–769.

Glass, John V. "Newell, Robert Henry." *Continuum Encyclopedia of American Literature*. Eds. Steven R. Serafin and Alfred Bendixen. New York: Continuum, 2003: 817–818.

Gould, Jenny. "Women's Military Services in First World War Britain." *Behind the Lines: Gender and the Two World Wars*. Eds. Margaret Randolph Higonnet et al. New Haven/London: Yale UP, 1987: 114–125.

Grayzel, Susan R. "Belonging to the Imperial Nation: Rethinking the History of the First World War in Britain and Its Empire." *The Journal of Modern History* 90.2 (June 2018): 383–405.

Green, Martin. *Seven Types of Adventure Tale: An Etiology of a Major Genre*. University Park: Penn State UP, 1991.

Gregory, James. *Of Victorians and Vegetarians: The Vegetarian Movement in Nineteenth- Century Britain*. London: Tauris, 2007.

Gubar, Marah. *Artful Dodgers: Reconceiving the Golden Age of Children's Literature*. Oxford: Oxford UP, 2009.

Hamilton-Honey, Emily. *Turning the Pages of American Girlhood: The Evolution of Girls' Series Fiction, 1865–1930*. Jefferson: McFarland, 2013.

Hammonds, Victoria, Tracey Handley, James Malley, and Rebecca Sturgess. "'Tickling Men to War': The White Feather Campaign." *Popular Experience and Cultural Representation of the Great War, 1914–1918*. Eds. Ruth Larsen and Ian Whitehead. Newcastle: Cambridge Scholars, 2017: 35–44.

Harris, Ruth. "The 'Child of the Barbarian': Rape, Race and Nationalism in France during the First World War." *Past & Present* 141 (November 1993): 170–206.

Hay, Marnie. "Scouting for Rebels: *Na Fianna Éireann* and Preparation for the Coming War, 1909–1918." *Children's Literature and Culture of the First World War*. Eds. Lissa Paul, Rosemary Ross Johnston, and Emma Short. New York: Routledge, 2016: 268–282.

Hendrick, Harry. *Child Welfare: Historical Dimensions, Contemporary Debate*. Bristol: Policy Press, 2003.

Hickel, K. Walter. "'Justice and the Highest Kind of Equality Require Discrimination': Citizenship, Dependency, and Conscription in the South, 1917–1919." *The Journal of Southern History* 66.4 (November 2000): 749–780.

Higate, Paul and John Hopton. "War, Militarism, and Masculinities." *Handbook of Studies on Men and Masculinities*. Eds. Michael Kimmel, Jeff Hearn, and R. W. Connell. Thousand Oaks: Sage, 2005: 432–447.

Higonnet, Margaret R. "Girl Soldiers in World War I: Marina Yurlova and Sofja Nowosielska." *Children and Armed Conflict: Cross-Disciplinary Investigations*. Eds. Daniel Thomas Cook and John Wall. New York: Palgrave Macmillan, 2011: 7–21.

Higonnet, Margaret R. "War Toys: Breaking and Remaking in Great War Narratives." *The Lion and the Unicorn* 31.2 (April 2007): 116–131.

Hillier, Mary. *Chloë Preston and the Peek-a-Boos*. Shepton Beuchamp/Somerset: Richard Dennis, 1998.

"History of *The Children's Newspaper*." *Look and Learn History Picture Archive*. <https://www.lookandlearn.com/childrens-newspaper/history.php>.

Horne, John and Alan Kramer. *German Atrocities, 1914: A History of Denial*. New Haven: Yale UP, 2002.

Hourihan, Margery. *Deconstructing the Hero: Literary Theory and Children's Literature*. London: Routledge, 1997.

Jackson, Ashley and James E. Kitchen. "Introduction. The British Empire and the First World War: Paradoxes and New Questions." *The British Empire and the First World War*. Ed. Ashley Jackson. London: Routledge, 2016: 1–18.

James, Kate. "Combatant Children: Ideologies and Experiences of Childhood in the Royal Navy and British Army, 1902–1918." *War and Childhood in the Era of Two World Wars*. Edited by Mischa Honeck and James Marten. Cambridge: Cambridge UP, 2019: 151–169.

Jenkinson, Jacqueline. "'All in the Same Uniform'? The Participation of Black Colonial Residents in the British Armed Forces in the First World War." *The Journal of Imperial and Commonwealth History* 40.2 (June 2012): 207–230.

"Junior Red Cross." *Our History: British Red Cross*. <http://www.redcross.org.uk/About-us/Who-we-are/Museum-and-archives/Historical-factsheets/Junior-Red-Cross>.

Karadzhov, Dimitar. "Assessing Resilience in War-Affected Children and Adolescents: A Critical Review." *Journal of European Psychology Students* 6.3 (2015): 1–13. <http://dx.doi.org/10.5334/jeps.dc>.

Keller, R. H. "The German Soldier in World War I. The Final 'Argument of Kings.'" *Great War Militaria*, 2009. <http://www.greatwar.com/scripts/openExtra.asp?extra=10>.

Kember, Joe. "Face Value: The Rhetoric of Facial Disfigurement in American Film and Popular Culture, 1917–1927." *Journal of War and Culture Studies* 10.1 (2017): 43–65.

Kennedy, David M. *Over Here: The First World War and American Society*. 25th anniversary ed. New York: Oxford UP, 2004.

Kennedy, Rosie. *The Children's War: Britain, 1914–1918*. Houndmills: Palgrave Macmillan, 2014.

Kennedy, Rosie. "'How Merrily the Battle Rages': Props for Make-Believe in the Edwardian Nursery." *Children's Literature and Culture of the First World War*. Eds. Lissa Paul, Rosemary Ross Johnston, and Emma Short. New York: Routledge, 2016: 226–238.

Kestner, Joseph A. *Masculinities in British Adventure Fiction, 1880–1915*. Farnham: Ashgate, 2010.

Kieran, David. 2012. "'What Young Men and Women Do When Their Country is Attacked': Interventionist Discourse and the Rewriting of Violence in Adolescent Literature of the Iraq War." *Children's Literature Association Quarterly* 37.1 (Spring): 4–26.

Kingsbury, Celia Malone. *For Home and Country: World War I Propaganda on the Home Front*. Lincoln/London: U of Nebraska P, 2010.

Kitchen, Martin. "The German Invasion of Canada in the First World War." *The International History Review* 7.2 (May 1985): 245–260.

Kokkola, Lydia. "The Embodied Child: An Introduction." *The Embodied Child: Readings in Children's Literature and Culture*. Eds Roxanne Harde and Lydia Kokkola. New York: Routledge, 2018: 1–20.

Kuhlman, Erika A. *Petticoats and White Feathers: Gender Conformity, Race, the Progressive Peace Movement, and the Debate Over War, 1895–1919*. Contributions in Women's Studies. Westport: Greenwood, 1997.

Kutzer, M. Daphne. *Empire's Children: Empire and Imperialism in Classic British Children's* Books. New York: Garland, 2000.

Lewis, Susan Ingalls. "Girls to the Rescue: The Impact of World War I on Girls' Series Books." *Dime Novel Roundup: A Magazine Devoted to the Collection, Preservation and Study of Old-Time Dime and Nickel Novels, Popular Story Papers, Series Books, and Pulp Magazines* 77.4 (August 2008): 131–140.

Lindenmeyer, Kriste. *"A Right to Childhood." The U.S. Children's Bureau and Child Welfare, 1912–46*. Urbana/Chicago: U of Illinois P, 1997.

Lindsay, Kate. "The She-Soldiers of World War One." <http://ww1centenary.oucs.ox.ac.uk/ unconventionalsoldiers/the-she-soldiers-of-world-war-one/>.

Little, Branden. "A Child's Army of Millions: The American Junior Red Cross." *Children's Literature and Culture of the First World War*. Eds. Lissa Paul,

Rosemary Ross Johnston, and Emma Short. New York: Routledge, 2016: 283–300.

MacLeod, Roy. "The Mobilisation of Minds and the Crisis in International Science: The *Krieg der Geister* and the *Manifesto of the 93*." *Journal of War & Culture Studies* 11.1 (2018): 58–78.

Madry, Anna. "Living on Borrowed Time: Brotherhood in *Private Peaceful* by Michael Morpurgo." *Re-Imagining the First World War: New Perspectives in Anglophone Literature and Culture*. Eds. Anna Branach-Kallas and Nelly Strehlau. Newcastle: Cambridge Scholars Publishing, 2015: 152–162.

Marquis, Alice Goldfarb. "Words as Weapons: Propaganda in Britain and Germany during the First World War." *Journal of Contemporary History* 13.3 (July 1978): 467–498.

McCrone, Kathleen E. "Play Up! Play Up! and Play the Game! Sport at the Late Victorian Girls' Public School." *Journal of British Studies* 23.2 (Spring 1984): 106–134.

McGeough, Kevin. "Esther the Hero: Going Beyond 'Wisdom' in Heroic Narratives." *The Catholic Biblical Quarterly* 70.1 (January 2008): 44–65.

McGetchin, Doug. "From *Ghadar* (Revolt) to Home Rule: Arguments about Violence, Nonviolence, and Race in the Struggle to Liberate India during the First World War." *World History Bulletin* 32.1 (Spring 2016): 18–23.

Medrich, Elliott A., Judith Roizen, Victor Rubin, and Stuart Buckley. *The Serious Business of Growing Up: A Study of Children's Lives Outside School*. Berkeley: U of California P, 1982.

Moruzi, Kristine. "Embodying the Healthy, Charitable Child in the Junior Red Cross." *The Embodied Child: Readings in Children's Literature and Culture*. Eds. Roxanne Harde and Lydia Kokkola. New York: Routledge, 2018: 113–126.

Moruzi, Kristine. "'A Very Cruel Thing': Canadian Children, The First World War, and the *Grain Grower's Guide*." *Children's Literature and Culture of the First World War*. Eds. Lissa Paul, Rosemary Ross Johnston, and Emma Short. New York: Routledge, 2016: 214–225.

Moss, Mark. *Manliness and Militarism: Educating Young Boys in Ontario for War*. Oxford: Oxford UP, 2001.

Nelson, Claudia. "Mixed Messages: Authoring and Authority in British Boys' Magazines." *Lion and the Unicorn* 21.1 (January 1997): 1–19.

Nodelman, Perry. *The Hidden Adult: Defining Children's Literature*. Baltimore: Johns Hopkins UP, 2008.

Nordstrom, Justin. "'A Salesman Soldier for Uncle Sam': Images of Childhood in US Food Conservation, 1914–1919." *Children's Literature and Culture of the First World War*. Eds. Lissa Paul, Rosemary Ross Johnston, and Emma Short. New York: Routledge, 2016: 179–193.

"Notable People." *Chudleigh History Group: Preserving Our Parish History*. <http://chudleighhistorygroup.uk/articles/notable_people.html>.

O'Connor, Karen Sands. "A Medal for Walter: Representations of Black Britons and World War I." *The Lion and the Unicorn* 41.2 (April 2017): 231–249.

Olsen, Stephanie. *Juvenile Nation: Youth, Emotions and the Making of the Modern British Citizen, 1880–1914*. London: Bloomsbury, 2014.

O'Sullivan, Emer. "Fun and Military Games: The War in German Picturebooks, 1914–1915." *Children's Literature and Culture of the First World*

War. Eds. Lissa Paul, Rosemary Ross Johnston, and Emma Short. New York: Routledge, 2016: 197–213.

Paris, Michael. *Over the Top: The Great War and Juvenile Literature in Britain*. Westport: Praeger, 2004.

Pattison, Robert. *The Child Figure in English Literature*. Athens: U of Georgia P, 1978/2008.

Pavlik, Anthony. "Viewing the Great War through American Series Fiction for Boys (1914–18)." *The Lion and the Unicorn* 41.2 (April 2017): 186–203.

Penn, Alan. *Targeting Schools: Drill, Militarism and Imperialism*. London: Woburn, 1999.

Pennell, Catriona. *A Kingdom United: Popular Responses to the Outbreak of the First World War and Ireland*. Oxford: Oxford UP, 2012.

Penner, Elizabeth. "'The Squire of Boyhood': G.A. Hutchison and the 'Boy's Own Paper'." *Victorian Periodicals Review* 47.4 (Winter 2014): 631–647.

Peppis, Paul. *Literature, Politics, and the English Avant-Garde: Nation and Empire, 1901–1918*. Cambridge: Cambridge UP, 2000.

Perkin, Harold. *The Rise of Professional Society: England since 1880*. 1989. London: Routledge, 2002.

Proctor, Tammy M. "Building an Empire of Youth: Scout and Guide History in Perspective." *Scouting Frontiers: Youth and the Scout Movement's First Century*. Eds. Nelson R. Block and Tammy M. Proctor. Newcastle: Cambridge Scholars, 2009: xxvi–xxxviii.

Proctor, Tammy M. "'Patriotic Enemies': Germans in the Americas, 1914–1920." *Germans as Minorities During the First World War: A Global Comparative Perspective*. Ed. Panikos Panayi. London: Routledge, 2014/2016: 213–234.

Read, Jane. "Gutter to Garden: Historical Discourses of Risk in Interventions in Working Class Children's Street Play." *Children and Society* 25 (2011): 421–434.

Reynolds, Kimberley. *Left Out: The Forgotten Tradition of Radical Publishing for Children in Britain 1910–1949*. Oxford: Oxford UP, 2016.

Reynolds, Kimberley. "Words about War for Boys: Representations of Soldiers and Conflict in Writing for Children before World War I." *Children's Literature Association Quarterly* 34.3 (Fall 2009): 255–271.

Robb, George. *British Culture and the First World War*. 2002. 2nd ed. London: Palgrave Macmillan, 2015.

Rose, Jonathan. *The Intellectual Life of the British Working Classes*. New Haven: Yale UP, 2001.

Rosen, David M. *Armies of the Young: Child Soldiers in War and Terrorism*. New Brunswick: Rutgers UP, 2005.

Rosen, David M. *Child Soldiers in the Western Imagination: From Patriots to Victims*. New Brunswick: Rutgers UP, 2015.

Sharp, Heather. "Representing Australia's Involvement in the First World War: Discrepancies between Public Discourses and School History Textbooks from 1916–1936." *Journal of Educational Media, Memory, and Society* 6.1 (Spring 2014): 1–23.

Shaw, Amy. *Crisis of Conscience: Conscientious Objection in Canada during the First World War*. Vancouver: UBC Press, 2009.

Sherington, Geoffrey E. "The 1918 Education Act: Origins, Aims and Development." *British Journal of Educational Studies* 24.1 (February 1976): 66–85.

Showalter, Elaine. "Rivers and Sassoon: The Inscription of Male Gender Anxieties." *Behind the Lines: Gender and the Two World Wars*. Eds. Margaret R. Higonnet et al. New Haven: Yale UP, 1987: 51–60.

Sim, Gary. "Ruiter Stinson Sherman." *The Homeroom*. <https://www2.viu.ca/homeroom/ content/Topics/People/sherman.htm>.

Sim, Gary. "School Days Magazine." *The Homeroom*. <https://www2.viu.ca/homeroom/ content/sdaysmag.htm>.

Sondhaus, Lawrence. *German Submarine Warfare in World War I: The Onset of Total War at Sea*. Lanham: Rowman and Littlefield, 2017.

Springhall, John. "Debate. Baden-Powell and the Scout Movement before 1920: Citizen Training or Soldiers of the Future?" *English Historical Review* 102.405 (October 1987): 934–942.

Stover, Allan C. *Underage and Under Fire: Accounts of the Youngest Americans in Military Service*. Jefferson: McFarland, 2014.

Strachan, Hew. "The First World War as a Global War." *First World War Studies* 1.1 (March 2010): 3–14. <https://doi.org/10.1080/19475021003621036>.

Strahan, Derek. "Herbert Myrick House, Springfield Mass." *Lost in New England: Exploring Historic and Modern Photos of New England and the Northeast* (May 23, 2017). <https://lostnewengland.com/2017/05/herbert-myrick-house-springfield-mass/>.

Sutherland, John. "The Bookman." *The Longman Companion to Victorian Fiction*. 2nd edition. Routledge 2013: 72.

Sutton-Smith, Brian. *The Ambiguity of Play*. Cambridge: Harvard UP, 1997.

Tait, Derek. *Plymouth in the Great War*. Barnsley: Pen and Sword, 2014.

Talley, Lee A. "Operation Pied Piper: Historical Texts and the CCSS." *The ALAN Review* 41.1 (Fall 2013): 26–32. <https://doi.org/10.21061/alan.v41i1.a.4>.

Tebbel, John. *The American Magazine: A Compact History*. New York: Hawthorn, 1969.

Thacker, Deborah. "Imagining the Child." *Introducing Children's Literature: From Romanticism to Postmodernism*. Eds. Deborah Cogan Thacker and Jean Webb. London: Routledge, 2002: 13–25.

Thompson, John Herd. *Ethnic Minorities during Two World Wars*. Canada's Ethnic Groups. Ottawa: Canadian Historical Association, 1991.

Towns, Jeff. "'Borrowed Plumes' – Requiem for a Plagiarist." *Dylan Thomas: A Centenary Celebration*. Ed. Hannah Ellis. London: Bloomsbury, 2014: 42–70.

"Townsend Evans '34." *Princeton Alumni Weekly* 60.21 (March 11, 1960): 33.

Tynan, Katherine. "Mrs. Belloc Lowndes." *America* 27.3 (May 6, 1922): 65–66.

Vance, Jonathan F. *Death So Noble: Memory, Meaning, and the First World War*. Vancouver: UBC Press, 1997.

Wallace, Jo-Ann. "The Very First Lady Chatterley? Mrs. Havelock Ellis's *Seaweed*." *English Literature in Transition, 1880–1920* 51.2 (2008): 123–137.

Warren, Allen. "Sir Robert Baden-Powell, the Scout Movement and Citizen Training in Great Britain, 1900–1920." *English Historical Review* 101.399 (April 1986): 376–398.

Wegs, Robert. "Youth Delinquency and 'Crime': The Perception and the Reality." *Journal of Social History* 32.3 (Spring 1999): 603–621.

Weikle-Mills, Courtney A. "The Child as (Potential) Citizen." Rev. of *Serialized Citizenships: Periodicals, Books, and American Boys, 1840–1911* by Lorinda Cohoon. *Children's Literature* 36 (2008): 214–219.

Weir, Erin M. K. "Using the Legacy of World War I to Evaluate Canadian Military Leadership in World War II." *Journal of Military and Strategic Studies* 7.1 (Fall 2004): 1–19. <https://jmss.org/article/view/57775??>.

Whitehead, Winifred. *Old Lies Revisited: Young Readers and the Literature of War and Violence.* London: Pluto, 1991.

Wingate, Jennifer. "Over the Top: The Doughboy in World War I Memorials and Visual Culture." *American Art* 19.2 (Summer 2005): 26–47.

Winter, J.M. "Military Fitness and Civilian Health in Britain during the First World War. *Journal of Contemporary History* 15.2 (April 1980): 211–244.

"Woman Journalist Dead: Mary Frances Billington." *The Argus* (August 29, 1925): 31.

"Women from Olean's Past." Olean Public Library. <https://oleanpubliclibrary.wordpress.com/category/local-history/>.

Yarrow, Andrew L. *History of U.S. Children's Policy, 1900-Present.* Washington: First Focus, 2009.

Index

Note: Bold page numbers refer to tables; page numbers followed by "n" denote endnotes.